FAITH IN REASON
PHILOSOPHICAL ENQUIRIES

Series Editors:
Laurence Paul Hemming and Susan Frank Parsons

The Politics of Human Frailty

A Theological Defence of Political Liberalism

Christopher J. Insole

scm press

British Library Cataloguing in Publication data

A catalogue record for this book is available
from the British Library

0 334 02957 0

First published in 2004 by SCM Press
9–17 St Albans Place, London N1 0NX

www.scm-canterburypress.co.uk

SCM Press is a division of
SCM-Canterbury Press Ltd

Printed and bound in Great Britain by
Biddles Ltd, www.biddles.co.uk

Contents

Acknowledgements

This book was the result of a Research Fellowship in Theology and Society at Heythrop College, University of London. Thanks should go first of all to Peter Askonas, whose generosity funded the Fellowship, and to Heythrop College for providing academic community and friendship for three years.

Many colleagues and friends have contributed to the process of preparing this book, through conversations, seminars and reading parts or (some brave souls) all of the manuscript in various stages. I would like to thank the following people: Oliver O'Donovan, David Fergusson, Ian Linden and John Gray for providing encouragement and judicious advice at an early stage of the project; anonymous readers for SCM Press for insightful suggestions on the manuscript; Giles Fraser for disagreeing with me so enjoyably throughout; Eddie Howells, Pierre Manent and James Hanvey for bringing their distinct expertise to bear on aspects of the book; Denys Turner and Douglas Hedley for stimulating conversations on Marx and Plotinus, that came too late to be part of the book, but have provided food for future thought; Nigel Biggar for his personal encouragement and sustained and detailed attention to the project, and David Dwan for constant intellectual friendship and his profound interrogation of an early draft of the manuscript. I should like to thank Barbara Laing of SCM Press for interest in the project and Roger Ruston for copyediting the manuscript so intelligently and courteously. Susan Parsons and Laurence Hemming have both been extraordinarily supportive, affirming and energetic in nurturing the interests of the project and its author, as series editors and fine friends.

Other people have been spared too much exposure to the hook, but have been vital over the course of writing the book for making my life larger than this project, and all the better for that. So thank you to Thomas Dixon, Kath O'Neill, Jude Bryson, Ferdinand von Knapp, Liz Gulliford, Anna Beer, Becca Williams and Phil Shiner. Friends on the Isle of Iona, both in the Iona Community, the

Columba and the village have provided vital renewal and inspiration, when the author, if not the project, was a little frayed at the edges.

Aspects of this book are informed by my involvement and engagement with Anglicanism. I have been fortunate to have so many kind and wise people who have nurtured me in this tradition. So for teaching me that gentleness, self-examination and tolerance can be the fruits of a strong, compassionate and confident faith I thank Michael Anderson, Robert Mitchell, Robert Fergusson, Giles Fraser, Trevor Williams, Liz Gulliford and Rachel Lawrence. A very practical and vital form of support was provided by the Church of England in the last year of writing this book, with accommodation provided by the Parish of Putney: thank you and sorry that I was such a poor gardener.

'Some of my best friends', as the saying goes, 'are Roman Catholics'; but in this case it is really true. Heythrop College and the Society of St Catherine of Siena have exhibited all the ancient confidence and inclusive generosity of the Roman Catholic tradition, by their preparedness to sponsor and promote a work concerned in part with the nature of Anglicanism. I owe them thanks and respect.

Towards the end of preparing this book the universe began to feel much more like home, when I began what I hope will be a long journey with Lisa Feeley. I would like to thank her for all the support and encouragement she has given in the final vital stages of producing the book.

Finally I should like to thank my parents, for constant and vociferous – if at times, I have felt, undeserved – pride in me and what I do. The pride is reciprocated and this book is dedicated to you.

Preface

This book provides a theological defence of a strand of political liberalism; a strand informed by the theological conviction that the human person is a creature incapable of its own perfection, although nonetheless called to and made for this perfection. My intention is to put a question-mark against easy caricatures of 'liberalism', which tend to describe it as individualistic, hubristic and relativist. By attending to figures such as Edmund Burke and Lord Acton in Chapter 1, I show that a passion to protect the individual within liberal institutions arises not from an illusory sense of self-sufficiency, but from an insight into our fallen condition, characterized by frailty, vulnerability, yet also a hope for, and intimation of, redemption and an eternal divine order. In Chapter 2 I take up the emphasis John Rawls places on the wars of religion in sixteenth- and seventeenth-century Europe as the historical impetus for an emerging political liberalism. The Anglican divine Richard Hooker was immersed in this context, addressing a Church riven by theological conflict; in so doing, I will suggest, Hooker provides a powerful articulation of our frailty, and shows how our need for generosity calls us to charity, reciprocity and self-examination, rather than persecuting zeal. In Richard Hooker's thought, one finds in the theologico-political seed-bed of liberalism a profound and moving theological sensitivity and motivation; one that is not lost in subsequent centuries, but reconfigured and interpreted.

In Chapter 3 I separate the political liberalism defended from theologically over-zealous appropriations of the notion of 'liberty' that emanate, for instance, from American presidents. I investigate how the notion of 'liberty' employed in America has a quite distinct theological lineage, rooted in the Calvinist notion of covenantal church government (liberty from Romish hierarchies) and Christian liberty from sin, guaranteed through the saint's pre-election, leading to activist projects to eliminate evil. Hooker's relevance is shown again, in that it is precisely the Puritan forebears of this tradition of talking about 'Christian liberty' that Hooker has in sight when writing the *Laws of Ecclesiastical Polity*.

On the basis of the defence of political liberalism I move on in Chapters 4 and 5 to critique utopian attempts to leap beyond liberalism to a more enchanted space. The critique of political liberalism found in Radical Orthodoxy writers is shown to be historically and conceptually impoverished, and their constructive solution – the assertion of a peaceful, teleological and analogically interrelated cosmos – is found to be politically naive and dangerous in ways well understood by the tradition of political liberalism that I defend.

I conclude by facing the charge that my approach has an inadequate ecclesiology, leading to an inability to resist evil.

Obscured Order, Human Frailty and the Liberal Tradition

There seems to be almost a consensus in theological circles concerning the nature of the problem with 'liberalism'.[1] Liberalism, according to this conception, is based upon an illusory human subject who constructs order and denies transcendence. The 'liberal' focuses on the will at the cost of attending to reason or order. This focus on the will engenders a fetish for freedom of choice and the removal of all impediments to human liberty; consequently, the notion of 'freedom/liberty' is emptied of any substantial historical, traditional or philosophical content. Flowing from this entirely stripped-down notion of freedom, liberalism has a voluntaristic account of values and meaning, with 'ethics' being a construction by the subject. This voluntarist meta-ethic fosters a destructive individualism and social atomism. In an attempt to distract from the poverty of the liberal conception of freedom, liberals tend to support a pseudo-Messianic/ Pelagian progressivism about history, often finding expression in a fixation with technology and economic growth. After relating this narrative, theology is called upon to judge this liberalism as a false and historically contingent religion masquerading as a secular, timeless and neutral framework. Although sometimes able to say a tentative 'yes' to some aspects of liberalism, there is usually also a trenchant call for the Church to stand as a counter-culture to the corrupt pseudo-religion of man which liberalism has become; 'modernity as Antichrist, a parodic and corrupt development of Christian social order',[2] as Oliver O'Donovan sternly phrases it.

The Radical Orthodoxy movement, which I treat extensively in

---

[1] A version of this chapter was presented at a conference organized by Heythrop College University of London, 'The Hidden City: a Theological Reflection on the Polis', held at Trinity College, Oxford, in September 2003.

[2] Oliver O'Donovan, *The Desire of the Nations: Rediscovering the Roots of Political Theology* (Cambridge: Cambridge University Press, 1996), p. 275.

Chapter 4, clearly flags its contempt of political liberalism. So John Milbank, in his recent *Being Reconciled: Ontology and Pardon*, comments that 'political liberalism itself engenders today an increasingly joyless and puritanical world' marked by a 'totalitarian drift ... its [political liberalism's] empty heart ... besieged by an irrational cult of race, science, style or belief'.[3] We find a more measured but not entirely dissimilar critique in Robert Song's *Christianity and Liberal Society*. Song's fine study is superior to many theological treatments of liberalism in that it does at least deny the possibility of a 'univocal definition of such an historically and conceptually complex phenomenon'[4] as liberalism. Nevertheless, Song identifies a 'pattern of characteristic family resemblances', of which the 'most central' are 'a voluntaristic conception of the human subject; a constructivist meta-ethics; an abstract, universalist, and individualistic mode of thought; and a broadly progressivist philosophy of history'.[5]

Song speaks of the 'political Messianism' of the 'doctrines of historical progress and implicit Pelagian theologies' behind liberalism,[6] which doctrines are now manifested in 'late twentieth-century dependencies on economic growth and technological progress'.[7] After identifying the centrality of the will, the loss of transcendence and the neglect of human limitations as defining features of this political Messianism,[8] Song states that 'theology must finally interpret politics, and not vice-versa',[9] with a special role for the Church to make 'declarations of moral truth in the public realm' being 'formed by a language which the world does not share'.[10] Although the Church can offer a tentative 'Yes' to some features of liberal society, in 'so far as it offers opportunities for contributing to social order less unjust than the alternatives',[11] nevertheless the Church with its 'orientation to eternity'[12] is there to 'signify the eschatological

---

[3] John Milbank, *Being Reconciled: Ontology and Pardon* (London: Routledge, 2003), p. 25.
[4] Robert Song, *Christianity and Liberal Society* (Oxford: Clarendon Press, 1997), p. 9.
[5] Song, *Christianity*, p. 9.
[6] Song, *Christianity*, p. 214.
[7] Song, *Christianity*, p. 214.
[8] Song, *Christianity*, pp. 216–20.
[9] Song, *Christianity*, p. 225.
[10] Song, *Christianity*, p. 231.
[11] Song, *Christianity*, p. 233.
[12] Song, *Christianity*, p. 231.

Kingdom',[13] and to register its 'No' to liberalism in so far as it is 'subservient to technology and oriented to historical utopianism'.[14]

O'Donovan identifies the 'series of self-interpreting doctrines' of liberalism 'which define metaphysical parameters for thought and action (even while innocently disavowing metaphysical intentions)'.[15] Liberalism emerges as a 'false posture of transcendence, an illusion that society may be organised on formal principles from the perspective of a "view from nowhere" (Nagel)'.[16] At the centre of the liberal moment is 'the notion of the abstract will, exercising choice prior to all reason and order, from whose *fiat lux* spring society, morality and rationality itself'.[17] Corresponding to this transcendent will who constructs meaning is 'an inert nature, lacking any given order that could make it good prior to the imposition of human purposes upon it'.[18] Drawing out the deep theological commitments of this position O'Donovan writes that 'the paradigm for the human presence in the world is creation *ex nihilo*, the absolute summoning of reason, order and beauty out of chaos and emptiness. This does not, of course, honour God's creative deed, but competes with it.'[19]

Such a critique of liberalism has venerable philosophical and theological roots. Heidegger's essay 'Die Frage nach der Technik' ('The Question of Technology')[20] identifies technology not as technical innovation but as an approach to practical reasoning that treats reason as an instrument which manipulates – to its own pre-conceived ends – the raw material around it. Such an ordering of reason to *techne* is understood by Heidegger to be behind humanism and liberalism,[21] binding it in the same ontological genealogy to Communism and Fascism. This binding is one which O'Donovan and Song are both happy to re-enact, with Song finding a 'similarity

---

[13] Song, *Christianity*, p. 231.
[14] Song, *Christianity*, p. 232.
[15] O'Donovan, *Desire*, p. 274.
[16] O'Donovan, *Desire*, p. 274.
[17] O'Donovan, *Desire*, p. 274.
[18] O'Donovan, *Desire*, p. 274.
[19] O'Donovan, *Desire*, p. 274.
[20] Martin Heidegger, 'The Question Concerning Technology' in trans. W. Lovitt, *The Question Concerning Technology and Other Essays* (1952–62) (New York: Harper and Row, 1977).
[21] See Martin Heidegger's 'Letter on Humanism' in *Pathmarks*, (ed.) W. McNeil (Cambridge: Cambridge University Press, 1998).

between liberal and national socialist rhetorics',[22] and O'Donovan drawing the more generalized and cautious parallel between liberalism and political structures that offer themselves as the 'sufficient and necessary condition of human welfare', and which as such are 'totalitarian'.[23] Bolstering the anti-liberal theological consensus we can perhaps also hear Karl Barth's characterization of the Enlightenment as the time of 'absolute man'. Barth's 'absolute man' is substantially the same as the 'liberal man' of theological consensus:

> Man, who discovers his own power and ability, the potentiality dormant in his humanity, that is, his human being as such, and looks upon it as the final, the real and absolute, I mean as something 'detached', self-justifying, with its own authority and power, which he can therefore set in motion in all directions and without any restraint – this man is absolute man.[24]

These theologians are not wrong about liberalism. There are certainly strands of liberalism which fit this characterization. Song, for instance, does a careful and effective job of showing these strands running through five liberal thinkers: Locke, Kant, Mill, Hobhouse and Hayek. Although not wrong about liberalism, Song, O'Donovan, Barth and their lesser imitators are not right about it either. Consider Song's 'family resemblance' description of liberalism, which is an entirely characteristic conception in the anti-liberal theological literature. Such liberalism is marked out, we remember, by: '. . . a voluntaristic conception of the human subject; a constructivist meta-ethics; an abstract, universalist, and individualistic mode

---

[22] Song, *Christianity*, p. 213. Based on Dr Goebbels' saying: 'You are at liberty to seek your salvation as you understand it, provided you do nothing to change the social order.' It is well known that totalitarian regimes commandeer the language of freedom; I would suggest that it should not be taken at face value that this reflects a deep conceptual fault line in liberalism, rather than a *kitsch* appropriation by totalitarians of antithetical principles.

[23] O'Donovan, *Desire*, p. 274.

[24] Karl Barth, *Protestant Theology in the Nineteenth Century*, trans. B. Cozens (London: SCM Press, 1972), p. 36. *Die Protestantische Theologie im 19 Jahrhundert* (Zollikon/Zürich: Evangelisher Verlag AG, 1952): 'Der Mensch, der seine eigene Fraft, sein Können, die in seiner Humanität, d.h. in seinem Menschein also solchem schlummerrule Potentialität entdeckt, der sie als Letzten, Eigentliches, Absolutes, will sagen: als ein Gelöstes, in sich selbst Berechtigtes und Bevollmächtigtes und Mächtiges versteht, der sie darum hemmungslos nach allen Seiten in Gang setzt, dieser Mensch ist der absolutische Mensch', p. 18.

of thought; and a broadly progressivist philosophy of history'.[25] The problem with this characterization is that it could have been delivered – almost point by point and *on the basis of his political liberalism* – by Edmund Burke as a summary of all that is wrong with projects and enthusiasms such as the French Revolution. The claim developed in this chapter is that proper attention to a figure such as Burke can challenge the anti-liberal consensus, indicating deep lines of theological compatibility between some aspects of political liberalism and the Christian tradition. Although the focus in this chapter will be on Burke – and to a lesser extent Lord Acton – the ramifications are much wider. By documenting a 'hidden' strand of political liberalism, theologians might be brought to think more generously about the possibilities and aspirations of political liberalism, as well as declaring its manifest failings, historical debasement and concrete problems. Christian theologians legitimately complain when 'Christianity' is judged by its worst historical and concrete moments, and ask for its higher aspirations and deepest truths to be reckoned with; we might do well to extend this courtesy to other traditions, such as political liberalism.

The term 'liberalism' was not used as a term in political contexts until the 1820s.[26] Considerable caution is required in 'back-projecting' the term to earlier periods. Nonetheless, a certain amount of 'back-projection' is legitimate if the term 'political liberalism' is used in a specified way to pick out themes that are unarguably part of political liberalism as we understand it, which themes are demonstrably developed in thinkers prior to 1820. So to be quite specific, by 'political liberalism' I mean the conviction that politics is ordered towards peaceful coexistence (the absence of conflict), and the preservation of the liberties of the individual within a pluralistic and tolerant framework, rather than by a search for truth (religious or otherwise), perfection and unity. The crucial ambition of this sort of 'political liberalism' is a refusal to allow public power to enforce on society a substantial and comprehensive conception of the good; driven as it is by its central passion for the liberties of individuals over and above the enthusiasms of other individuals or collectivities. Political authority is wielded on behalf of the people it protects, and is derived ultimately from their consent.

---

[25] Song, *Christianity*, p. 9.
[26] I am grateful to Matthew Grimley for drawing my attention to this.

Burke (1729–97), inasmuch as he endorses each of these features of political liberalism, represents a 'politically liberal' position. Striking for our purposes here, Burke defends these politically liberal elements whilst critiquing everything to which anti-liberal theologians are allergic: the voluntaristic, abstract, formal, universalizing, self-transcendent will who constructs all order, meaning and beauty. This 'liberal' (from now on I will drop the scare marks, with the understanding that I mean by 'liberalism' the specified elements outlined above) tradition is driven by a sense of the frailty and limitations of individuals and a sense of the difficulty and dangers of discerning and imposing order given our fallen and complex condition.

There is something ironic about the charge that liberalism has 'become' a pseudo-religion, that it has – in Song's words – 'take[n] on Messianic form, in its philosophy of history and tendency to progressivism'.[27] As will become clear in my discussion of 'crusading liberalism' (Chapter 3), this progressivist and eschatologically ambitious liberalism is entirely the child of certain theological presuppositions. There is no need for theology to intervene or come in judgement, or for liberal society to be 'sacralized' (Song);[28] there is already too much theology of too specific a nature directly behind some of the most objectionable features of crusading liberalism. These features spring from an attempt to separate in history the saints from the damned, and to purify the visible historical institution of the Church so that it becomes, through human activism, the eschatological gathering in glory of all the saints. The visible Church was to be transformed into the invisible (the impure into the pure) by the regeneration of the saints. Once this regeneration was complete, the saints could take their activist part in inaugurating the Kingdom by the confident identification and elimination of evil.

There is perhaps a trace – no more than this, and subject to qualification given below – of something depressingly familiar in the way the Church is invoked by O'Donovan and Song. It has echoes at least of the pure, transforming, politically activist Church of sixteenth- and seventeenth-century radical Protestants, who we will see are behind some of the most depressing features of modern triumphalist liberalism. There is an intimation of the same movement of thought. The Church is pure, the world (liberalism) impure;

---

[27] Song, *Christianity*, p. 229.
[28] Song, *Christianity*, p. 229.

through salvation of its members the Church is then called to prophetic action and judgement of the world and the elimination of evil, leading to the inauguration of the Kingdom on earth. So Song writes of the 'Church as the unique eschatological sign of the coming Kingdom . . . that which, by its existence, defines the world as world, and by its life, shows to the world its worldly nature . . . a living demonstration of the relativity and transient nature of politics'.[29] O'Donovan tells us that the church is the 'only . . . society which is incorporated into the Kingdom of God and which recapitulates the narrative of the Christ event'.[30]

Is this the visible or the invisible Church? If the visible, *where* is the Church which is not – for all its glories – like every human institution bogged down in conflict, complacency, corruption, mediocrity and self-deception? Sometimes it seems that 'the Church' being spoken of is not tainted, fallen and complex in the same way as all human institutions, but that the visible Church has already been transformed into the invisible, and needs to maintain purity of witness and action before a world cast in darkness. It is not confidence in human activism and voluntarism *per se* that seems to be problematized, but human activism and voluntarism outside of the Church. How else can we make sense of the rather odd feature of Oliver O'Donovan's magnificent *Desire of the Nations*, that after a sustained scholarly polemic against the notion of voluntarism and the will, we are brought in the ultimate paragraph before a 'moment of *decision*', between the 'two loves which made the two cities',[31] as if – after all – human decision-making is the key.

Limited theological appreciation of liberalism

With these reservations emphatically made, it is nevertheless important to record that the theological treatments of liberalism presented by O'Donovan and Song are more subtle and nuanced than some of the passages quoted above would suggest. We have already seen how Song's 'family resemblance' account of liberalism avoids the fruitless drawing-up of necessary and sufficient conditions for liberalism, and so avoids a crude caricature. Song's approach is valuable, for

---

[29] Song, *Christianity*, p. 229.
[30] O'Donovan, *Desire*, p. 251.
[31] O'Donovan, *Desire*, p. 284.

instance, in being able to distinguish constitutional liberalism (Locke and Kant), 'rooted in opposition to arbitrary, personal, or unlimited power', *laissez-faire* liberalism (Hayek) emphasizing 'freedom of trade internationally and minimal government domestically' and welfare/revisionist liberalism (Hobhouse) stressing 'the importance of social justice and equitable material distribution' within a framework 'which guarantees civil liberties and the rights of the individual'.[32] Such a differentiation of the liberal tradition is invaluable in that it helps Song to see how one can criticize one form of liberalism on the basis of another. So, for instance, in his discussion of Reinhold Niebuhr, Song notes how Niebuhr's critical attitude to certain strands of liberalism was only possible because he was a 'chastened welfare liberal with a strong commitment to liberal constitutionalism'.[33]

Song's subtlety about liberalism comes out at another point in his discussion of Niebuhr. Niebuhr draws a connection between what he understands to be the optimistic, liberal view of man and progressivist notions of history and Pelagianism, writing for instance that the 'belief that man could solve his problem . . . by the historical process itself is a mistake which is partly prompted by the most universal of all "ideological" taints: the pride, not of particular men and cultures, but of man as man'.[34] Song's entirely apposite comment here is that Niebuhr 'sometimes talked of liberalism when properly he meant optimism . . . clearly regarding the former as a species of the latter'.[35] Song correctly points out that 'not all liberals have been naive progressivists'.[36] Even where some notion of progress is in play, it need not have the perfectibilist implausibility that Niebuhr claims. So Kant hoped for perpetual peace and the unity of mankind, 'but was relatively pessimistic about human perfectibility';[37] Mill was dispositionally a perfectibilist ('the general tendency is . . . a tendency towards a better and happier state'[38]), but as Song points out, Mill

---

[32] Song, *Christianity*, pp. 38–9.

[33] Song, *Christianity*, p. 50.

[34] Song, *Christianity*, p. 64. Reinhold Niebuhr, *The Nature and Destiny of Man* (London: Nisbet, 1943), ii, 331.

[35] Song, *Christianity*, p. 71.

[36] Song, *Christianity*, p. 71.

[37] Song, *Christianity*, p. 72.

[38] Ibid. The Mill reference is, 'A System of Logic Ratiocinative and Inductive', in *The Collected Works of John Stuart Mill*, ed. J. M. Robson (London: Routledge, 1974), Vol. VI, p. 3.

also feared the coming of democracy, and 'hardly owned to a massive historical idealism'.[39]

O'Donovan's strictures against liberalism are counter-balanced with his acknowledgement that 'the liberal tradition . . . has right of possession . . . we cannot simply go behind it; it has the status of a church tradition, and demands to be treated with respect'.[40] O'Donovan, like Song, has a rich appreciation of the different strands that make up modernity:

> As it has gained in sophistication, modernity-criticism has shown more clearly the multiplicity of threads from which the fabric is woven, and so has allowed us to think of other liberalisms, different possibilities of combination and development from those which have woven our contemporary bondage. By way of this closer view of the weaving of modernity, we are free to discern both the triumph of Christ in liberal institutions and the coming of the Antichrist.[41]

It is precisely this 'closer view of the weaving of modernity' which I am engaged upon in this book, and I attach myself emphatically to O'Donovan's observation that 'the liberal tradition is not homogenous or unchanging, and its central Christian witness does not always lie on the surface'.[42] O'Donovan's most severe judgements, the outline of which I gave above, are reserved more for 'late-modern' liberalism, with its confidence in the human will, constructivism and technology. O'Donovan provides a more mixed report for the 'early modern liberalism' of Locke, Hobbes and Kant, 'a composite of rationalist, romantic and sceptical influences as well as Christian, some of them tending to subvert, some to strengthen the Christian contribution'.[43] Early modern liberalism has the watermark of Christendom running through it.

There are at least three areas in which O'Donovan perceives the legacy of Christendom in early modern liberalism: the responsibility of rulers; the rule of law and tolerance. On the first motif O'Donovan comments that 'the political doctrine that emerged from

---

[39] Song, *Christianity*, p. 72.
[40] O'Donovan, *Desire*, p. 229.
[41] O'Donovan, *Desire*, p. 228.
[42] O'Donovan, *Desire*, p. 229.
[43] O'Donovan, *Desire*, p. 229.

Christendom is characterised by a notion that government is responsible'.[44] Because of the division between the two Kingdoms, the lack
of identification between the two Cities, 'rulers, overcome by Christ's
victory, exist provisionally and on sufferance for specific purposes. In
the church they have to confront a society which witnesses to the
Kingdom under which they stand and before which they must dis-
appear. It is to that conception we refer when we describe political
authority in terms of "the state".' This was a concept unknown to
the ancient world, describing something new, 'a form of political
authority which has come to understand itself differently as a result
of Christ's triumph'.[45] The notion that rulers are provisional and on
sufferance for specific purposes – vehicles of an authority which is
not intrinsic to them – is broadly what makes possible the liberal conception of power invested in government: provisional, instrumental,
answerable. Furthermore, the influence of Christendom is to be
discerned in the liberal emphasis on law. Under Christendom the
'state exists in order to give judgement; but under the authority of
Christ's rule it gives judgement *under law*, never as its own law. One
might say that the only sense of political authority acknowledged
within Christendom was the law of the ascended Christ, and that all
political authority was the authority of that law.'[46]

A third 'Christian' feature of early modern liberalism discussed by
O'Donovan – tolerance – owes less to Christendom than a certain
Protestant understanding of the relationship between an individual's
faith and reason. So for early liberals

> the dialectical struggle of rational debate, in which each side
> marshals arguments to bring the other to agreement, seemed . . . a
> healthy thing, the proper alternative to violent struggle. In an
> argument which had currency from Milton to Mill, they pleaded
> for the toleration of erroneous beliefs precisely on the ground that
> they stimulated rational discussion and so assisted the common
> quest for truth without approving the hope that common persua-
> sions may emerge from it. They thought there was nothing to
> fear from shared convictions if they were rationally reached and
> rationally held.[47]

This theological resonance of early modern liberalism has been

---

[44] O'Donovan, *Desire*, p. 231.
[45] O'Donovan, *Desire*, p. 231.
[46] O'Donovan, *Desire*, p. 233.
[47] O'Donovan, *Desire*, p. 221.

of interest to David Fergusson also, whose work is exemplary for a subtle appreciation of the strengths of liberalism. So Fergusson outlines the theological case for tolerance in the early modern period as being 'based on a cluster of related arguments – the example of Christ and the early church, the limits of state power, the irrationality of coercion, the sanctity of each person's faith commitment, the need for peace and social cohesion, and the promotion of conversation and debate amongst those who differ for the sake of a greater approximation to God's truth'.[48] The truth of Fergusson's claim about the theological origins of 'liberal' toleration can be shown strictly and biographically by looking at Locke's *Four Letters on Toleration*,[49] where we find Locke stating that 'the toleration of those that differ from others in matters of religion, is so agreeable to the Gospel of Jesus Christ, and to the genuine reason of mankind, that it seems monstrous for men to be so blind, as not to perceive the necessity and advantage of it, in so clear a light'.[50] The theological non-intervention of the state, and the tolerance of religious diversity, are absolutely necessary given the nature of faith as autonomous, reasoned and individual:

> All the life and power of true religion consists in the outward and full persuasion of the mind; and faith is not faith without believing. Whatever profession we make, to whatever outward worship we conform, if we are not fully satisfied in our own mind that the one is true, and the other well pleasing unto God, such profession and such practice, far from being any furtherance, are indeed great obstacles to our salvation. For in this manner, instead of expiating other sins by the exercise of religion, I say, in offering thus unto God Almighty such a worship as we esteem to be displeasing unto him, we add unto the number of our other sins, those also of hypocrisy, and contempt of his Divine Majesty.[51]

Fergusson draws contemporary lessons from this theological lineage, that 'these arguments' concerning the relationship between non-coercion, tolerance and faith, 'retain their validity even if more

---

[48] David Fergusson, 'The Reformed Tradition and the Virtue of Tolerance', in *Public Theology for the 21st Century*, ed. William Storrar and Andrew Morton (London: T. & T. Clark International, forthcoming 2004). See also *Community, Liberalism and Christian Ethics* (Cambridge: Cambridge University Press, 1998).

[49] John Locke, *Four Letters on Toleration* (London: Ward, Lock, 1899).

[50] Locke, *Toleration*, p. 5.

[51] Locke, *Toleration*, p. 6.

modern claims for autonomy are found increasingly suspect. At a time when liberalism is under attack, we may need to be reminded of the preceding theological case of toleration.'[52]

Attending to the best contemporary theological treatments of political liberalism – as found in Oliver O'Donovan, Robert Song and David Fergusson – we may be able to discern a new wind, more favourable to liberalism than the likes of Heidegger and Karl Barth. Any enthusiasm for liberalism is muted, reserved, partial and specifically theological, tending to focus on earlier strands of the liberal tradition which are seen to preserve something of their Christian inheritance: the responsibility of rulers, the rule of law and the importance of toleration and freedom of conscience as a necessary but not sufficient pre-condition for faith and salvation. There is, as we have seen, a sense that as time moves on the theological impulses behind liberalism get watered down and corrupted with more dubious preoccupations. The concern of critics such as Song and O'Donovan is that the responsibility of rulers becomes reduced to their instrumental and unprincipled slavery to the ballot box and the stock market. The rule of law is no longer subservient to Christ, but is conceived within a framework where the conventional and constructed nature of order and truth is taken for granted. Tolerance becomes either an indifferent relativism, or itself a paradoxically intolerant ideology which makes impossible more 'coercive' forms of life and traditional communities. But nonetheless, there is an appreciation of the impossibility of simply leaping over liberalism, and the stirrings of an appreciation of its complex conceptual, historical and theological motivations.

I conceive the thesis being argued for here as is in some ways attached to, and in sympathy with, this more considered re-appreciation of aspects of liberalism. Where I would depart significantly from the contemporary literature is in a conviction that it has not in several respects gone far enough. First of all, there is almost no attempt to face with repentance and self-reflexiveness the fairly direct theological responsibility which the Christian tradition has for some of the worst features of crusading liberalism. This narrative, traced especially in Chapter 3, shows that the most divisive, activist and intolerant strands of liberalism arise historically from a too close identification of the visible and invisible Church, and a subsequent anthropology which verges on the perfectibilist and Manichean.

---

[52] Fergusson, 'Reformed Tradition', p. 11.

Theological accounts of liberalism can be very keen to take responsibility for the prettier aspects of liberalism (the responsibility of rulers and freedom of conscience), with the less attractive aspects being ascribed to liberalism's falling away from whatever Christian origins it may have had. On the other hand, there is some reluctance to perceive that the 'pseudo-Messianism' which can be found in liberal progressivist views of history has not *become* superficially attached through a kitsch secular appropriation of theological themes, but was in fact a generating and theological principle of this 'liberal' movement, which can drop the explicit theological reference and then appropriate more 'secular' themes (such as technology or global free-markets).

The second respect in which I would claim that the contemporary re-evaluation of liberalism does not go far enough, is that it fails to see that there is a healthy strand of liberalism – running through the early modern period and still alive in the present day – which is informed by, or at the very least powerfully compatible with, a theological tradition of reckoning with our status as creatures. Even the most appreciative approaches that we have considered are wedded to a characterization of liberalism as voluntaristic, constructivist and broadly progressivist. This critique remains in place, even where some credit is given to liberalism for its emphasis on non-coercive faith, or the de-sacralization of power. So liberalism is held to be 'voluntaristic', in that the individual is conceived as the fundamental ontological unit. The individual, so conceived, is abstracted from contingency, context and history, failing to acknowledge our thrown-projection, our embodiment, or in a more theological key, our createdness. It is 'constructivist' in that all order and value are constructed by the subject, either individually or collectively. It is 'progressivist' in that – even if in a broad and complicated way – history is moving towards a better organization of society and fulfilment of human potential, with liberalism being instrumentally necessary for this progress. This characterization of liberalism is sometimes described as an aspect of the 'modern turn', given powerful philosophical expression by thinkers such as Heidegger and Leo Strauss. In spite of more nuanced appreciations of the virtues of 'early-modern' liberalism, the sense that liberalism belongs on the wrong side of this turn seems always to remain. Where there is divergence, it concerns what we can hope to do about this 'modern turn', of which political liberalism is a symptom, ranging from the 'participatory universe' of Radical Orthodoxy, through to the evangelical-prophetic, eschatological Church uttering its considered 'yes' and 'no' to liberalism.

This characterization of liberalism needs to be challenged. I will present a strand of liberal political thought, focusing in this chapter on Edmund Burke and to a lesser extent Lord Acton, which is in crucial respects anti-voluntaristic, anti-constructivist and anti-progressivist; in short, a strand of liberalism opposed to all those features that are supposed – even on the most generous interpretation – to belong to liberalism, as liberalism in turn belongs to the 'modern turn'. We will find that where the individual is conceived as the basic ontological unit, this is entirely because of a sense of the frailty and createdness of individuals. In these thinkers there is a powerful sense of given and created order, along with a caution which arises from an equally urgent sense of the importance and difficulty of fallen humans reading this order. Will and construction are always balanced by an integrated account of reason, tradition and order. Burkean liberalism is rooted in an Augustinian sense of the complexity and fallenness of history, with no whiff of progressivism or Pelagianism. In showing this tradition of liberalism, I will be challenging the pervasive 'fits all' hermeneutic value of the 'modern turn', and arguing for a much more theologically resounding endorsement of specific liberal movements of thought.

It will also be necessary to show that this theologically subtle and informed liberal tradition did not exhaust itself – as O'Donovan suggests – in an 'early modern period' leading to a monopoly of a much more pernicious voluntaristic liberalism. I argue against this theological narrative by attending in the next chapter to John Rawls, and the debate generated by Rawls. I will suggest that a proper consideration of Rawls shows that there are places where the finest ideals of political liberalism are as alive today as they ever have been. The theological narrative that liberalism has 'fallen' from an early modern state of grace is likely to be as historically unfounded as the inverse Whig narrative of progress. To judge the demise of political liberalism by its worst debasements – hawkish American administrations, corrupt global corporations and popular TV shows – is to invite a similarly ungenerous and unscholarly announcement of the fall of 'Christianity' (in its entirety) on the basis of its worst debasements, for instance, sectarian terrorism, white supremacist groups who appropriate Christian vocabulary, and slick television evangelists.

Edmund Burke and obscured order

My discussion of Burke will move through four stages. First of all, I will demonstrate the unequivocal sense in which Burke is a liberal in the specified sense, accounting at the same time for his trenchant anti-democratic stance, and his apparent inegalitarianism. Second, I will demonstrate Burke's committment to the notion of created order and harmony; at this point I will suggest that the 'modern turn' posited in politics by Leo Strauss would seem not to pertain in crucial respects to Burkean liberalism. This is no insignificant conclusion, as it indicates that there can be non-voluntaristic and non-constructivist insights within the liberal tradition, and so that the hermeneutic value of speaking in blanket terms of the 'modern turn' is too crude and alarmist. The third phase of the discussion shows how Burke has a profound and compassionate sense of human imperfectibility, frailty and complexity, which lends his political thought an allergy to abstraction, metaphysical generalization, extremism and progressivism. We will see how this sense of human imperfectibility is a generating motivation for Burke's liberalism and individualism; although there is unconstructed order and harmony, it is hard – but not impossible – to read it, owing to the obscured quality of the order. Finally, I show how this draws together to produce Burke's spirit of loving reformation: an active and principled commitment to resist abuses of power, but within a framework of constant caution about human nature and action. The City of God is hidden amid the City of Man: attempts to render the heavenly city visible or construct it on earth through human activity, Burke fears, are steeped in blood, the product of a hubristic metaphysical frenzy leading to vast human misery.

Burke's liberalism and Lord Acton

For Burke the centrality of 'liberty' and its inherent relationship to given order is made clear in his *Appeal from the Old to the New Whigs*, where he writes that 'the *distinguishing* part of our constitution . . . is its liberty':

> To preserve that liberty inviolate, is the *peculiar* duty and *proper* trust of a member of the House of Commons. But the liberty, the *only* liberty I mean, is a liberty connected with *order*, and that not

only exists *with* order and virtue, but cannot exist at all *without* them. It inheres in good and steady government, as in *its substance and vital principle*.[53]

Burke's attachment to ordered, rational liberty preserved within historical constitutions makes him hostile to what he understands to be the vacuous formulaic calls for liberty heard in the French Revolution. At the same time, it makes him supportive of the Glorious Revolution of 1688 and the American move to independence: both were, as he understood them, in some sense attempts to protect ancient liberties enjoyed by English subjects from innovation and tyranny imposed by the Government. So Burke appeals to British colonists in North America as fellow 'men of liberal minds',[54] who enjoy the 'large and liberal platform of common liberty'[55] which unites the Americans and the 'largest and soundest' part of 'this kingdom' (England), where originated the 'very liberty which you (the Americans) so justly prize'.[56] The Americans were increasingly unhappy with insensitive colonial rule, featuring oppressive taxation without consent or representation. Burke concedes that the behaviour of the English administration has been so bad that even a revolution and subsequent 'series of wars and contentions amongst yourselves . . . might be worth the risk to men of honour, when rational liberty is at stake'.[57] The revolutionaries, provoked by an illiberal British administration, '*have and . . . hold* to that foundation of common liberty' and as such are 'the only true Englishmen', with the English administration of Lord North and others being 'corrupted in blood, and wholly fallen from their original rank and value' being the 'real rebels to the fair constitution and just supremacy of England'.[58]

Already we see that Burke's position is subtle enough to support reform of a significant kind – to the point of revolution – and is far from being a eulogy to the powers that be, with it being possible to castigate British prime ministers as 'rebels' when they threaten the

---

[53] Edmund Burke, 'Appeal from the New to the Old Whigs', in *The Works and Correspondence of the Rt. Hon. Edmund Burke*, Vol. iv (London: Francis and John Rivington, 1852), p. 417.

[54] Edmund Burke, 'An Address to the British Colonists in North America', in *Works and Correspondence*, Vol. v, p. 544.

[55] Burke, 'Address', p. 540.

[56] Burke, 'Address', p. 544.

[57] Burke, 'Address', p. 544.

[58] Burke, 'Address', pp. 543–4.

common liberties of the subject. The popular image of Burke – as a Tory defender of an oppressive status quo – can be an impediment to serious consideration of his stature and thought, and a little background here may be helpful. In fact Burke was a Whig and spent most of his active political life opposing the Tories, and in his own words in 'constant attempts to reform abuses in government'.[59] Burke may have in mind his piloting of the Catholic Relief Act though the Commons in 1778; his spirited attacks on the oppressive taxation enforced by the American Stamp Act and the Massachusetts Bay Regulation Bill; attempts up to and through the American War of Independence to get the House to grant American independence, and his attempt to impeach Warren Hastings, Director of the East India Company, for British atrocities in India. So in speeches before Parliament Burke accused Hastings and his agents of showing 'the avarice of English dominion' with an 'unbounded license to plunder'. Burke complained that they built no schools, no hospitals, no bridges, but were merely out for 'profit' and 'the transmission of great wealth to this country'.[60] On Britain's responsibilities in America, India and Ireland, Burke is a more nuanced figure than in his pontifications on France – for which he is best known – where his genuinely interesting critique of the Revolution is at times alarmingly and gratuitously tied up with a romantic, chivalrously blinkered, and almost nauseating defence of the *ancien régime*.

Another clear indication of Burke's political liberalism is his attitude to religion. The state must be silent about religious truth, not because there is none, but because it is hard to discern, and the attempt to impose upon others leads to conflict and oppression. So we have the characteristic liberal call to religious tolerance, based first of all upon a sense of a lack of certainty in religious matters, but then justified in terms of the Christian virtue of charity: 'Perhaps [religious] truth may be far better [than social peace]. But as we have scarcely ever the same certainty in the one that we have in the other, I would, unless the truth were evident indeed, hold fast to peace, which has in her company charity, the highest of virtues.'[61] Burke is explicit that authority derives from consent, expressed over time

[59] Burke, 'Appeal', p. 422.

[60] Edmund Burke, 'Speech on the Impeachment of Warren Hastings' (3rd Day, 18 February 1788), in *The Works of the Right Honourable Edmund Burke* (London: Bohn Standard Library, 1877–84), Vol. 7, pp. 43–5.

[61] Edmund Burke, 'A Letter on the Affairs of Ireland, written in the year 1797', in *Works and Correspondence*, Vol. VI, pp. 75–6.

within a mixed constitution. A certain amount of relearning of the 'conservative' Burke might be required to see this point. Burke does not believe in democratic elections as the effective mechanism for representing the people and protecting their ancient liberties (the purpose of government, in Burke's view). He believes, as we may not, in custom, tradition, history and the common law, and in the representation of the people in a largely undemocratic mixed constitution. But the crucial liberal point is that authority is derived by popular consent, and is ordered towards the preservation of the subject's life, liberty and property. How that consent is registered is another matter; elective democratic representation is not necessary to political liberalism. Rather democratic representation through elections is thought by some to be the only effective guarantor of liberalism, or to be a legitimate expression of it; by others, such as Burke, democratic representation through polling is conceived to be a dangerous threat to political liberalism.

The greatest danger to the liberties of individuals is arbitrary rule, the overpowering of rational government. Burke considers that democracy is a great danger to liberalism – indeed 'the most false, wicked, and mischievous doctrine that ever could be preached to [the people]' – because it fosters and nourishes a desire for arbitrary power:

> . . . arbitrary power is so much to the depraved taste of the vulgar, of the vulgar of every description, that almost all the dissensions, which lacerate the commonwealth, are not concerning the manner in which it is to be exercised, but concerning the hands in which it is to be placed. Somewhere they are resolved to have it. Whether they desire it to be vested in the many or the few, depends with most men upon the chance which they imagine they themselves may have or partaking in the exercise of that arbitrary sway, in the one mode or in the other.[62]

The broader lesson to be learnt from Burke's anti-democratic stance is that attitudes to representative mechanisms of democracy are no litmus test for a thinker's political liberalism, especially where there is a concern about the frailty and fallenness of individuals, and the potential tyranny of majorities over the liberties of individuals (the great liberal passion).

---

[62] Burke, 'Appeal', p. 459.

This passion comes to the fore where Burke expresses his concern about the ambitions of the post-revolutionary French state:

> Individuality is left out of their scheme of Government. The state is all in all. Everything is referred to the production of force; afterwards everything is entrusted to the use of it. It is military in its principle, in its maxims, in its spirit, and in all its movements. The state has dominion and conquest for its sole object; dominion over minds by proselytism, over bodies by arms.[63]

This violates the principle that the state 'has been made to the people, not the people conformed to the state'. Not only should the state seek 'every sort of social advantage', but it should also cultivate 'the welfare of every individual'. Countries that value liberty are such that 'the objects (the ends) which they embrace are of the greatest possible variety, and have become in a manner infinite'. This means necessarily that no one plan or end will be pursued, for the ends of individuals are various and not to be lightly trampled upon. Burke fears the way in which the French state is 'considered as a great machine' which operates 'for some one great end'. Burke is more comfortable with the British state, because in his view it 'pursues the greatest variety of ends, and is the least disposed to sacrifice any one of them to another, or to the whole':

> It aims at taking in the entire circle of human desires, and securing for them their fair enjoyment. Our legislature has been ever closely connected, in its most efficient part, with individual feeling, and individual interest. Personal liberty, the most lively of these feelings and the most important of these interests, which in other European countries has rather arisen from the system of manners and the habitudes of life, than from the laws of the state, (in which it flourished more from neglect than attention) in England, has been a direct object of government.[64]

Whatever we make of the comparative politics here, these comments underline the importance to Burke of the personal liberty of subjects to frame and pursue – without state interference – their own ends,

---

[63] Edmund Burke, 'Second Letter on a Regicide Peace', in *Works and Correspondence*, Vol. V, p. 340.

[64] Burke, 'Second Letter', pp. 339–40.

various and incompatible as these may be. This must be one of the
enduring pedal notes of all variations of political liberalism, and
Burke's political thought at points resonates deeply with it.

A feature of Burke's thinking which might be thought to be in
tension with other aspects of the liberal tradition is his hostility to
calls for equality, compounded by his troublesome and at times
effusive affection for aristocracy. The liberal tradition is usually com-
mited to some notion of the equality of citizens. There can be no
doubt that aspects of Burke's thought are in tension with a more
developed and egalitarian liberalism; Burke is a multi-valenced
thinker who became important for traditions other than the liberal
one that I am highlighting. Nonetheless, there is something which
can be said to mitigate the 'offence' (in politically liberal terms) of
Burke's apparent inegalitarianism.

Taking an unambiguously political liberal thinker such as John
Rawls – whom I will discuss extensively in the next chapter – we find
that he is able to endorse a 'complex egalitarianism' when unpacking
what is involved in a society of 'free and equal citizens'. A complex
egalitarianism does not call for a levelling of all resources, wealth and
symbolic power. Rather the maxim is that inequalities are justified
inasmuch as the least advantaged are better off with them than they
would be without them. Although Rawls comments that contemporary American culture is a long way from being in such a position,
some inequality is in principle acceptable, if it is to the 'greatest
benefit of the least-advantaged members of society'.[65] Burke's position is in fact not so different, in that he certainly considers the least
advantaged to be better off with the inequalities than without them.
He makes a distinction between 'levelling' and 'equalizing', where
the former is a blanket reduction of all to the same estate, and the
latter is more like a just distribution of resources (material and
symbolic) according to – as Burke sees it – merit, need (widely understood) and overall utility. Burke's conviction is that 'those who
attempt to level, never equalize', for 'in all societies, consisting
of various descriptions of citizens, some description must be
upper-most'.[66]

Although we may not agree with Burke's view here, that he
defends an unequal distribution of resources and power hardly dis-

---

[65] John Rawls, *Justice as Fairness: A Restatement*, ed. Erin Kelly (Cambridge,
Mass.: Harvard University Press, 2001), p. 43.
[66] Edmund Burke, 'Reflections on the Revolution in France', in *Works and
Correspondence*, Vol. IV, p. 190.

qualifies him from being a 'liberal'. Otherwise seminally liberal thinkers such as Locke and Hayek would be disqualified, supporting as they do unequal distribution of resources for a mixture of reasons to do with merit, need and overall utility. Burke's aversion to levelling programmes is made more comprehensible in the light of his attachment to 'order', and his wariness about the 'tricks and devices of human skill', both of which I will go on to discuss.

Even the impact of Burke's interest in the aristocracy can be mitigated by reflecting on the intentions behind both Burke's endorsement and Rawlsian 'complex egalitarianism'. The importance Burke places in aristocrats does not arise from any sense that the aristocrat is necessarily a more excellent human being (although he *should* have certain virtues attendant upon his birth and education, as each of the estates should), or deserves more protection under the law; Burke is not inegalitarian in that sense. Rather, Burke considers that the historical institution of aristocracy is a vital protection of certain basic liberties of the subject. This argument was prevalent in an English republican tradition, with Milton praising 'those faithful and courageous barons' of the Middle Ages 'who lost their lives in the field, making glorious war against the tyrants for the common liberty'.[67] A similar expectation of the nobility was espoused after the Restoration by the republican writer Algernon Sidney who recalled the 'ancient', 'warlike', 'powerful, gallant nobility' who had spirits 'suitable to their births' and who had been able to protect the liberties of the subject, 'to restrain the exorbitances that either the king, or the commons might run into'.[68] Burke is less convinced about the personal merits of aristocrats, commenting that the House of Lords were 'in general, languid, scrupulous, and unsystematic', although 'on the whole' Burke inclines to the view that 'the faults in . . . [the Lords] . . . are no more than the ordinary frailties of human nature'.[69] Nonetheless, that the nobles had something of a protective national role for Burke is made clear, for instance, in a letter to the Duke of Richmond where he instructs his grace that 'you, if you are what you

---

[67] John Milton, *The Complete Prose Works of John Milton*, ed. D. M. Wolfe, 8 vols. (New Haven: Yale University Press, 1952–82), Vol. III, p. 343. My comments on the English republican tradition are indebted to Blair Worden's article 'English Republicanism' in J. H. Burns (ed.), *The Cambridge History of Political Thought 1450–1700* (Cambridge: Cambridge University Press, 1991), pp. 443–75. For the discussion of Milton and Sidney see p. 459.

[68] Robert Molesworth, *An Account of Denmark* (London: 1694), p. 70.

[69] Edmund Burke, *Letter to the Duke of Richmond Nov 17 1772*, in *Works and Correspondence*, Vol. I, p. 187.

ought to be, are the great oaks that shade a country and perpetuate your benefits from Generation to Generation'.[70]

Nevertheless, the aristocrat is often not what he ought to be, and Burke is frequently exhausted and exasperated by the behaviour of actual nobility. So in 1795 Burke complained of how the Duke of Bedford oppressed the industry of the 'common man', by which Burke meant himself, being as he was of fairly humble origins: 'The Duke of Bedford is the leviathan among all the creatures of the crown. He tumbles about his unwieldy bulk, he plays and frolics in the ocean of royal bounty. Huge as he is . . . he is still a creature.'[71] Burke goes on to describe his grace's 'ribs, his fins, his whale bone, his blubber, the very spiracles through which he spouts a torrent of brine against his origin, and covers me all over with the spray'.[72]

So Burke's affection for aristocracy is not straightforward. He tends to demand from aristocrats the stability and protections we would expect from more democratic institutions. The difference between a thinker like Burke and John Rawls is less a substantial one concerning the intrinsic excellence of persons, leading to a different standing before the law; the concern is more how best to preserve (as we would understand them) liberal protections. For Rawls, inequalities are justified if under them the least advantaged are still better off than they would be with greater equality; this, however erroneous, would be the grounds of Burke's defence of aristocracy.

Lord Acton, the nineteenth-century liberal, was so explicitly concerned with the theological basis of his political liberalism, that he proclaimed to have 'renounced everything in Catholicism which was not compatible with Liberty, and everything in Politics which was not compatible with Catholicity'.[73] Although Acton conceded that 'liberty' was 'an idea of which there are two hundred definitions',[74] it was recognizable most of all by the absence of arbitrary rule and the protection of the liberties of individuals: 'you will know it by outward signs: Representation, the extinction of slavery . . . and the like;

---

[70] Burke, 'Richmond', p. 190.

[71] Edmund Burke, 'A Letter to a Noble Lord', in *Works and Correspondence*, Vol. v, pp. 215–50.

[72] Burke, 'Letter', pp. 215–50.

[73] Lord Acton, *Essays on Freedom and Power* (Boston, Mass.: The Beacon Press, 1948), p. lvi.

[74] From his Inaugural Lecture delivered at Cambridge, 11 June 1895, reprinted in *Lectures on Modern History* (London and New York: Macmillan, 1906), pp. 12–13.

better still by less apparent evidences: the security of the weaker groups and the liberty of conscience, which, effectually secured, secures the rest'.[75] Acton was convinced that 'politics is an affair of principle, that it is an affair of morality, that it touches eternal interests as much as vices and virtues do in public life'.[76] Concerning Burke, Acton wrote to Gladstone 'some day, I shall say to a pupil: Read Burke night and day. He is our best political writer, and the deepest of all Whigs.'[77] No one could deny the 'liberal' credentials of Acton and Gladstone (if they are not liberals, the category is an empty one); Acton's deep admiration of Burke, and his proclaiming Burke as 'the deepest of all Whigs', with Whiggery to an extent becoming nineteenth-century Gladstonian liberalism,[78] is perhaps a testimony to the possibilities of a liberal reading of Burke.

Acton, like Burke, had a theological appreciation of the need to protect individuals both because of the dignity of our freedom, and the wretchedness of our fallen condition: 'now as heretofore, the Men of the Time are, in most cases, unprincipled, and act from motives of interest, of passion, of prejudice cherished and unchecked, of selfish hope or unworthy fear'.[79] This criticism is rooted explicitly in Acton's Christian beliefs:

> The Christian is bound by his very creed to suspect evil, and cannot release himself . . . religion has brought evil to light in a way in which it never was before; it has shown its depth, subtlety, ubiquity; and a revelation, full of mercy on the one hand, is terrible in its exposure of the world's real state on the other. The Gospel fastens the sense of evil upon the mind; a Christian is enlightened, hardened, sharpened, as to evil; he sees it where others do not . . . He owns the doctrine of original sin; that doctrine puts him necessarily on his guard against all appearances,

---

[75] Acton, *Lectures*, pp. 12–13.

[76] *Letters of Lord Acton to Mary Gladstone*, ed. Herbert Paul (London and New York: Macmillan, 1904), p. 105.

[77] Scholarly integrity demands that I complete Acton's sentence: '. . . and he (the student) will answer: Dear Me! I thought he broke up the party, carried it over to the Tories, admired the despotism of the Bourbons, and trained no end of men towards Conservatism? I shall have to answer: So he did. Both sayings are true.' In *Lord Acton and His Circle*, ed. G. Abbot (London and New York: Gasquet, 1906, p. 60).

[78] Which is not to under-emphasize the importance of other traditions that fed into Gladstonian liberalism, such as the Peelites and Radicals.

[79] *Letters to Mary Gladstone*, p. 228.

sustains his apprehension under perplexity, and prepares him for recognizing anywhere what he knows to be everywhere.[80]

Here we have a liberal denying the supposedly 'liberal' conviction that evils can be eliminated by education, social programmes or better government. In Acton's famous dictums that 'progress is the religion of those who have none'[81] and 'power tends to corrupt and absolute power corrupts absolutely',[82] we have a sense that there is an irreducible wickedness in human nature, a general, basic and radical evil. Himmelfarb comments that this sense 'depended upon the paradoxical insight that men are sinful creatures, not to be confused with God, and that, created in the likeness of God, they have spiritual needs that no amount of material well-being can satisfy'.[83] As with Burke there is a sense that human nature is both created and fallen, and that liberal political institutions that protect the frail and dependent individual must contain this wickedness.

At the same time, Acton disagrees with Burke's prescription as to how these protections are to be maintained. Although both fear the tyranny of the majority, Acton's suspicion of human nature is more consistently applied across the board than Burke's, and lacks the latter's high expectations of aristocrats and the *ancien régime*. Consequently Acton supports the expansion of democracy in the form of the Reform Acts of the 1830s, commenting that 'the danger is not that a particular class is unfit to govern. Every class is unfit to govern.'[84] We would endorse Acton's censure of Burke, and the recognition of the vital role of democracy as one of the protections of liberal democracy within a mixed constitution.

Leo Strauss: order and nature

Leo Strauss tells a story about the demise of the notion of natural law in political philosophy. It is my conviction that Burke creates problems for this story, and that once the narrative framework has been pierced in one place, other fragments seem to fit the accepted picture less comfortably. The story Strauss tells goes something like this. In the eighteenth century modern natural science destroyed 'the

---

[80] Acton, 'Study of History', in *Essays*, p. 28.
[81] Acton, *Essays*, p. xxxviii. Quoting from Add. MSS., 5648.
[82] 'Acton–Creighton Correspondence' in Acton, *Essays*, p. 364.
[83] Acton, 'Introduction', *Essays*, p. l.
[84] Acton, *Letters to Mary Gladstone*, p. 196.

teleological view of the universe, of which the teleological view of man forms a part'.[85] It was found to be unpalatable to follow up the non-teleological conception of the universe with a similarly non-teleological account of human life as 'it seemed to be impossible to give an adequate account of human ends by conceiving of them merely as posited by desires or impulses'.[86] The unstable solution found was 'to accept a fundamental, typically modern, dualism of a nonteleological natural science and a teleological science of man'.[87] An attempt was made to locate the difference between man and non-human nature in the dimension of history, 'history was thought to supply the only empirical, and hence the only solid, knowledge of what is truly human, of man as man: of his greatness and misery'.[88] At the same time, empirical historical study revealed a great diversity and plurality of forms of life, challenging the very notion that there is anything at all which constitutes man's nature, 'man as man'.[89] This presented a challenge to natural right doctrines, which 'claim that the fundamentals of justice are, in principle, accessible to man as man. They presuppose, therefore, that a most important truth can, in principle, be accessible to man as man.'[90] What started as an attempt to mark out the teleological nature of man within an historical dimension becomes a 'radical historicism' which 'asserts that the basic insight into the essential limitation of all human thought is not accessible to man as man, or that it is not the result of the progress of the labor of human thought, but that it is an unforeseeable gift of unfathomable fate'.[91] 'Fate' stands for all the contingency of our thrownness in the world, rendering us incapable of speaking about any 'essential' nature, rather than our constructed social roles and identities. Radical historicism, coupled with the supposed impossibility of going from factual statements to value judgements, led to the demise of natural right doctrines, and the death of any notion of unconstructed, given order.

Ultimately responsible for this demise of the natural law tradition is the modern turn away from attending to eternal order, towards

---

[85] Leo Strauss, *Natural Right and Reason* (Chicago: University of Chicago Press, 1953), p. 8.
[86] Strauss, *Natural Right*, p. 8.
[87] Strauss, *Natural Right*, p. 8.
[88] Strauss, *Natural Right*, p. 17.
[89] Strauss, *Natural Right*, p. 28.
[90] Strauss, *Natural Right*, p. 28.
[91] Strauss, *Natural Right*, p. 28.

attending to human construction. The account of how this happens given by Strauss is complex, and needs some unteasing. First of all, the difference between the modern and the pre-modern is distinctly *not*, for Strauss, that the moderns are sceptical about natural law, whereas the pre-moderns thought it possible to read the natural law, the purposes of creation from creation itself. Strauss insists that being bewildered by the 'variety of notions of right' and so moving towards the 'nonexistence of natural right' 'is as old as political philosophy itself'.[92] Rather, the difference between classical and modern approaches for Strauss seems to be the following.

The classical approach

Even where there is not a sense of natural law, there is nevertheless a view that there is a natural and eternal order, not constructed by human convention. Because of the epistemological difficulty of reading this order, in human and political affairs it may be that we have little to go on except convention, an 'agreement which may produce peace' but 'not truth'.[93] The crucial difficulty here is epistemological. There is an eternal and natural order, which in principle could be known, but in practice this is so difficult that we must rely on convention, although 'nature is of incomparably higher dignity than convention of the fiat of society'.[94] Although convention can be given an important role, it is 'originally an inadequate attempt to answer the question of the all-comprehensive truth of the eternal order . . . The fundamental premise of conventionalism is, then, nothing other than the idea of philosophy as the attempt to grasp the eternal.'[95]

The 'modern turn' and the modern denial of natural right takes the following form:

The modern approach

The difficulty with natural right – and its associated notions of order, law and harmony – for the modern approach is not epistemological but ontological. There is no sense that it is 'difficult' to discern order, in that there just is no natural and eternal order which it could be

---

[92] Strauss, *Natural Right*, p. 10.
[93] Strauss, *Natural Right*, p. 11.
[94] Strauss, *Natural Right*, p. 11.
[95] Strauss, *Natural Right*, p. 12.

difficult to read. So 'the adherents of the modern historical view . . .
reject as mythical the premise that nature is the norm; they reject the
premise that nature is of higher dignity than any works of man'.[96]
This lends an importance to convention that was not there on the
classical view. On the classical view, convention is in principle
answerable to a non-constructed order; whereas on the modern view
there is no ontological lever with which one can be sceptical about
human conventions. Where grasping the eternal is in principle
impossible (because of its completely noumenal status, or because
everything is a human construction), the 'eternal' becomes in practice
irrelevant. Where the classical approach sees 'philosophy as the
attempt to grasp the eternal', 'the modern opponents of natural right
reject precisely this idea. According to them, all human thought is
historical and hence unable ever to grasp anything eternal.'[97] 'The
contemporary rejection of natural right in the name of history is
based', writes Strauss 'not on historical evidence, but on a philosophical critique of the possibility or knowability of natural right.'[98]
This 'critique of the possibility or knowability' of natural right goes
beyond the epistemological difficulties of the classical approach.
Rather it asserts that it is in principle impossible to know, just
because there is nothing to know.

Some attention to crucial passages in Burke reveal that he fits
Strauss's 'classical' model much more closely than the 'modern'.
Burke it seems, and Burkean liberalism, is on the wrong side of the
modern turn. And if Burkean liberalism is, what else might be?
The 'modern turn' has something of the status of a Kuhnian paradigm. A certain amount of marginal counter evidence can be accommodated, and the paradigm can remain because of its overall utility
and persuasiveness. But if the evidence against the paradigm is too
great, then it can be toppled. Then fragmented pieces, which previously might have been easily ignored, can begin to assume their own
pattern and centrality. There is, of course, no intention to replace one
monolithic impression of liberalism with another one, and there are
features of liberalism that the 'modern turn' explains well, just as
there were features of the universe explained well by the Ptolemaic
world-view.

The Straussian paradigm begins to be stretched, then, when we

---

[96] Strauss, *Natural Right*, p. 11.
[97] Strauss, *Natural Right*, p. 12.
[98] Strauss, *Natural Right*, p. 12.

hear Burke proclaim that 'I love order . . . for the universe is order'.[99] God is 'the awful Author of our being' and 'the Author of our place in the order of existence'. Burke finds that order is 'made to us, and we are made to it'. We are all bound by the law that God has pre-scribed for us. This 'great immutable, pre-existent law' connects us with the 'eternal frame of the universe'.[100] This eternal law gives our conventions 'all the force and sanction they can have'.[101] It simply cannot be said that Burke has no sense of the answerability of human convention to the 'eternal law' when we hear him say such things as 'each contract of each particular state is but a clause in the great primeval contract of eternal society, linking the lower with the higher natures, connecting the visible and invisible world, according to a fixed compact sanctioned by the inviolable oath which holds all physical and all moral natures, each in their appointed place'.[102] The different contracts made by political societies are as 'municipal corporations' of a 'universal kingdom'. There is certainly none of the 'liberal' or 'modern' confidence in human ability to freely construct order and meaning when Burke tells us that these 'municipal corpo-rations' are 'not morally at liberty at their pleasure, and on their speculations of a contingent improvement, wholly to separate and tear asunder the bands of their subordinate community, and to dis-solve it into an unsocial, uncivil, unconnected chaos of elementary principles'.[103]

For Burke there is an eternal order – it is hard to read, but human convention is answerable to it. This is essentially the 'classical' point of view on Strauss's scheme. There is in political and moral matters 'a necessity that is not chosen, but chooses, a necessity paramount to deliberation, that admits no discussion, and demands no evi-dence'.[104] Burke considers political society to be ordered, by the consent of the people, for the preservation of the liberty of indi-viduals. At the same time he has a powerful sense of our thrownness, the contingency and createdness of the human condition, 'this neces-sity . . . is part . . . of that moral and physical disposition of things, to

---

[99] Edmund Burke, *The Correspondence of Edmund Burke* (Chicago and Cambridge University Presses, 1958–70), Vol. VI, p. 460.

[100] Burke, *Correspondence*, Vol. VI, p. 75.

[101] Burke, *Correspondence*, Vol. VI, p. 75.

[102] Burke, 'Reflections on the Revolution in France', in *Works and Corre-spondence*, Vol. IV, p. 230.

[103] Burke, 'Reflections', p. 230.

[104] Burke, 'Reflections', p. 230.

which man must be obedient by consent of force'.[105] When human hubris leads man to break away from his createdness – as Burke understands it – and to treat the eternal law as an 'object of choice' then 'the law is broken, nature is disobeyed, and the rebellious are outlawed, cast forth, and exiled, from this world of reason, and order, and peace, and virtue, and fruitful penitence, into the antagonist world of madness, discord, vice, confusion, and unavailing sorrow'.[106]

Now it is true that Burke places a high importance on convention, custom, prescription and artifice in political affairs. This in no way contradicts his reverence for the natural order; rather it is an intense expression of it. The human mind and human reason are part of the natural order, and nature – richly understood as a continuity running through all of creation – commands that we obey convention, custom and prescription. So Burke tells us that 'in all things whatever, the mind is the most valuable and the most important'.[107] We then have a classically Aristotelian expression of reason as the informing principle, just as 'the beast is an informing principle to the plough and cart, the labourer is as reason to the beast; and the farmer is as a thinking and presiding principle to the labourer'.[108] In a crucial passage linking Burke's understanding of artificiality and 'natural law', we see that there is no tension between the two, just because art is 'man's nature':

> The state of civil society . . . is a state of nature; and much more truly so than a savage and incoherent mode of life. For man is by nature reasonable; and he is never perfectly in his natural state, but when he is placed where reason may be best cultivated, and most predominates. Art is man's nature. We are as much, at least, in a state of nature in formed manhood, as in immature and helpless infancy. Men, qualified in the manner I have just described, form in nature, as she operates in the common modification of society, the leading, guiding and governing part. It is the soul to the body, without which the man does not exist. To give therefore no more

---

[105] Burke, 'Reflections', p. 230.
[106] Burke, 'Reflections', p. 230.
[107] Burke, 'Reflections', p. 230.
[108] Burke, 'Thoughts and Details on Scarcity', in *Works and Correspondence*, Vol. v, p. 193.

importance, in the social order, to such descriptions of men, than that of so many units, is a horrible usurpation.[109]

So there is a natural law basis to Burke's doctrine of prescription, convention and tradition. Remember that this natural law connects us ultimately to the eternal created order, and so is answerable to that. There is a high importance for convention in Burke, but again, it resembles more the classical view, where the natural order is something apart from and prior to the human, but in which the human participates by virtue of our rational nature. Where there is a difficulty in talking of the natural law – again as with Strauss's classical view – it is in terms of the epistemological difficulty of knowing what it is, given our 'fallible and feeble' natures. Hence, for Burke, the need for institutions and traditions rich in memory and experience:

> Through the same plan of a conformity to nature in our artificial institutions, and by calling in the aid of her unerring and powerful instincts, to fortify the fallible and feeble contrivances of our reason, we have derived several other, and those no small benefits, from considering our liberties in the light of an inheritance.[110]

Burke combines an orientation to the eternal divine law with an endorsement of the local particularity of different forms of government and convention, depending upon the customs and history of various societies. This way of conceiving the relationship between local particularity and divine law is not evidence of a 'modern' constructivism or a creeping relativism, but goes back to a distinction drawn by Augustine between the eternal and temporal law. In *De libero arbitrio* Augustine gives an example of a law which deserves to be called 'eternal':

> . . . consider the law that is called the highest reason, which must always be obeyed, and by which the wicked deserve misery and the good deserve a happy life and by which the law that we agreed to call 'temporal' is rightly enacted and rightly changed. Can anyone of sense deny that this law is unchangeable and eternal?[111]

---

[109] Burke, 'Appeal', p. 467.
[110] Burke, 'Reflections', p. 178.
[111] The translation used is by T. Williams, Augustine, *On Free Choice of the Will*, (Indianapolis/Cambridge: Hackett Publishing Company, 1993), Bk I.6,

As human beings are 'changeable and subject to time',[112] there must also be temporal law 'promulgated in writing helpful to human beings living in this present life'.[113] This law is 'temporal', for 'although it is just, it can justly be changed in the course of time'.[114] These temporal laws, although changeable over time, and variable from people to people, nonetheless gain whatever validity they do from their service to the eternal law. The eternal law that 'is stamped upon our minds is the law according to which it is just that all things be perfectly ordered' and is that 'by which all temporal laws regarding human government can be changed'.[115] Burke is a perfect Augustinian when writing, as quoted above, that 'each contract of each particular state is but a clause in the great primeval contract of eternal society, linking the lower with the higher natures, connecting the visible and invisible world, according to a fixed compact sanctioned by the inviolable oath which holds all physical and all moral natures, each in their appointed place'.[116]

The final nail in the coffin of any attempt to place Burke in the modern 'historical' camp must be his strictures against the importance of the historical dimension. Burke is strong on time, and the frailties and contingencies which belong to our temporal nature, but there is not in Burke any sense that 'history' yields the key to man's unique nature, nor that in any sense it is a progressive or dynamic concept. The crucial category for Burke is constantly temporal nature, rather than a dynamic historical progress or awareness. So

---

p. 11. The original text is as follows: '. . . illa lex quae summa ratio nominatur, cui semper obtemperandum est et per quam mali miseram, boni beatam uitam merentur, per quam denique illa, quam temporalem uocandam diximus, recte fertur recteque mutatur, potestne cuipiam intellegenti non incommutabilis aeternaque uideri?', *De Libero Arbitrio*, Bk I.6, p. 220, in *Aurelii Augustini Opera, Pars I:2: Contra Academicos* in *Corpus Christianorum, Series Latina* 29 (Typographi Brepols Editores Pontificii, 1970).

[112] Augustine, *Free Choice*, p. 10. '. . . Mutabiles temporibusque subjecti . . .', *De Libero Arbitrio*, p. 219.

[113] Augustine, *Free Choice*, p. 10. '. . . Utrum lex quae litteris promulgator hominibus hanc uitam uiuentibus opituletor', *De Libero Arbitrio*, p. 220.

[114] Augustine, *Free Choice*, p. 11. 'Appellemus ergo istam legem . . . temporalem quae quamquam iusta sit, commutari tamen per tempora iuste potest', *De Libero Arbitrio*, p. 220.

[115] Augustine, *Free Choice*, p. 11. 'Cum ergo sit una lex, ex qua illae omnes temporales ad homines regendos uariantur, num ideo ipsa uariari ullo modo potest?', *De Libero Arbitrio*, p. 220.

[116] Burke, 'Reflections', p. 230.

after reaffirming again that 'our political system is placed in a just correspondence and symmetry with the order of the world, and with the mode of existence decreed to a permanent body composed of transitory parts wherein', Burke informs us that:

> . . . the great mysterious incorporation of the human race, the whole, at one time, is never old, or middle-aged, or young, but, in a condition of unchangeable constancy, moves on through the varied tenor of perpetual decay, fall, renovation, and progression. Thus, by preserving the method of nature in the conduct of the state, in what we improve, we are never wholly new; in what we retain, we are never wholly obsolete. By adhering in this manner and on those principles to our forefathers, we are guided not by the superstition of antiquarians, but by the spirit of philosophic analogy.[117]

This passage also explodes the consensus that liberalism is necessarily attached to at least a broad sense of progress; there could be no more perfect expression of the classical Augustinian view of history than Burke's invocation of the 'varied tenor of perpetual decay, fall, renovation, and progression'.[118]

Where there is a difference between Burke and the classical tradition, it lies in the enormous emphasis Burke can put on the individual and the liberties of the individual. Strauss correctly picks up on this, but goes on to draw the wrong implication when he comments that for Burke, 'naturalness and free flowering of individuality are the same',[119] as if Burke is somehow taken in by the 'modern turn' and announces that order and meaning arise from the free construction and expression of individuals. Burke emphasizes the individual not because of the individual's potency and creative constructive abilities, but precisely because of the individual's created, fallen, thrown, frail and complex condition. The protection of individuals needs to be the lynch-pin of political liberalism, just because individuals, taken singly or collectively, are dangerous and fallen. There is such a thing as human wisdom, but it is so obscured and delicate, that it needs to be read off generations, rather than individuals or committees.

---

[117] Burke, 'Reflections', p. 178.
[118] Burke, 'Reflections', p. 178.
[119] Burke, 'Reflections', p. 178.

So the difference between Burke and the 'classical view' as outlined by Strauss is not at all that Burke thinks that there is no eternal order, or that we construct such order that there is, but rather that Burkean liberalism elaborates on a *classical* theme – the epistemological difficulty of reading this order – and adds a theological richness to this in terms of his compassionate sense of human fallenness. There is a greater emphasis on the individual in Burkean liberalism than in Straussian classicism, but this is due to an even more pronounced sense of our created, fallen and thrown condition, answerable to the eternal order which it sees but through a glass darkly. It is certainly not ascribable to the modern disease of believing that individual expressivity, creativity and construction is salvific in itself.

Burke and the politics of fallenness

The third phase of the discussion shows how Burke has a profound and compassionate sense of human imperfectibility, frailty and complexity, which gives his political thought an allergy to abstraction, metaphysical generalization, extremism and progressivism. We will see how this sense of human imperfectibility is a generating motivation for Burke's liberalism and individualism; although there is order and harmony, it is hard – but not impossible – to read it, owing to the obscured quality of the order.

Burke's view is that a tendency towards oversimplistic extremism, generalization and metaphysical abstractions arises from failing to reckon with our complexity, fallenness and fallibility – very similar, as we will see, to the anxieties expressed by Hooker in relation to Puritanism. Failing to account for 'the concerns, the actions' and 'the passions' of men leads thinkers to attempt to treat social knowledge as a species of technical or scientific knowledge, exactly the tendency in 'liberalism' identified by theologians in the wake of Heidegger:

> These philosophers consider men in their experiments, not more than they do mice in an air pump, or in a recipient of mephitic gas . . . It is remarkable, that, in a great arrangement of mankind, not one reference whatsoever is to be found to anything moral or anything politic; nothing that relates to the concerns, the actions, the passions, the interests of men.[120]

---

[120] Burke, 'Letter to a Noble Lord', p. 246.

The need for caution in politics is brought about because of our frail and complex condition. Burke is subtle here, both celebrating our createdness, and lamenting our fallen frailty. So, on the one hand, we find Burke discouraging a lament at the created human condition, stating that 'he censures God who quarrels with the imperfections of man':[121] 'There is no part of our condition, but we ought to submit to with cheerfulness. Why should I desire to be more than man? I have too much reverence for our nature to wish myself divested even of the weak parts of it.'[122] On the other hand the invocation to 'submit . . . with cheerfulness' has to be read against Burke's cautionary stricture that 'the natural progress of the passions, from frailty to vice, ought to be prevented by a watchful eye and a firm hand'.[123] In history 'a great volume is unrolled for our instruction' consisting 'for the greater part' of humanity's slippage from frailty to vice, of the 'miseries brought upon the world by pride, ambition, avarice, revenge, lust, sedition, hypocrisy, ungoverned zeal, and all the train of disorderly appetites, which shake the public with the same'.[124] This is not so different from Richard Hooker's observation that faults that arise 'from the root of human frailty and corruption . . . not only are, but have been always more or less, yea . . . will be till the world's end complained of'.[125] Human nature is imperfect; therefore we should be practical, realistic and compassionate, rather than full of righteousness, pride, extreme idealism or indignation. But there is something from which we have fallen, something we should have been, a moral order exemplifying goodness, beauty and harmony, and we should still orientate ourselves as much as possible to this order.

So Burke sees the need for the irreducible wickedness of the human condition to be contained within stable structures, rather than attempting to eliminate it through radical measures, for

> you would not cure the evil by resolving, that there should be no more monarchs, nor ministers of state, nor of the Gospel; no interpreters of law; no general officers; no public councils. You

---

[121] H. V. F. Somerset (ed.), *A Notebook of Edmund Burke* (Cambridge: Cambridge University Press, 1957), p. 92.

[122] Burke, 'Speech at Bristol, previous to the Election, 1780', in *Works and Correspondence*, Vol. III, p. 411.

[123] Burke, 'Reflections', p. 269.

[124] Burke, 'Reflections', p. 267.

[125] Richard Hooker, 'Laws of Ecclesiastical Polity', preface, ch. III. 7, p. 147.

might change the names. The things in some shape must remain. A certain *quantum* of power must always exist in the community, in some hands, and under some appellation. Wise men will apply their remedies to vices, not to occasional organs by which they act, and the transitory modes in which they appear. Otherwise you will be wise historically, a fool in practice.[126]

If one reacts only to the 'transitory organ' by which 'vice' acts, one will fall foul of the fact that

seldom have two ages the same fashion in their pretexts and the same modes of mischief. Wickedness is a little more inventive. Whilst you are discussing fashion, the fashion is gone by. The very same vice assumes a new body . . . You are terrifying yourselves with ghosts and apparitions, whilst your house is a haunt of robbers. It is thus with all those, who, attending only to the shell and husk of history, think they are waging war with intolerance, pride and cruelty, whilst, under colour of abhorring the ill principles of antiquated parties, they are authorizing and feeding the same odious vices in different factions, and perhaps in worse.[127]

The political implications of Burke's understanding of human weakness contained within a moral framework are well understood by the commentator Michael Freeman:

Men who hate vice too much, says Burke, love men too little. Men of excessive virtue may take excessive measures to bring ordinary men into the path of virtue. In the womb of moral puritanism lies the seed of political authoritarianism. Fanaticism, even if altruistic, perhaps especially when altruistic, poses a greater threat to freedom and humanity than ordinary selfishness. Paradoxically, extreme virtue turns into extreme vice.[128]

Anticipating the Manichaean tendencies of crusading liberalism, which will be discussed in Chapter 3, it is interesting to find Freeman using a similar vocabulary for Burke's critique: 'Burke . . . accused

---

[126] Burke, 'Reflections', p. 267.
[127] Burke, 'Reflections', p. 267.
[128] Michael Freeman, *Burke and the Critique of Political Radicalism* (Oxford: Blackwell, 1980), p. 41.

revolutionaries of Manichaeanism, the belief that the world is divided between the forces of Good and Evil'.[129]

The spirit of loving reformation

A sense of human frailty does not lead into a moral or political nihilism, but rather lends itself naturally to a reforming nature, but reform enacted out of a sense of caution about oneself, compassion for others and a sense of the frailty and limitations of human agency. Burke cautions against a 'mode of arguing from your having done *any* thing in a certain line, to the necessity of doing *every* thing'. Such an approach 'has political consequences of other moment than those of a logical fallacy'.[130]

In his efforts for reform Burke aims to act towards the constitution – 'no simple, no superficial thing, nor to be estimated by superficial understandings'[131] – on the analogy of a 'friend with frailties':[132]

> I think it a duty, in that case, not to inflame the public mind against the obnoxious person, by any exaggeration of his faults. It is our duty rather to palliate his errors and defects, or to cast them into the shade, and industriously to bring forward any good qualities that he may happen to possess.[133]

So, contrary to what is sometimes thought, Burke did not think the British constitution was perfect; it had, he acknowledged, obnoxious elements and faults. Taking the friend analogy further, Burke gives us an account of what the 'spirit of reformation' consists in:

> . . . it then becomes the office of a friend to urge his faults and vices with all the energy of enlightened affection, to paint them in their most vivid colours, and to bring the moral patient to a better habit. Thus I think with regard to individuals; thus I think with regard to ancient and respected governments and orders of men. A spirit of reformation is never more consistent with itself, than when it refuses to be rendered the means of destruction.[134]

---

[129] Freeman, *Burke*, p. 51.
[130] Burke, 'Appeal', p. 422.
[131] Burke, 'Appeal', p. 487.
[132] Burke, 'Appeal', p. 426.
[133] Burke, 'Appeal', p. 426.
[134] Burke, 'Appeal', p. 426.

Destruction, Burke considers, is the likely result when we turn our hand to the transforming – the 'demolition and construction' – of human nature. Here we have a fine statement of the danger of constructionism and the view that the subject can construct itself and society:

> If circumspection and caution are a part of wisdom, when we work only upon inanimate matter, surely they become a part of duty too, when the subject of our demolition and construction is not brick and timber, but sentient beings, by the sudden alteration of whose state, condition, and habits, multitudes may be rendered miserable.[135]

The spirit of loving reformation, which refuses to be 'the means of destruction' is the only approach which recognizes that 'the nature of man is intricate; the objects of society are of the greatest possible complexity; and therefore no simple disposition or direction of power can be suitable either to man's nature, or to the quality of his affairs'.[136] So from considerations to do with human createdness within a moral order, and fallenness from this order, we derive a warning concerning political simplifications and metaphysical generalization, for 'circumstances are infinite, and infinitely combined', they are ' are variable and transient' and 'he, who does not take them into consideration is not erroneous, but stark mad . . . A statesman, never losing sight of principles, is to be guided by circumstances; and judging contrary to the exigencies of the moment he may ruin his country for ever.'[137] In this last sentence we have the createdness and fallenness perfectly poised: the statesman must never lose 'sight of principles', the eternal moral order, but must also be 'guided by circumstances . . . the exigencies of the moment'.

Contrary to the spirit of loving reformation within a framework of obscured order, is a simplistic and metaphysically abstract way of proceeding, such as Burke considered to be at work in the French Revolution. In a sentiment reminiscent of Hooker's warning, which we will come to in the next chapter, against the Puritans who

---

[135] Burke, 'A Letter from Mr. Burke to the Sheriffs of Bristol, on the Affairs of America', in *Works and Correspondence*, Vol. III, p. 322.

[136] Burke, 'Reflections', p. 201.

[137] Burke, 'Letters on a Regicide Peace', in *Works and Correspondence*, Vol. V, p. 307.

'endeavour to purge the earth of all manner of evil',[138] Burke complains about the 'clumsy subtlety' of the revolutionaries' 'political metaphysics',[139] warning of the way in which it can 'sweep the earth with their hurricane, and . . . break up the fountains of the great deep to overwhelm us'.[140] Simplistic abstractions and universal political norms cannot be framed, not because there is no moral order, but because 'the lines of morality are not like ideal lines of mathematics':

> It is not worth our while to discuss, like sophisters, whether, in no case, some evil, for the sake of some benefit, is to be tolerated. Nothing universal can be rationally affirmed on any moral, or any political subject. Pure metaphysical abstraction does not belong to these matters. The lines of morality are not like ideal lines of mathematics. They are broad and deep as well as long. They admit of exceptions; they demand modifications. These exceptions and modifications are not made by the process of logic, but by the rules of prudence. Prudence is not only the first in rank of the virtues political and moral, but she is the director, the regulator, the standard of them all. Metaphysics cannot live without definition; but prudence is cautious how she defines.[141]

As we saw above in Burke's attitude to the 'rebellious' Lord North, we cannot even state universally and in all instances that revolutions are illegitimate. There is just a cautious presumption against them on the basis of a 'parsimony' when it comes to the 'voluntary production of evil':

> Without attempting therefore to define, what never can be defined, the case of a revolution in government, this, I think, may be safely affirmed, that a sore and pressing evil is to be removed, and that a good, great in its amount, and unequivocal in its nature, must be probable almost to certainty, before the inestimable price of our own morals, and the well-being of a number of our fellow-citizens, is paid for a revolution. If ever we ought to be economists even to parsimony, it is in the voluntary production of evil. Every revolution contains in it something of evil.[142]

---

[138] Richard Hooker, *Laws of Ecclesiastical Polity*, preface, Ch. VIII. 6, p. 41.
[139] Burke, 'Reflections', p. 198.
[140] Burke, 'Reflections', p. 198.
[141] Burke, 'Appeal', p. 407.
[142] Burke, 'Appeal', p. 407.

This degree of certainty before radical action is required, for the reason that 'very plausible schemes, with very pleasing commencements, have often shameful and lamentable conclusions. In states there are often some obscure and almost latent causes, things which appear at first view of little moment, on which a very great part of its prosperity or adversity may most essentially depend.'[143] There is a tendency with extreme action to resemble the man 'that sets his house on fire because his fingers are frost-bitten'; such a man, Burke comments, 'can never be a fit instructor in the method of providing our habitations with a cheerful and salutary warmth'.[144]

The problem with 'rights' language – as invoked, for instance, in the French Revolution – is not so much that there is an appeal to nature, or natural purposes and order, but that the appeal is too simplistic, overlooking the way in which 'nature' when it reaches the heights of humanity, is complex, artificial (remember 'art is man's nature') and diverse:

> These metaphysic rights entering into common life, like rays of light which pierce into a dense medium, are, by the laws of nature, refracted from their straight line. Indeed, in the gross and complicated mass of human passions and concerns, the primitive rights of men undergo such a variety of refractions and reflections, that it becomes absurd to talk of them as if they continued in the simplicity of their original direction.[145]

Burke's political instincts are constantly informed by his sense of the frailty and complexity of the human condition, leading to vigilance, caution, self-interrogation and discerning reform: '. . . the nature of man is intricate; the objects of society are of the greatest possible complexity: and therefore no simple disposition or direction of power can be suitable either to man's nature, or to the quality of his affairs'.[146]

Conclusion

In certain specifiable respects, Burke is unequivocally a liberal. Political society is ordered towards the protection of the liberties of

---

[143] Burke, 'Reflections', p. 200.
[144] Burke, 'Appeal', p. 487.
[145] Burke, 'Reflections', p. 201.
[146] Burke, 'Reflections', p. 201.

individuals; authority is derived by the consent of the people within a mixed constitution, and the state must be tolerant of religious diversity, favouring peace over truth. At the same time, the motivating force for his liberal individualism within a mixed constitution is his theological anthropology of the human being as constructed, created, thrown, contingent and fallen. In a more contemporary idiom we might comment that Burke is aware of the subject not as the transcendent source of its own identity and value, but as a site for a complex interweaving of discourses, social, historical and political, which constitute the subject. He is individualistic not because he thinks the individual is self-contained or the ultimate ontological unit. It is *because* the individual is so powerless in the face of her construction amidst a range of discourses over which she has no control, that the political subject must be protected – as much as possible – from the violence and intrusion of other subjects *qua* their life together in the polis.

So, to move back into a theological idiom, we find that Burke exemplifies exactly the sort of 'faith in creation' which O'Donovan can find missing in liberal 'voluntarism':

> Faith in creation means accepting the world downstream of the Arbitrary Original, justified to us in being, goodness and order. Voluntarism, on the other hand, situates the agent at the source; it offers mystical access to the moment of origination, and leads the spirit to the rapture of pure terror before the arbitrariness of its own choice.[147]

Burke speaks of created 'reason, and order, and peace'[148] and 'a necessity that is not chosen, but chooses',[149] combining this with his abhorrence 'since the first dawn of my understanding to this its obscure twilight' of 'all the operations of opinion, fancy, inclination, and will, in the affairs of government'.[150] We could not have a more compelling flesh-and-blood proof of the compatibility, even the binding conceptual momentum, which runs between a strand of political liberalism and a theological critique of voluntarism, constructivism and progressivism.

---

147 O'Donovan, *Desire*, p. 274.
148 Burke, 'Reflections', p. 230.
149 Burke, 'Reflections', p. 230.
150 Burke, 'Letter to a Noble Lord', p. 225.

2

Reciprocity and the Burdens
of Judgement:
Political Liberalism and the Invisible Church

The conception of liberalism which I defend, and find early intimations of in Edmund Burke, is a distinctly political conception, concerned primarily with limiting the scope of the use of public power, given certain general assumptions about the human being: that we are frail, imperfect, complex and that we are neither angels nor demons. The characterization I gave in the last chapter read as follows:

> [Political liberalism] is the conviction that politics is ordered towards peaceful co-existence (the absence of conflict), and the preservation of the liberties of the individual within a pluralistic and tolerant framework, rather than by a search for truth (religious or otherwise), perfection and unity. The crucial ambition of this sort of 'political liberalism' is a refusal to allow public power to enforce on society a substantial and comprehensive conception of the good; driven as it is by its central passion for the liberties of individuals over and above the enthusiasms of other individuals or collectivities. Political authority is wielded on behalf of the people it protects, and is derived ultimately from their consent.

So society is not mandated to attempt to save human souls by the use of public power: whether that be negatively through punishment and sanctions, or positively through incentives and special privileges made dependent upon one adopting a certain comprehensive and substantial conception of the good. By a 'comprehensive conception of the good' I mean a view which covers much more than the framework of laws which govern our life together as citizens. A comprehensive conception would have implications for all manner of concerns about human relationships, human fulfilment and

purposes. It is worth noting here that political liberalism rules out
using public power to support what might be called more comprehensive 'liberalisms'. So, for instance, it would rule out using public
power to impose or promote a notion of Kantian autonomy, or J. S.
Mill's notion of utility.

The contemporary thinker who has most clearly given a conceptual articulation of this distinctly political conception of liberalism is John Rawls. At the same time, I do not consider Rawls to be
the first thinker ever to have articulated such a 'political' conception,
as some of the more enthusiastic Rawlsians tend to claim. So consider Burton Dreben's commentary on the following passage from
Rawls:

> In the society of the Middle Ages, more or less united in affirming
> the Catholic faith, the Inquisition was not an accident. The sup-
> pression of heresy was needed to preserve that shared religious
> belief . . . The same holds, I believe, for any reasonable compre-
> hensive philosophical and moral doctrine, whether religious or
> nonreligious. A society united on a reasonable form of utilitarian-
> ism, or on the reasonable liberalisms of Kant or Mill, will likewise
> require the sanctions of state power to remain so. Call this 'the fact
> of oppression'.[1]

Dreben goes too far when he goes on to claim that 'this . . . has never
been said in the history of philosophy. It is a totally radical view.'[2] In
the rather too rigorous sense that we can never step twice in the same
river, Dreben may speak the truth: no one has said precisely the same
thing within the same theoretical framework, within the same context. But the broadly drawn insight that state power should not be
used to assert or promote religious or moral truth because of the
likelihood of oppression, without prejudging whether there is religious or moral truth, is certainly found in Burke. Remember Burke's
comment in the 'Letter on the Affairs of Ireland': 'Perhaps [religious]
truth may be far better [than social peace]. But as we have scarcely
ever the same certainty in the one that we have in the other, I would,

---

[1] John Rawls, *Political Liberalism* (New York: Columbia University Press,
1993), p. 37.
[2] Burton Dreben, 'On Rawls and Political Liberalism', in *The Cambridge
Companion to Rawls*, ed. S. Freeman (Cambridge: Cambridge University Press,
2003), p. 319.

unless the truth were evident indeed, hold fast to peace, which has in her company charity, the highest of virtues.'[3] The concern about the 'fact of oppression' is clearly in place when Burke expresses unease with the ambitions of the post-revolutionary French state, writing that 'the state has dominion and conquest for its sole object, dominion over minds by proselytism, over bodies by arms'.[4]

The nineteenth-century liberal, Lord Acton, also expresses a caution against using public power to assert a comprehensive conception of the good, whilst robustly holding one of the conceptions which – according to the same view – should not be promoted (in Acton's case Catholicism):

> The state is competent to assign duties and draw the line between good and evil only in its immediate sphere. Beyond the limits of things necessary for its well-being, it can only give indirect help to fight the battle of life by promoting the influences which prevail against temptation, – religion, education, and the distribution of wealth. In ancient times the state absorbed authorities not its own, and intruded on the domain of personal freedom. In the Middle Ages it possessed too little authority, and suffered others to intrude. Modern states fall habitually into both excesses. The most certain test by which we judge whether a country is really free is the amount of security enjoyed by minorities. Liberty, by this definition, is the essential condition and guardian of religion.[5]

The 'others' operative in the Middle Ages include the Roman Catholic Church; Acton was one of Victorian Britain's most distinguished Catholic laymen. If one re-reads the supposedly unprecedented Rawls' quote above, it could almost stand as an acceptable paraphrase of the passage from Acton. One would expect an analytical philosopher to be more wary of negative existentials ('there are no black swans'), especially where history is concerned; Dreben may

---

[3] Burke, 'A Letter on the Affairs of Ireland, written in the year 1797', in *The Works and Correspondence of the Rt. Hon Edmund Burke* (London: John and Francis Rivington, 1852), Vol. VI, pp. 75–6.

[4] Edmund Burke, 'Second Letter on a Regicide Peace', in *Writings and Speeches*, Vol. 9, ed. P. Langford, R. B. MacDowell and William B. Todd (Oxford: Clarendon Press, 1991), pp. 264–96, p. 288.

[5] Lord Acton, 'The History of Freedom in Antiquity', in *Essays on Freedom and Power* (Boston, Mass.: The Beacon Press, 1948), p. 33.

never have read anything like Rawls before, but this is distinct from nothing like it ever having been said.

Rawls in this regard is more humble than the Rawlsians, never making such bold claims. Rawls is framing in an analytically precise idiom insights which he is happy to ascribe to a wide and deep liberal tradition. In this chapter I will relate Rawls' account of political liberalism to the case argued in the last chapter for the compatibility – conceptual and historical – of political liberalism and Christian theology. This will lead me to consider Rawls' own stated interest in the sixteenth- and seventeenth-century wars of religion in Europe as the politico-religious seed-bed of liberalism. In further elaborating upon the theological depths of the liberal tradition, I will look at how a thinker such as Richard Hooker, writing within the context of Reformation disputes, develops themes with striking relevance for our consideration of political liberalism.

Rawlsian political liberalism

Rawls describes the task of political liberalism as one of answering the question 'how it is possible that there may exist over time a stable and just society of free and equal citizens profoundly divided by reasonable though incompatible religious, philosophical, and moral doctrines?'.[6] The very way the question is set up indicates that there is no presumption that 'liberalism' entails secularism or atheism: indeed 'secularism' would count as one of the comprehensive conceptions of the good which should be facilitated within a political structure, but not promoted or imposed. Rather 'political liberalism assumes that, for political purposes, a plurality of reasonable yet incompatible comprehensive doctrines is the normal result of the exercise of human reason within the framework of the free institutions of a constitutional democratic regime'.[7]

It is crucial to Rawls' thought that citizens will and should endorse a range of comprehensive and substantial conceptions of the good over and above their commitment to political liberalism. Rawls' hope is that citizens can embrace self-restraint with regard to the use of public power, while acting with integrity in relation to their own more substantial commitments:

---

[6] Rawls, *Political Liberalism*, p. xx.
[7] Rawls, *Political Liberalism*, p. xx.

... it is important to stress that ... [political liberalism] ... does not say, for example, that the doctrine *extra ecclesiam nulla salus* is not true. Rather, it says that those who want to use the public's political power to enforce it are being unreasonable. That does not mean that what they believe is false ... in saying it is unreasonable to enforce a doctrine, while we may reject that doctrine as incorrect, we do not necessarily do so. Quite the contrary: it is vital to the idea of political liberalism that we may with perfect consistency hold that it would be unreasonable to use political power to enforce our own comprehensive view, which we must, of course, affirm as either reasonable or true.[8]

Rawls suggests that a notion of 'public reason' can foster a stable and just society of free and equal citizens even among profound differences of 'religious, philosophical, and moral doctrines'.[9] The content of 'public reason' is provided by a broadly liberal 'political conception of justice'[10] which has three features: first of all it specifies certain

basic rights, liberties, and opportunities (of the kind familiar from constitutional democratic regimes); second, it assigns a special priority to these rights, liberties and opportunities, especially with respect to claims of the general good and of perfectionist values; and third, it affirms measures assuring all citizens adequate all-purpose means to make effective use of their basic liberties and opportunities.[11]

As each of these elements 'can be seen in different ways, so there are many liberalisms' such that the content of public reason is given by the principles and values of a family of liberal political conceptions of justice such that 'to engage in public reason is to appeal to one of these conceptions – to their ideals and principles, standards and values – when debating fundamental political questions'.[12] Crucially, Rawls is not aiming to silence religious voices within the public forum, a point demonstrated when he writes that 'this [public

---

[8] Rawls, *Political Liberalism*, p. 138.
[9] Rawls, *Political Liberalism*, p. xx.
[10] Rawls, *Political Liberalism*, p. 223.
[11] Rawls, *Political Liberalism*, p. 223.
[12] John Rawls, 'The Idea of Public Reason Revisited', in *Collected Papers*, ed. Samuel Freeman (Cambridge, Mass.: Harvard University Press, 1999), p. 583.

reason] . . . still allows us to introduce into political discussion at any time our comprehensive doctrine – religious or nonreligious, provided that, in due course, we give properly public reasons to support the principles and policies our comprehensive doctrine is said to support. I refer to this requirement as the *proviso*.'[13]

A vital sub-clause here is 'in due course': this may in fact never come, in which case citizens need never resort to a (broadly defined) public reason. There is no clear-cut way to determine when the due time is reached, and so when the proviso is required, and how the proviso is to be satisfied. Rawls embraces this lack of any *a priori* necessary and sufficient conditions for the use of public reason, drawing a comparison between the process of discerning the role of public reason with judgements made in common law, which must proceed on a case-by-case basis, with attention to precedence and the particular: 'the details about how to satisfy this proviso must be worked out in practice and cannot feasibly be governed by a clear family of rules given in advance'.[14] This principled pragmatism – we might say a theoretically justified stance against the use of abstract theory – is not so far removed from Burke, for whom the process of interpreting the common law was also a model of prudential political judgement. With both Burke and Rawls the lack of abstract certainty faithfully reflects political realities which would be distorted rather than clarified by greater precision and universality. Or as Wittgenstein put it, a precise picture of a vague reality is a distortion, rather than a clarification.[15] I take it that Burton Dreben has Wittgenstein's attention to the particular, and allergy to *a priori* and universalizing philosophical theory in mind when he alludes to the

---

[13] Rawls, 'Public Reason', p. 584.

[14] Rawls, 'Public Reason', p. 592.

[15] See L. Wittgenstein, *Philosophical Investigations* (Oxford: Basil Blackwell, 1994), sections 76–7. Wittgenstein is considering 'two pictures, one of which consists of colour patches with vague contours, the other of patches similarly shaped and distributed, but with clear contours'. Of the two pictures Wittgenstein comments that 'the degree to which the sharp picture *can* resemble the blurred one depends on the latter's degree of vagueness . . . if the colours in the original merge without a hint of any outline won't it become a hopeless task to draw a sharp picture corresponding to the blurred one? Won't you just have to say: "Here I might just as well draw a circle or heart as a rectangle, for all the colours merge. Anything – and nothing – is right." And this is the position you are in if you look for definitions corresponding to our concepts in aesthetics or ethics.' Following Dreben's reading of Rawls, and mine of Burke, we might add 'politics' to Wittgenstein's list.

'very close connection' which he perceives between 'Wittgenstein on (the) one hand, and Rawls, on the other',[16] a connection which we would suggest extents to features of Burke's political thought.

Where it is judged that the proviso applies, say in the case of a stand-off between citizens using their comprehensive conceptions of the good, Rawls calls for a certain 'civility' in the public forum. Two questions immediately present themselves: what such a 'civility' consists of, and why it should be shown. The same answer addresses both questions: civility is both marked out and justified by its respect for reciprocity and the burdens of judgement. 'Reciprocity' arises from our sense that just as we would not like to be coerced into a course of life or action without being able to accept the reasons given, so we should not expect others to tolerate such coercion. So Rawls explains the 'criterion of reciprocity' in the following terms: 'our exercise of political power is proper only when we sincerely believe that the reasons we offer for our political action may reasonably be accepted by other citizens as a justification of those actions'.[17] Rawls is explicit that the criterion of reciprocity presupposes a certain anthropology, where

> citizens are viewed as having the (appropriate) intellectual and moral powers . . . such as a capacity to form, follow and revise their individual doctrines of the good, and capable also of the political virtues necessary for them to cooperate in maintaining a just political society. Their capacity for other virtues and moral motives beyond this is not of course denied.[18]

Where issues of basic justice are at stake, just as judges cannot resolve difficult cases by appealing to their own political views, so 'if when stand-offs occur, citizens invoke the grounding reasons of their comprehensive views, then the principle of reciprocity is violated'.[19]

The second feature and justification of public reason is a respect for the 'burdens of judgement'. Here the resonances with Burke's observations about the complexity and obscurity of political judgement is very clear, with Rawls commenting that 'the evidence . . . bearing on the case is conflicting and complex, and thus hard to

16 Dreben, 'On Rawls and Political Liberalism', p. 316.
17 Rawls, *Political Liberalism*, p. xlvi.
18 Rawls, *Political Liberalism*, pp. xlvi–xlvii.
19 Rawls, *Political Liberalism*, pp. lv–lvi.

assess and evaluate', such that 'even where we agree fully about the kinds of consideration that are relevant, we may disagree about their weight, and so arrive at different judgements'.[20] Remember Burke's comment that 'the nature of man is intricate; the objects of society are of the greatest possible complexity; and therefore no simple disposition or direction of power can be suitable either to man's nature, or to the quality of his affairs';[21] turning back to Rawls we find a similar sentiment in a different idiom, with Rawls commenting that 'moral and political concepts' are 'vague and subject to hard cases' leading to an 'indeterminacy' which 'means that we must rely on judgement and interpretation (and on judgements about interpretations) within some range (not sharply specifiable) where reasonable persons may differ'.[22] The way in which we weigh moral and political values is shaped by 'our total experience, our whole life up to now'. As 'our total experience must always differ' from that of another, it is consequently difficult to make an 'overall assessment' where there are 'different kinds of normative considerations of different sorts on both sides of an issue'.[23]

Of most interest to us here is Rawls' claim that citizens can come to accept the content (the priority of basic liberties) and the procedural principles (reciprocity and the burdens of judgement) of public reason on the basis of reasons from within their own comprehensive conception of the good:

> . . . all those who affirm the [liberal] political conception start from within their own comprehensive view and draw on the religious, philosophical, and moral grounds it provides. The fact that people affirm the same political conception on those grounds does not make their affirming it any less religious, philosophical, or moral, as the case may be, since the grounds sincerely held determine the nature of their affirmation.[24]

Indeed, it seems to be the test – for Rawls – as to whether a comprehensive conception of the good is 'reasonable', whether or not it does so accept the demands of public reason. In the last chapter, I

---

[20] Rawls, *Political Liberalism*, p. 56.
[21] Burke, 'Reflections', p. 201.
[22] Rawls, *Political Liberalism*, p. 56.
[23] Rawls, *Political Liberalism*, p. 57.
[24] Rawls, *Political Liberalism*, pp. 147–8.

demonstrated the way in which Christian and politically liberal commitments had a mutually supportive conceptual relationship in Burke and Acton. The previous chapter can be read as an attempt to flesh out Rawls' rather abstract claim that citizens can come to accept a liberal endorsement of public reason from within their own comprehensive conception of the good, and from within their conception of the good find motivation for self-restraint about imposing that same legitimate conception of the good upon others.

Fleshing out this abstract claim, I have indicated, as a citizen in a politically liberal society and as a Christian theologian, how politically liberal principles are compatible with a full-blooded and theologically main-stream Christian commitment: one which holds that the human creature is incapable of its own perfection, although made for and called to that perfection by a gracious God who is the creator, sustainer and redeemer of time and space. Both Burke and Acton are committed to the notion of a divine purpose for human nature, but also its obscuring owing to sin, and the need to form a framework of government which respects the dignity and ultimate purpose of our freedom, while being cautious about the destructive possibilities that arise from the same source. These theological commitments lead them in different ways to endorse political judgements which in qualified senses – and I have tried to give the qualifications at each turn – are legitimately called 'politically liberal'.

I find myself in sympathy with an already well-developed literature which has sought to demonstrate the compatibility of Christianity with Rawlsian liberalism. The focus here tends to be on Rawls' notion of the 'original position' as first developed in *The Theory of Justice*,[25] and modified in *Political Liberalism*. In brief, this approach involves interlocutors imagining themselves behind a 'veil of ignorance'. They must imagine that they are in a sort of 'pre-born' state and know nothing about what position, gender, role or gifts they will be 'born with'. The subjects behind the veil of ignorance are also to imagine an ignorance about what their conceptions of the good will be, which is to say, that the individuals behind the veil of ignorance will not know what their beliefs are about how they should lead their lives. From this hypothetical position, citizens are supposed to be able to move towards a consensus about what the basic framework

---

[25] John Rawls, *A Theory of Justice* (Cambridge, Mass.: Harvard University Press, 1971).

of law should be in a society, in order to protect basic liberties necessary to enable free and equal citizens with different comprehensive
conceptions of the good to co-exist peacefully.

Now there is a critique of Rawls which goes something like this:
the hypothetical contract drawn up behind the veil of ignorance is
neither possible nor desirable because it overlooks the extent to
which people (1) are shaped by their 'circumstances', and (2) identified by their conceptions of the good. This critique is made forcefully by Charles Taylor who argues that Rawls' approach represses
the dependence of conceptions of the good and the self upon social
matrices.[26] In a more theological register the critique against Rawls
is that he has a faulty anthropology ignoring the extent to which
people are thrown into their embodied and created situations,
complete with both fatal limitations and immortal longings.

But this critique would not have got Rawls quite right.[27] As
becomes clear in his *Political Liberalism*,[28] it is not that Rawls is
somehow unaware of our social and historical conditioning, but
rather that he is all too aware of it, and the difficulties it engenders
when trying to frame laws of fairness within a diverse and pluralistic
culture. Rawls is aware of our constructedness within discourses,
and of our diverse comprehensive conceptions of the good. It is precisely this awareness which motivates, as a 'device of representation',[29] the artificial exercise of attempting to abstract from those
thicker discourses *when, and only when, framing the laws of the
polis.* We might say that it is because of Rawls' sense of the frailty,
createdness and complexity of human agency that he sees the need
for the artificial exercise of framing laws behind the veil of ignorance;
it is because the imagined life behind the veil of ignorance is so *unlike*
our actual condition, that it can help us – heuristically – to frame
laws and institutions which facilitate a diverse and pluralistic
society, with voluntary public association between people who share
comprehensive and substantial conceptions of the good.

A defence of Rawls along these lines is mounted by Daniel A. Dombrowski in *Rawls and Religion: The Case for Political Liberalism.*[30]

---

[26] Charles Taylor, *Philosophy and the Human Sciences: Philosophical Papers
2* (Cambridge: Cambridge University Press, 1999), pp. 289–317.
[27] For an excellent discussion of this point, to which I am much indebted, see
Stephen Mulhall and Adam Swift, *Liberals and Communitarians* (Oxford:
Blackwell, 1992), Ch. 6.
[28] Rawls, *Political Liberalism.*
[29] Rawls, *Political Liberalism*, p. 24.

Dombrowski does a superb job of surveying the developments in Rawls' thought, and arguing for the way in which many of Rawls' key devices and notions (particularly the original position, but also reciprocity and the burdens of judgement) are compatible with Christian instincts about the irreducible dignity of the individual. In a similar vein Werpehowski argues that the 'abstract' nature of Rawls' thought (the way in which individuals in the original position are hypothetically removed from the normal weave of human existence) is necessary to overcome sinful human tendencies to ensure fairness and respect for all.[31]

The strength of the existing literature lies in its superb Rawls scholarship, and the conceptual clarity which tends imitatively to mirror the thinker under scrutiny. Although appreciative of, and in broad sympathy with Dombrowski, Werpehowski and Beckley, I consider that my approach differs in some crucial respects. The 'Christian' defence of Rawls tends to be rather historically thin and aphoristic, relying on a few – in my view correct but underdeveloped – intuitions about the 'dignity' of the human individual or the problem of human sinfulness. It may be the rather bloodless and un-textured nature of the Christianity invoked which makes it so hard to know what is going on when another Christian theologian such as Nicholas Wolterstorff reports that *he* finds that Rawlsian political liberalism stops him from saying things he wants to say in the public forum. In that Rawls attempts to prevent Wolterstorff from saying these things, Rawls is creating an implicit political community (of Rawlsians) with their own 'unspoken' comprehensive conception of the good which coerces Wolterstorff out of the public forum. Wolterstorff exposes what he considers to be Rawls' premise that religious people can divide 'their life into a religious component and a non-religious component'. Against this Wolterstorff wants to say that 'when we bring into the picture persons for whom it is a matter

---

[30] Daniel A. Dombrowski, *Rawls and Religion: The Case for Political Liberalism* (New York: State University of New York Press, 2001).

[31] See William Werpehowski, 'Political Liberalism and Christian Ethics', *The Thomist* 48 (1984), pp. 81–115. See also Harlan Beckley, 'A Christian Affirmation of Rawl's Idea of Justice as Fairness: Part I', *Journal of Religious Ethics* 13 (1985), pp. 210–42 and 'A Christian Affirmation of Rawl's Idea of Justice as Fairness: Part II', *Journal of Religious Ethics* 14 (1986), pp. 229–46. Beckley does a careful job of showing how the notion of distributive justice employed in *The Theory of Justice* is compatible with a particular understanding of Christian ethics.

of religious conviction that they ought to strive for a religiously integrated existence – it's then, especially, though not only then, that the
unfairness of liberalism to religion comes to light'.[32]

Wolterstorff's objection is a coherent and deeply felt one, and
deserves a serious answer. I consider that an answer can be given, one
that is supportive of political liberalism, whilst remaining entirely
'integrated' in Wolterstorff's sense. But to get to that answer we
need to move deeper than the rather aphoristic nature of Christian
defences or critiques of political liberalism (a sort of ping-pong with
both sides claiming 'I want to say *this* and political liberalism
will/won't let me'), to consider more theologically systematic and
historically textured factors. The treatment of Burke was a move
towards this. It seemed appropriate that a claim for the conceptual
compatibility of Christianity and aspects of political liberalism
should be made with reference to an historical thinker with – in
Burke's case – a fairly well-developed Augustinian theology. In this
way the compatibility is unearthed, and demonstrated as being
already in place, rather than being coerced by radically reconceiving
either political liberalism or Christianity. In this chapter I want to
move the theological parameters deeper and further back to the
sixteenth-century Anglican divine Richard Hooker. His location as a
Reformation thinker attempting to discern theological grounds for
national peace and unity in the midst of competing comprehensive
conceptions of the good, provides the link with the debate around
Rawls, which I read as a particularly perspicuous and articulate
flashpoint for wider issues surrounding Christianity's attitude to
political liberalism.

Richard Hooker and the invisible Church

Rawls identifies 'the historical origin of political liberalism' as being
'the Reformation and its aftermath, with the long controversies over
religious toleration in the sixteenth and seventeenth centuries'.[33]
Medieval Christianity was 'authoritative, salvationist, and expansionist', such that when 'within the same society' a 'rival authoritative

---

[32] Nicholas Wolterstorff, 'Why We Should Reject What Liberalism Tells Us
about Speaking and Acting in Public for Religious Reasons', in Paul Weithman
(ed.), *Religion and Contemporary Liberalism* (South Bend, Ind.: University of
Notre Dame Press, 1997), pp. 162–81, p. 177.
[33] Rawls, *Political Liberalism*, p. xxvi.

and salvationist religion' appears, 'different in some ways from the original religion from which it split off, but having for a certain period of time many of the same features', it is inevitable that division and conflict will occur. Rawls is not sectarian on this issue, characterizing Luther and Calvin as being 'as dogmatic and intolerant as the Roman Church had been'.[34] Trenchant religious division, the source of conflict and bloodshed, led eventually to a serious acknowledgement that there was no alternative to a 'reasonable . . . pluralism of comprehensive doctrines'. The acknowledgement of this fact gives rise to the question we remember Rawls posing above as the generating problem of political liberalism of 'how is it possible that there may exist over time a stable and just society of free and equal citizens profoundly divided by reasonable religious, philosophical and moral doctrines?'[35] The possibility realized in the Reformation was the 'clash between salvationist, creedal and expansionist religions', a 'clash . . . that introduced into people's conceptions of their good a transcendent element not admitting of compromise':[36]

> This element forces either mortal conflict moderated only by circumstance and exhaustion, or equal liberty of conscience and freedom of thought. Except on the basis of these last, firmly founded and publicly recognized, no reasonable political conception of justice is possible. Political liberalism starts by taking to heart the absolute depth of that irreconcilable latent conflict.[37]

The answer which begins to be formed in this period is 'liberty of conscience and freedom of thought', such that 'to see reasonable pluralism as a disaster is to see the exercise of reason under the conditions of freedom itself as a disaster'.[38] Rawls then moves fairly swiftly on to discuss the 'new social possibility' of a 'reasonably harmonious and stable pluralist society',[39] through the (explicitly at least) non-religious theories of Hume and Kant, and then in terms of his own framework. It may pay us to linger a little longer in this period, and consider an explicitly theological treatment of the problems posed by the aftermath of the Reformation. My contention is that a figure such as Richard Hooker also took to heart the

---

[34] Rawls, *Political Liberalism*, p. xxv.
[35] Rawls, *Political Liberalism*, p. xx.
[36] Rawls, *Political Liberalism*, p. xxviii.
[37] Rawls, *Political Liberalism*, p. xxviii.
[38] Rawls, *Political Liberalism*, p. xxvi–xxvii.
[39] Rawls, *Political Liberalism*, p. xxvii.

'absolute depth of that irreconcilable latent conflict', and that
although he can in no meaningful sense be called a political liberal,
his theological reflection amidst the politico-religious seedbed of
political liberalism (as identified by Rawls) commands our attention.

The immediate context of Hooker's *Laws of Ecclesiastical Polity*
was an attempt, coming to a head in the 1590s, by radical Protestant
elements to 'purify' the Church of England, discontent as they were
with the remaining Catholic remnants of the Church (for instance,
the episcopal structure to high liturgy). As it stood, the visible
Church of England reflected all the ambiguities of being the national
Church. Rather than being a unified Church founded upon a systematic and comprehensive conception of the good (for instance
Calvinism or Roman Catholicism), it contained within its structure
those who were doctrinally Catholic, and those who identified much
more with the continental Reformation led by Calvin and Luther.
Radical presbyterian elements in the Elizabethan Church wished to
reform the Chuch along 'scriptural lines' thus enabling the 'visible'
Church (the actual concrete historical Church, constituted by a complex mixture of doctrinal Catholics and Protestants) to become,
within history, the 'invisible' Church (the eschatological gathering
in glory of all the saints, who in this case would certainly be
Protestants). The fallen institution could be regenerated this side of
the Kingdom. This transformation of the national Church would
effect a whole-scale conversion of England, making it a close
approximation to, and inauguration of, the Kingdom of God.

A typical statement of this attempt to transform the visible Church
into the community of the saints can be found in the sixteenth-
century Puritan theologian Thomas Cartwright. Cartwright saw
reform of the Church's government, and purification of its discipline
as a means by which England could be in covenant with God.
Imperfection, compromise and corruption should be weeded out,
separating in history good from evil and casting out evil. Cartwright
expected a golden age, immanent within history, to be achieved by
human action and righteousness, when 'our saviour Christ sitteth
wholly and fully not only in his chair to teach but also in his throne
to rule, not alone in the hearts of everyone by the spirit, but also
generally and in the visible government of the church, by those laws
of discipline he hath prescribed'.[40]

---

[40] Peter Lake, *Anglicans and Puritans: Presbyterian and Conformist Thought
from Whitgift to Hooker* (London: Unwin, 1988), p. 31. The Cartwright refer-

With the visible and the invisible Church so closely identified – after a process of reform, purification and expulsion to ensure only the elect were in the visible Church – language normally appropriate to individual sanctification and transformation could be applied at the national and political level. The historian Peter Lake comments of Cartwright that it was 'the . . . slippage between the two realms which allowed him to attach such golden visions of reformed purity to the discipline'.[41] It was this slippage which enabled the 'presbyterian platform' to be 'transformed from just another shopping list of projected reforms and institutional adjustments' into a movement 'of world-historical significance'.[42]

What we have in Hooker's Elizabethan Church is an attempt to use public power to effect, by political means, a perfectionist and coercive programme for the salvation of souls. Hooker resists this salvific us of public power in the midst of controversy, for theological reasons. I will suggest that Hooker's position resonates with our own situation, where the political liberal faces irreconcilable reasonable conceptions of the good, and refuses to use public power to achieve consensus or unity around any one conception. Hooker's critique of perfectionist programmes is based upon the conviction that the visible Church cannot be reformed by activism within history into the invisible Church, just because good and evil are too intermingled. So he writes that 'many things exclude from the kingdom of God, although from the Church they separate not', entailing that the visible Church must live out her intermingled existence 'till the final consummation of the world'.[43] Hooker steers the debate about the relationship between the visible and invisible Church away from the prevalent fixation on predestination and the elect, and turns towards a Christological vision of the Church as a participatory

---

ence is to be found in J. Ayre (ed.), *The Works of John Whitgift* (Cambridge: Parker Society, 1851–3), Vol. 3, p. 315.

[41] Lake, *Anglicans and Puritans*, p. 31.

[42] Lake, *Anglicans and Puritans*, p. 31.

[43] Lake, *Anglicans and Puritans*, p. 161. The Hooker reference is *Of the Laws of Ecclesiastical Polity*, Bk. III, Ch. 1.7. See also, Bk. v, Ch. 1.18. Where possible page references are given to Richard Hooker, *Of the Laws of Ecclesiastical Polity* (Cambridge: Cambridge University Press, 1989), ed. A. S. McGrade. The Cambridge edition contains the preface, and books 1 and 8, from which nearly all the material cited comes. Occasional references outside of these sections are taken from Richard Hooker, 'Laws of Ecclesiastical Polity' in *The Works of that Learned and Judicious Divine Mr. Richard Hooker*, ed. John Keble, 7th edn. revised by R. Church and F. Paget (Oxford: Clarendon Press, 1888).

body within which we can hope for the gradual sanctification of all. We begin to harbour the suggestion – endorsed as we will see by both Barth and Balthasar – that the entire historical visible Church may actually be *smaller* than the invisible; or at least, that in its glory and consummation in Christ, the invisible Church may be more universal and inclusive than we might dare to hope. So we find Hooker answering Puritan objections to a passage in the prayer-book that all may be saved, by emphasizing that Christ died as: '. . . the price of redemption for all and a forcible mean to procure the conversion of all such as are not yet acquainted with the mysteries of that truth which must save their souls'.[44] Although 'there is, in the knowledge both of God and man, this certainty, that life and death have divided between them the whole body of mankind', 'what portion either of the two hath, God himself knoweth; for us he hath left no sufficient means to comprehend and for that cause neither given any leave to search in particular who are infallibly the heirs of the kingdom of God, who castaways'. In a sentiment which will be echoed by Barth's declarations on the openness of the Church and the sinful pride of human judgement between good and evil, Hooker tells us that the

> safest axioms for charity to rest itself upon are these 'he which already believeth is' and 'he which believeth not as yet may be the child of God'. It becometh not us 'during life altogether to condemn any man seeing that' (for anything we know) 'there is hope of every man's forgiveness the possibility of whose repentance is not yet cut off by death'. And therefore charity 'which hopeth all things' prayeth also for all men.[45]

This charity which 'hopeth all things' does not do so in vain, theologically speaking. Hooker's vision of the Church is one which expresses the desire for participation found at every level of creation, finding its ultimate consummation in infinite desire for God. It cannot be in vain to hope for 'every man's forgiveness' if one's anthropology inclines one to the view that the deepest satisfaction, the end of all the yearning of creation, is to move towards the creative centre. Peter Lake gives a beautiful evocation of Hooker's vision, showing how in the 'face of the Puritans' inherently subversive view

---

[44] Hooker, *Laws*, Bk. v, Ch. 49.1–2.
[45] Lake, *Anglicans and Puritans*, p. 162. The Hooker reference is *Laws*, Bk. v, Ch. 49.1–2.

of the community of Christians, permanently fractured by division between the godly and ungodly' one has Hooker's 'more restful vision of a visible church which included everyone within the slow-moving cycle of its outward observances, while the slow trickle of sacramental grace performed its subtly ameliorative work and the mystical body of Christ grew with glacial slowness and a soothing lack of conflict'.[46]

Hooker would regard human intentions and actions as too ambivalent, frail and unpredictable to trust a single individual or collective to inaugurate the Kingdom within which all must enjoy being subjects or be expelled. Hooker considers that the Puritans notice sin and fallenness, and leap to the confident conclusion that they are the ones to do something – everything even – about it. Hooker complains that the Puritans 'impute all faults and corruptions, wherewith the world aboundeth, unto the kind of ecclesiastical government established'.[47] When noticing the 'stains and blemishes in our state' – which Hooker concedes are there – the Puritans fail to understand that they spring 'from the root of human frailty and corruption' and 'not only are, but have been always more or less, yea and (for any thing we know to the contrary) will be till the world's end complained of, what form of government soever take place'.[48] The Puritans' error is to believe that through their righteous action they can hope to identify and eliminate evil. Hooker's critique of this belief has resonances for our own time, as we will see in the next chapter, when we consider the political rhetoric of American presidents who promise to eliminate evil by righteous (military) action.

Puritans combine a black and white ability to see the evil of the rest of the world, along with a confidence in their own regeneration, leading them to a straightforward and naive political application of scripture. So Hooker complains that the Puritans are 'taught to apply all things spoken of' in the Bible such as the ' repairing the walls and decayed parts of the city and temple of God, by Esdras, Nehemias, and the rest' as if 'the Holy Ghost had therein meant to foresignify' contemporary events such as 'Admonitions to the Parliament . . . Supplications to the Council . . . Petitions to her Majesty, and . . . other writs' which are offered in 'behalf of this their cause'.[49]

---

[46] Lake, *Anglicans and Puritans*, p. 196.
[47] Hooker, *Laws*, Preface, Ch. 3.7, pp. 15–16.
[48] Hooker, *Laws*, Preface, Ch. 3.7, pp. 15–16.
[49] Hooker, *Laws*, Preface, Ch. 3.7, pp. 15–16.

From Hooker we have a picture of the Puritan – a lovable, forgivable figure to whom he wishes to be reconciled – who is nonetheless carried away by a false certainty, an insufferable desire to divide the world into good and evil, and to rebuild it in the confidence of his or her own salvation. So Hooker complains of the way in which the Puritan fancies that 'the Spirit . . . [is] . . . the author of . . . persuasions concerning discipline', whereby a preference for a non-episcopal form of church government is taken to be the Spirit that seals 'them to be God's children'. This conviction leads to 'high terms of separation between such and the rest of the world; whereby the one sort are named The breathren, The godly, and so forth; the other, worldlings time-servers, pleasers of men not of God, with such like'.[50]

This conviction makes the Puritans intransigent to criticism and debate, such that if any man of 'contrary opinion open his mouth to persuade them, they close up their ears, his reasons they weigh not, all is answered with rehearsal of the words of John, "We are of God; he that knoweth God heareth us: as for the rest, ye are of the world; for this world's pomp and vanity it is that ye speak, and the world, whose ye are, heareth you."'[51] Even where one can demonstrate the stupidness or ineptness of an argument, Hooker complains that the Puritan can make the response that 'God hath chosen the simple', with the weakness of their arguments being a symptom of discipleship in that ' "Christ's own apostle was accounted mad: the best men evermore by the sentence of the world have been judged to be out of their right minds" '.[52]

Disturbed by the Puritans' desire to jettison history, custom and tradition, Hooker comments that it is a

> very strange thing . . . that such discipline as ye speak of should be taught by Christ and his apostles in the word of God, and no church ever have found it out, nor received it till this present time; contrariwise, the government against which ye bend yourselves be observed every where throughout all generations and ages of the Christian world, no church ever perceiving the word of God to be against it.[53]

---

[50] Hooker, *Laws*, Preface, Ch. 3.11, pp. 16–17.
[51] Hooker, *Laws*, Preface, Ch. 3.14, p. 18.
[52] Hooker, *Laws*, Preface, Ch. 3.14, p. 18.
[53] Hooker, *Laws*, Preface, Ch. 4.2, p. 20.

Hooker's critique of the Puritans targets their 'endeavour to purge the earth of all manner evil, to the end there might follow a new world afterward, wherein righteousness only should dwell'.[54]

The heart of the theological defence of political liberalism is a sense of the danger and hubris involved in such projects, which inevitably arise from and provoke a conflation of the invisible and the visible Church. Hooker saw this danger with unusal acuity at a crucial historical moment, but we will see this insight does not belong to Anglicanism, but can be found at work in theologians such as Karl Barth and Hans Urs von Balthasar. This is what one would expect of truth; if it is true, it will be discerned in different ways, at different times, from within different traditions.

We find that the Elizabethan Puritan can stand for a more timeless pheonomenon: the citizen who expects and claims political actions to be justified by distinctively and irreducibly religious reasons. By 'distinctively and irreducibly' religious reasons I mean not only reasons that have been generated by deep religious convictions, which can – according to the principle of reciprocity – be justified to citizens who do not share this comprehensive conception of the good, but reasons that arise from a special authority supposed to derive from scripture or inspiration and that cannot be assented to by someone who does not assent to this authority. Rawls' (non-religious) objection to such a procedure, as we have seen, is that it violates the norms of reciprocity and the burdens of judgement. Hooker's call to self-examination, moderation and charity provides a theological reason for the sort of self-restraint and consideration to others fostered in Rawls' approach.

A reckoning with something like the 'burdens of judgement' is manifest in Hooker's sense of the enormous complexity of framing good laws, and the need for even scripture and inspiration to be interpreted through (fallible) reason and tradition. In a tight and effective argument – which would engage powerfully with contemporary biblical fundamentalism – Hooker complains that the Puritan fails to appreciate that reading and intepreting scripture involves complex presuppositions which are mediated through reason and tradition, which is constantly dependent, as Rawl would put it, 'on judgement and interpretation (and on judgements about interpretations) within some range (not sharply specifiable) where reasonable

---

[54] Hooker, *Laws*, Preface, Ch. 8.6, p. 41.

persons may differ'.[55] Hooker comments that just as every 'Art and Science . . . presupposeth many necessary things learned in other sciences and known beforehand', so also scripture which contains 'all things which are necessary to salvation' nonetheless can only be read and understood 'with presupposal of knowledge concerning certain principles wherof it receiveth us already persuaded'.[56] One of the presuppositions necessary is 'the sacred authority of scripture',[57] a presupposition which we take to the scriptures, but which does not come out of scripture. Rather we are 'persuaded by other means that these scriptures are the oracles of God', giving reason and tradition a vital hermeneutical role in scriptural devotion. The importance of balancing scripture with reason and tradition is clearly seen if one accepts Hooker's observation that ' . . . our belief in the Trinity, the Coeternity of the Son of God with his Father, the proceeding of the Spirit from the Father and the Son, the duty of baptizing infants . . . are notwithstanding in scripture nowhere to be found by express literal mention, only deduced they are out of scripture by collection', a 'collection' that is never complete or definitive for 'let us not think that as long as the world doth endure, the wit of man shall be able to sound the bottom of that which may be concluded out of the scripture, especially if things contained by collection do so far extend, as to draw in whatsoever may be at any time out of scripture but probably and conjecturally surmised'.[58]

'Reciprocity' is supported by Hooker on the basis of two Christian convictions: on the one hand our created dignity which bestows us with freedom and the use of reason, and on the other hand, the frailty and vulnerability of our shared human condition, all of us complicit in sin, and dependent upon the grace of God. Rawls' hypothetical 'original position', where citizens are supposed to be able to reach a reasonable consensus on the just principles of a basic framework of laws given certain assumptions about human nature, can be read theologically in terms of Hooker's 'law of reason or human nature' which is 'investigable . . . without the help of revelation supernatural and divine', just because such an understanding of human nature is 'that which men by discourse of natural reason have rightly found out themselves to be all forever bound unto in their actions'.[59] Rawls'

---

55 Rawls, *Political Liberalism*, p. 56.
56 Hooker, *Laws*, Bk. 1, Ch. 14.1, pp. 112–13.
57 Hooker, *Laws*, pp. 112–13.
58 Hooker, *Laws*, Bk. 1, Ch. 14.2, p. 113.
59 Hooker, *Laws*, Bk. 1, Ch. 8.9, p. 82.

suggestion that certain principles of justice can be discerned without a comprehensive (religious) conception of the good need not be hostile to a theologically robust position. We can read this claim in theological terms as involving a commitment to the goodness of our created nature, where God has bestowed us with a certain capacity for self-understanding, for the 'law which human nature knoweth itself in reason universally bound unto . . . this law, I say, comprehendeth all those things which men by the light of their natural understanding evidently know, to be beseeming or unbeseeming, virtuous or vicious, good or evil for them to do'.[60] Hooker immediately follows on with an example of one of the great truths that is available to all humans by virtue of their created reason: 'Do as thou wouldest be done unto, is a sentence which all nations under heaven are agreed upon. Refer this sentence to the love of God, and it extinguisheth all heinous crimes: refer it to the love of thy neighbour, and all grievous wrongs it banisheth out of the world.'[61] The theological claim that this truth is universally binding, and universally accessible to human reason, is germane to Rawls' claim that reciprocity should always be valued by citizens, who must not expect other citizens to tolerate coercive programmes of a salvationist or perfectionist nature, when they themselves would resist any coercive measures taken against them as part of a salvationist programme to which they themselves could not assent. Or more succinctly, citizens should do as they would be done to.

Now we are in a position to answer Wolterstorff's objection. Wolterstorff objects to the way in which religious believers had to 'shape-up' within a politically liberal system and be prepared to give 'non-religious' reasons in the public forum. His complaint was that religious people desire an integrated existence, and would be coerced by any attempt to separate their lives into religious (non-public) and non-religious (public) components. We already note Rawls' qualification concerning the proviso, indicating that religious believers need only use 'non-religious' reasons (respecting reciprocity and the burdens of judgement) in the case of a stand-off. So Wolterstorff's objection must be that religious believers should not have to use non-religious reasons at any point, even in the case of a stand-off: there must be no proviso. We should also note that at no point is it said by the Rawlsian liberal that the religious believer should not ultimately

---

[60] Hooker, *Laws*, Bk. I, Ch. 8.9, p. 82.
[61] Hooker, *Laws*, Bk. I, Ch. 8.10, pp. 82–3.

be motivated by the religious reason. The only requirement is that in communicating with a fellow citizen who does not share this reason, other non-religious reasons be brought forward as well. So Wolterstorff's objection needs to be strengthened again, to the claim that a religious believer should not, in any circumstances – even in a pluralistic culture when discussing the use of public power in the case of a stand-off – be required to introduce non-religious reasons when communicating with citizens who do not share those reasons.

It may be that this is a much stronger claim than Wolterstorff wants to be committed to. Nonetheless, the point is that to stand as an effective objection to Rawlsian liberalism it needs *to be at least this strong*; anything more measured can be accommodated within the liberal framework. Wolterstorff seems to be aware of this when giving his revised 'formulation . . . of *the liberal position* as incorporating the following as one of its core theses':

> . . . citizens and officials are to base their discussions concerning (at least fundamental) political issues, and their discussion of those issues in the public space, on the principles yielded by some source independent of any and all of the religions found in society. This thesis . . . is silent on whether citizens and officials may *also* base their decisions and public discussions on *religious* considerations.[62]

This account of political liberalism seems to appreciate the accommodations made to the religious believer. Nonetheless, Wolterstorff pushes his objection, justifying the strong interpretation made of his position.

Once sufficiently strengthened to take account of all Rawls' qualifications, Wolterstorff's position begins to resemble that of the Elizabethan Puritan discussed above: the citizen who expects and claims political actions to be justified by distinctively and irreducibly religious reasons, reasons that arise from a special authority supposed to derive from scripture, a particular tradition or inspiration, and which cannot be assented to by someone who does not assent to this authority. Wolterstorff objects to Rawls' non-religious objection to such a procedure, claiming that it exemplifies the very coercive use of power the liberal is supposed to resist. My main objection to what

---

[62] Nicholas Wolterstorff in R. Audi and N. Wolterstorff (eds.), *Religion in the Public Square* (Lanham, Md.: Rowman and Littlefield, 1997), p. 147.

Wolterstorff might be read as wanting is not non-religious and political, but theological: from a sense of humility and fellowship in sin, we are called to show love to our neighbour by exemplifying self-restraint, self-examination and charity. In this context it is Hooker who articulates my theological objection to Wolterstorff's desire to be able to use always irreducibly religious reasons when discussing the use of public power. Such a desire tramples upon the frailty and vulnerability of our shared human condition, all of us complicit in sin, and dependent upon the grace of God; our fallen vision of the Kingdom, through a glass darkly, should lead us to an appreciation of the enormous complexity of framing good laws, and the need for even scripture and inspiration to be interpreted through (fallible) reason and tradition. The heart of the problem with Wolterstorff is his conflation of the visible and the invisible Church; the theological insight of political liberalism is that these must never be conflated. 'Religiously integrated' citizens who see the dangers of this conflation will be able, for religious reasons, to assent to the need to give non-religious reasons in the public forum, in the case of a stand-off where it is judged that the proviso applies. Their preparedness to withhold religious reasons in the public square is itself an act of witness arising from humility, their sense of common complicity in sin, and the giving of all glory and judgement to God alone.

Rome and Geneva on the invisible Church

Although I have chosen to look at Hooker when considering the dangers of identifying the visible and invisible Church, it is not an exclusively Anglican insight. A resounding warning against such a conflation can be found in the twentieth century from both Rome and Geneva, we might say, in the thought of Hans Urs von Balthasar and Karl Barth respectively. Again, this is what we would expect of truth when it is true: that it is articulated in different times and in different vocabularies. In fact, all the themes I have drawn out of Richard Hooker and Edmund Burke are found in Barth and Balthasar also. Partly reacting against perfectionist and salvationist totalitarian projects of the twentieth century, both Barth and Balthasar stress the impossibility of self-perfection, the dangers of political projects that promise the realization of the absolute on earth, the hubris in declaring knowledge of good and evil, and the difficulty of identifying any earthly, visible Church with the invisible Church, the eschatological gathering in glory of all the saved.

So we find Balthasar refusing to draw a boundary between the righteous and unrighteous, calling us to see things from ' the highest angle' which involves reckoning with 'our solidarity in sin' as 'the necessary condition if God's last and final initiative for his entire mankind is to be revealed. For he did not take upon himself the sin of chosen individuals, but the sin of all, without selectivity. This is the heart of the theo-drama.'[63] So Balthasar warns and promises that 'the boundaries of the visible Church do not correspond to those of the living Mystical Body of Christ, for the latter can have true members outside the *Catholica* and many dead members within her'.[64]

The heart of Balthasar's theo-drama is concerned with the relationship between the visible and the invisible, or in Balthasar's vocabulary, the meeting of man's finitude with the infinity of the creator. This meeting of the finite and the infinite leads to a terrible pathos: man desires to be absolute, but cannot be, and must live out his time in creatureliness and transience. So we learn that 'man can neither throw off his vertical relationship to the absolute nor entrap the absolute within his own finitude by his own', so he becomes, 'right from the start, a figure of pathos on the world stage':

> . . . this yearning for the absolute is at the very heart of man; it is the source of his search for meaning as such, including the meaning that he tries to discern in horizontal history. However, none of the passing moments of the world of time can encapsulate that desired absolute meaning . . . As a result, the pathos of the world stage becomes grotesque, grimacing and demonic.[65]

---

[63] Hans Urs von Balthasar, *Theo-Drama: Theological Dramatic Theory*, Vol. IV 'The Action' (San Francisco: Ignatius Press, 1981), pt. II, p. 191; '. . . aus höchster Perspektive (ist) unsere Schuldsolidarität die Bedingung der Möglichkeit für die Offenbarung des letztmöglichen Einsatzes Gottes für seine ganze Menschheit, da er nicht die Schuld einzelner Auserwählter, sondern wahloss aller auf sich genommen har. Hierin liegt der Kern des Theodramus', *Theo-Dramatik III: Die Handlung* (Einsiedeln: Johannes Verlag, 1980), p. 177.

[64] von Balthasar, *Theo-Drama*, Vol. IV, pt. IV, pp. 453–4; '. . . die Grenzen der sichtbaren Kirche nicht überein fallen mit denen des lebendigen mystichen Leibes Christi, der wahre Glieder ausserhalb der Catholika haben kann, und viele erstobene in ihr', *Theo-Dramatik*, Vol. III, pt. IV, p. 424.

[65] von Balthasar, *Theo-Drama*, p. 73; '. . . der Mensch sich seiner vertikalen Beziehung zum Absoluten nicht entschlagen, aber das Absolute auch nicht durch

So we have a creature who 'cannot cease puzzling over himself, for he knows what meaning is (even if he can no longer find it) and because meaning lays claim to a certain absoluteness. Yet, in the face of time and death, he can never show this absolute claim to have been fulfilled. This is the pathetic dimension that informs everything that happens on the world stage.'[66]

I would suggest that political liberalism, in refusing to identify the visible with the invisible, is able to reckon with the depth of the pathos articulated by Balthasar. In its fundamental respect for the liberties of the individual, political liberalism also opens a space for Balthasar's proper appreciation of the possibilities of created freedom, for in itself created freedom is 'man's openness to the good as such; it is the power of self-determination, the highest and noblest form of power'.[67]

The Elizabethan Puritan (in the wide heuristic sense employed here), we would suggest, stands under the theological judgement made by Balthasar of those who wish, within history, to achieve a 'synthesis' of finitude and infinity. All alike, from the powerful who erect monuments, to the least powerful, wish to 'scratch something true, something valid, into the face of the dwindling day'.[68] But this synthesis will not be achieved by our efforts, but is known only to God. 'The all-encompassing reality that is manifested in all particular action' does not come to us whole and transparent; rather 'fragments

---

eigenes (magisches Tun) in seine Endlichkeit hinein bannen kann, wird er von vornherein zu einer pathetischen Gestalt auf seiner Weltbühne . . .'; '. . . diese Sehnsucht ist das Herzstück des Menschen und der Quellpunkt, von dem aus das Postular von Sinn überhaupt, ja von Sinn schlechtin auch in die horizontale Geschichte hinein ergeht. Da aber keiner der innerzeitlich zerfliessenden Augenblicke den geforderten absoluten Sinn bergen kann . . . doch . . . wird die Pathetik auf der Weltbühne nunmehr grotesk, fratzenhaft, dämonish', *Theo-Dramatik*, Vol. III, pt. 2, p. 69.

[66] von Balthasar, *Theo-Drama*, pp. 73–4; 'Er Kann deschalb nicht aufhören, über sich zu rätseln, weil er weiss, was Sinn ist (auch wenn er ihn nicht mehr findet), weil Sinn einen Anspruch von Absolutheit in sich hat, we aber die Erfüllung dieses Anspruchs angesichts von Zeit and Tod nie vorweisen kann. Das ist das Pathetische an allem, was auf Weltbühne vor sich geht', *Theo-Dramatik*, Vol. III, pt. 2, p. 72.

[67] von Balthasar, *Theo-Drama*, p. 77; '. . . Freiheit als Eröffnetsein des Menchen für das Gute überhaupt, Freiheit als die Macht der Selbstbestimmung und damit als die höchste, edelste Form von Macht überhaupt', *Theo-Dramatik*, Vol. III, pt. 2, p. 72.

[68] von Balthasar, *Theo-Drama*, p. 82; '. . . in den zerrinnenden Tag etwas Wahres und Gültiges einzuritzen . . .', *Theo-Dramatik*, Vol. III, pt. 2, p. 75.

of meaning flash and sparkle everywhere in the life of the individual and of the community but . . . these fragments are limited and hence relative, creating contradictory antinomies'.[69] We see fragments of this synthesis, this order, as our 'finitude has a reflex consciousness of itself, that is, is illuminated by a spark of the absolute'.[70] We have here a familiar theological moment, as identified in Hooker and Burke: a gesturing towards an obscured order, that which is hidden, yet which permeates and illuminates all things:

> The point of absoluteness – reason's openness to the totality of being, of the true and the good, and its innate necessity to orientate itself to that totality and to be judged by it – can be conceived in manifold ways . . . it is both hidden (the 'good beyond all *ousia*') and yet illuminates and permeates all finite reality . . . [71]

Barth similarly resists a conflation of the visible and invisible Church. The real Church is not to be identified with a space and time, but exists only in Christ, in moments of grace fragmented throughout creation by God in God's sovereign and gracious freedom:

> The real Church therefore lives as it constantly held and sustained over an abyss. When it imagines it can find comfort and encouragement in itself it is certainly not the real Church. The real Church lives on the comfort and exhortation which it is allowed to receive despite the folly and perversity of man . . . It lives by allowing itself to be shamed by His (its Lord's) goodness. It lives only in so far as its own religiosity and pious habits, its whole ritual,

---

[69] von Balthasar, *Theo-Drama*, Vol. IV, pt. 2, p. 72; '. . . oder ist es nicht vielmehr so, dass überall, im individuellen wie im gesellschaftlichen Leben Sinnfragmente aufblitzen, die aber in sich begenzt und deshalb relativ und deshalb antinomisch gegeneinanderstehen . . .', *Theo-Dramatik*, Vol. III, pt. 2, p. 68.

[70] von Balthasar, *Theo-Drama*, p. 96; '. . . dass diese Endlichkeit reflex bewusst, also von einem Lichtfunken des Absoluted erleuchtet wird', *Theo-Dramatik*, Vol. III, pt. 2, p. 96.

[71] von Balthasar, *Theo-Drama*, p. 104; 'Der Absolutpunkt – Offenheit der Vernunft auf das Ganze des Seins, des Wahren und Guten, Notwendigkeit, sich aufgrund des eigenen Wesens danach auszurichten und davon richten zu lassen – kann in seiner Entzogenheit (das "Gute jenseits aller *Ousia*") aber mit seinem Hineinscheinen in alles Endliche durch vielfältige Denk-Projektiones vorgestellt werden . . .', *Theo-Dramatik*, Vol. III, pt. 2, pp. 96–7.

ordinary as well as extraordinary, are constantly being reduced to dust and ashes in the fire of His word and Spirit.[72]

It is clear for Barth that the lordship of Christ has and does operate outside of the visible Church:

> In all ages the will of God has been fulfilled outside the Church as well. Indeed, to the shame of the Church, it has often been better fulfilled outside the Church than in it. This is . . . because Jesus, as the One who has risen from the dead and sits at the right hand of God, is in fact the Lord of the whole World, who has His servants even where His name is not yet or no longer known and praised.[73]

Members of the Church are not distinguished by their superior virtue – they are not a moral elite – but by their awareness of their own human guilt and the indissoluble solidarity of all humans as sinners.[74] We saw that Balthasar called us to loving fellowship with all in the solidarity of our sin; similarly Barth tells us that to participate in real humanity is to be free from the sin of pride. When the human creature gives itself over to self-righteousness, ideological thinking and strife he fails to understand 'the language of others because he is too much convinced of the soundness of his own

---

[72] Karl Barth, 'The Real Church', in *Against the Stream*, ed. R. G. Smith, trans. E. M. Delacour and Stanley Godman (London: SCM Press, 1954), pp. 67–8; 'Die Wirkliche Kirche', in *Christliche Gemeinde im Wechsel der Staatsordnungen, Dokumente einer Ungarnreise 1948* (Zollikon: Evangelisher Verlag , 1948), pp. 15–29. The original German reads as follows: 'Die Wirkliche Kirche lebt also in der Weise, dass sie fort und fort wie über einem Abgrund gehalten und getragen ist. Wo sie sich selbst zu trösten und zu ermuntern weiss, da ist sie bestimmt nicht die wirkliche Kirche. Die wirkliche Kirche lebt von dem Trost und von der Mahnung, die sie der menschlichen Torheit und Verkehrheit, an der auch sie teilnimmt, zum Trotz empfangen darf. . . . Sie lebt, indem sie sich durch seine Güte beschämen lässt. Sie lebt, indem ihre Religiosität und fromme Gewohnheit, ihre ganz ordentliche und ausserordentliche Feierlichkeit immer wieder zu Staub und Asche werden müssen im Feuer seines Wortes und Geistes', p. 20.
[73] Karl Barth, *Church Dogmatics*, in 4 vols., ed. G. W. Bromiley and T. F. Torrance (Edinburgh: T. & T. Clark, 1936–77), Vol. II, pt. 2, p. 569; 'Der Wille Gottes ist zu allen Zeiten auch ausserhalb der Kirche erfüllt worden und zu deren Beschämung ausserhalb der Kirche oft besser als immerhalb . . . weil Jesus als der von den Toten Auferstandene, sitzend zur Rechten Gottes, faktisch der Herr der ganzen Welt ist, der auch da seine Diener hat, wo sein Name noch nicht oder nicht mehr erkannt und gepriesen ist', *Die Kirchliche Dogmatik* (Zollikon: Evangelischer Verlag, 1940–42), p. 632.
[74] Barth, *Church Dogmatics*, Vol. II, pt. 2, p. 569.

seriously to want to understand the others'.[75] This is the strident theological ban on self-righteousness which was heard forcefully in the thought of Richard Hooker and Edmund Burke, and which I have claimed to be at the core of a theological appreciation of the humility and self-restraint of political liberalism.

In an intriguing passage, Barth describes the serpent's invitation to Eve to become like God as the 'establishment of ethics'.[76] He has in mind the sinful self-sufficiency with which man, turned away from the creator, has pretences to judge good from evil, and to set up human systems of ethics. By so doing the creature attempts to control and bypass the sovereign freedom and judgement of God. The fallen human creature sets herself up as 'an Atlas bearing and holding together the great building of the universe'.[77] The human will to self-justification through judgement of others leads to a 'fanatical self-instruction',[78] which destroys moral fellowship:

> I am already putting myself in the wrong with others, and doing them wrong, when – it makes no odds how gently or vigorously I do it – I confront them as one who is right, wanting to break over them as a great crisis. For when I do this I divide myself and I break the fellowship between myself and others. I can only live at unity with myself, and we can only live in fellowship with one another, when I and we subject ourselves to the right which does not dwell in us and is not manifested by us, but which is over me and us as the right of God above, and manifested to me and us only from God.[79]

---

[75] Barth, *Church Dogmatics*, Vol. IV, pt. 1, p. 447; '. . . keiner auch nur die Sprache des Anderen versteht, weil er von der Güte seiner eigenen viel zu sehr überzeugt ist', *Kirchliche Dogmatik*, p. 496.

[76] Barth, *Church Dogmatics*, Vol. IV, pt. 1, p. 448; '. . . die Begründung der Ethik . . .', *Kirchliche Dogmatik*, p. 497.

[77] Barth, *Church Dogmatics*, Vol. IV, pt. 1, p. 450; '. . . das grosse Weltgebäude tragenden und zusammenhaltenden Atlas ausüben könne . . .', *Kirchliche Dogmatik*, p. 499.

[78] Barth, *Church Dogmatics* Vol. IV, pt. 2, p. 374; '. . . scwärmerischen Selbstunterweisung', *Kirchliche Dogmatik*, p. 374.

[79] Barth, *Church Dogmatics* Vol. IV, pt. 1, p. 451; 'Damit setzte ich mich auch den Anderen gegenüber sofort ins Unrecht und tue ich ihnen Unrecht, dass ich mich ihnen als der, der Recht hat – ob ich das in Sanftmut oder in Heftigkeit tue, spielt keine Rolle! – gegenüber stelle, als die grosse Krisis über hereinbrechen will. Damit spalte ich mich selbst auf und damit zerbreche ich die Gemeinshaft zwischen mir und den Anderen. Denn in Einheit mit mir selbst könnte ich – und in Gemeinschaft untereinander könnten wir gerade nur dann leben, wenn ich und

When the human creature sets out 'to exercise his own power to judge',[80] we arrive at 'the formation both microcosmically and macrocosmically of a world which is darkened and disrupted and bedevilled by its own self-righteousness'.[81] It is heartening to see how a burning zeal for the freedom and sovereignty of God can act not as a rigid and iron tool of self-righteousness, but as a lever from which all self-righteousness is destabilized.

Barth issues a stern warning against the pride of the creature who would be judge in place of God, out of 'a desire to be God and lord instead of man and servant'.[82] When Barth sees creatures setting themselves up as participants in a battle of good against evil, he notices that 'in this battle all parties . . . think that they are the friends of what is good and the enemies of what is evil':

> Therefore, quite contrary to the purpose and intention of those who take part in it, the more seriously this battle is waged, the more certainly it will lead to pain and tears and crying, so that at the end we have to ask seriously whether the upshot of it all is not a fresh triumph, not for a supposed evil, but for one which is very real. From this final result the theory and practice of what we call tolerance seem to be the final refuge and one which we have to discover again and again . . .[83]

---

wenn wir uns unter das Recht beugen würden, das nicht in uns wohnt und nicht aus uns heraus offenbar wird, sondern als das Recht Gottes in der Höhe über mir und über uns ist und das mir und uns aus dieser Höhe Gottes herunter immer wieder offenbar werden will . . .', *Kirchliche Dogmatik*, p. 501.

[80] Barth, *Church Dogmatics*, Vol. IV, pt. 1, p. 447; '. . . in Ausüben seiner eigenen Gerichtsbarkeit ausrichten kann . . .', *Kirchliche Dogmatik*, p. 496.

[81] Barth, *Church Dogmatics*, Vol. IV, pt. 1, p. 447; '. . . mikrokosmisch und makrokosmisch der Aufbau einer gerade durch ihre Selbstgerichtigkeit verfinsterten, zerrissenen und verteufelten Welt', *Kirchliche Dogmatik*, p. 496.

[82] Barth, *Church Dogmatics*, Vol. IV, pt. 1, p. 447; 'dass er selbst Gott und Herr, statt schlicht Mensch und Knecht sein will', *Kirchliche Dogmatik*, p. 495.

[83] Barth, *Church Dogmatics*, Vol. IV, pt. 1, p. 447; 'der Kampf . . . in welchem sich Alle . . . für die Freunde des Guten und Feinde des Bösen halten: der Kampf, der dann merkwürdigerweise sehr gegen die Meinung und Absicht aller Beteiligten, je ernster er hüben und drüben genommen wird, umso sicherer in allerlei Leid, Tränen und Geschrei – und wie oft so endigen wird, dass man sich ernstlich fragen muss: ob nicht irgend ein neuer Triumph nicht eines angeblichen, sondern das jetzt sehr wirklich Bösen das letzte und eigentliche Ergebnis der Sache gewesen sein möchte? Jenseits dieses Endes und Ergebnisses erscheint dann wohl als letzte, je und je neu zu entdeckende Zuflucht die Theorie und Praxis der sog. Toleranz, d.h. der allgemeinen Müdigkeit, der sich die Menschen jeweils wieder eine Zeitlang hingeben mögen . . .', *Kirchliche Dogmatik*, p. 496.

I would suggest that there is a strand of political liberalism which withdraws from using public power in instigating perfectionist and salvationist programmes, precisely because of a sense of our complicity in sin, the conviction that judgement belongs to God, and a desire to show the charity, toleration and generosity towards our neighbour which we ourselves so painfully need, and at times, so little deserve.

I have no doubt that both Barth and Balthasar would be surprised to see their thought referred to as part of a case for political liberalism. As we saw in the last chapter, Barth's critique of 'absolute man' was directed at – as he understood it – the 'liberal' subject posited by Rousseau, whose 'power and ability' is conceived as 'self-justifying' and 'without any restraint'. Barth is pleased to speak of the 'abandonment by evangelical theology at least in some fields of the traditional liberalism and individualism of the fathers of the eighteenth and nineteenth centuries'.[84] It has been part of the intention of this book to challenge this single characterization of the 'liberal'project, and in so doing, to put a question mark against the monolithic and largely negative notion of the 'modern turn' which was supposed to have occurred between the sixteenth and eighteenth centuries. In exploring the thought of Hooker, Burke and Acton we have been able to suggest that there is what might be called an 'anti-modern' critique of the subject woven in to the very fabric of 'modern' political thought, and that this critique is motivated by theological convictions. So whilst endorsing the theological convictions of Barth and Balthasar, when they condemn the hubris of human self-righteousness and self-perfection, I would want to question what can feel like a judgement against a whole 'post-Enlightenment' project; a judgement sometimes characterized by the very self-righteousness that is being so effectively resisted.

---

[84] Barth, 'The Real Church', p. 63; '. . . die wenigstens in gewissen Bereichen vollzogene Abkehr der evangelischen Theologie von dem überkommenen Liberalismus und Individualismus der Väter des 18. und 19. Jahrhunderts', 'Die Wirkliche Kirche', p. 16.

Constructivism, law and purposive self-limitation

Barth's unease with Rousseau takes us to the source of a deep theological anxiety about 'liberalism': that according to liberalism, the human creature creates order out of chaos, by determining by herself, among other creatures, what this order is, and how it is to be sustained. In contrast the Christian theologian should speak of how God creates order out of nothingness and chaos, with the human constantly owing to God all life, order and meaning. The element in liberal thought where this anxiety seems most justified is the emphasis that can be placed upon what can be broadly called 'constructivism', whereby agents are able to make initially arbitrary – but then binding – determinations about the framework of laws in which they live. So for Rawls, 'political constructivism' provides the nearest that political liberalism has to a 'conception of objectivity': 'Political constructivism is a view about the structure and content of a political conception. It says that once . . . the principles of political justice (content) may be represented as the outcome of a certain procedure of construction.'[85] Rawls' constructivist procedure is given by his original position, already discussed above, where citizens are to form the framework of laws for a just society by imagining themselves behind a veil of ignorance, where they do not know what their specific interests, needs, or conception of the good will be. From behind this veil of ignorance citizens construct the principles and laws of a just society. As we have already seen, this model has been criticized for its abstraction from more full-blooded human commitments. Another charge against it might be its hubris and denial of any element of transcendence or giveness when framing human laws. It is the constructivist nature of liberalism that theologians can have in sight when criticizing 'voluntarism', whereby the human agent, as O'Donovan puts it, is situated at the 'source' with a 'mystical access to the moment of origination' which leads 'the spirit to the rapture of pure terror before the arbitrariness of its own choice'.[86] On this picture the human agent faces pure chaos, nothingness, and creates his or her own arbitrary meaning *ex nihilo*. Robert Kraynak expresses a typical theological judgement when writing that the 'state of nature' out of which liberal philosophers attempt to construct

---

[85] Rawls, *Political Liberalism*, pp. 89–90.
[86] O'Donovan, *The Desire of the Nations*, p. 274.

order is 'a description of human beings . . . living in a chaotic and iso-
lated condition . . . the implication is that God and nature are so
uncaring and stingy that men must construct political authority on
their own through an artificial social contract'.[87]

Such a characterization is plausible if our attention is on a thinker
such as Hobbes, who does indeed see political authority as arising by
human construction out of a chaotic materialistic universe. At the
same time I want to suggest, by looking at Hooker, that there is
another interpretation of constructivism, which is quite compatible,
driven even, by a profound reckoning with our status as creatures.
Again this can be read as taking up the suggestion made by Rawls
that 'political constructivism neither denies nor asserts' that there is
an 'order of moral values' which is 'independent and constitutes
itself'.[88] In that givenness and transcendence is not denied, and if
citizens with comprehensive conceptions of the good are supposed to
be able to affirm political constructivism for reasons from within
their own conceptions, then theologians can address themselves to
the question of what the Christian tradition has to say about 'political constructivism'.

Hooker must always have in view, in the *Laws of Ecclesiastical
Polity*, the Calvinist convictions of his more radical brethren. One of
the glories of Calvinism is its clear witness to the sovereign freedom
of God, leading to an anxiety that in liturgies, institutions or hierarchies we make, as Calvin says, 'golden chains . . . with which to
bind Him'.[89] An aspect of Hooker's task can be understood as an
attempt to reckon both with this sovereign freedom of God, as well
as with the law-governed patterns of order and regularity in which
we live. These law-governed patterns include the natural, the political and the ecclesiastical (in Hooker's case the Church of England).
Hooker finds that this tension is resolved by attending to the very
origin of law in the Godhead. Law arises from the voluntary and
purposive self-limitation of God:

> If therefore it be demanded, why God having power and ability
> infinite, the effects notwithstanding of that power are all so limited
> as we see they are: the reason hereof is the end which he hath

---

[87] Robert P. Kraynak, *Christian Faith and Modern Democracy* (Notre Dame,
Indiana: University of Notre Dame Press, 2001), pp. 31–2.

[88] Rawls, *Political Liberalism*, p. 95.

[89] John Calvin, *Concerning the Eternal Predestination of God*, trans. J. K. S.
Reid (London: James Clark, 1961), p. 170.

proposed, and the law whereby his wisdom hath stinted the effects of his power in such sort, that it doth not work infinitely but correspondently unto that end for which it worketh, even all things in most decent and comely sort, all things in measure, number and weight.[90]

All law to some extent derives from and imitates this divine self-limitation. The law which is 'laid up in the bosom of God, they call eternal'. This eternal law 'receiveth according unto the different kinds of things which are subject unto it different and sundry kind of names'.[91] The laws which are subject in different ways to the eternal law include natural laws ('which ordereth natural agents'), celestial laws ('which Angels do clearly behold'), laws of reasons ('which bindeth creatures reasonable in this world'), divine law ('not known but by special revelation from God'), and *human* law, which 'out of the law either of reason or of God, men probably gathering to be expedient, they make it a law'.[92]

Human law, although arising out of the law of reason or of God, need not be directly determined in its content by either of these things, but by the 'probabilistic' judgement that something is expedient, and should be a law. Human law, no less than natural, celestial or divine law, is ultimately derived from the initial divine self-limitation. Hooker talks of a two-fold eternal law. The first law eternal is the direct result of God's self-limitation; the second law eternal is what arises from human self-limitation, which is only possible in that it is the glory of the human creature to be created with the capability of (divine-like) self-limitation:

All things therefore, which are as they ought to be, are conformed unto *this second law eternal*, and even those things which to this *eternal* law are not conformable, are notwithstanding in some sort ordered by the *first eternal law*. For what good or evil under the sun, what action correspondent or repugnant unto the law which God hath imposed upon his creatures, but in or upon it God doth work according to the law which himself hath eternally purposed to keep, that is to say, the *first law eternal*.[93]

---

90 Hooker, *Laws*, Bk. I, 2.3–4, p. 56.
91 Hooker, *Laws*, Bk. I, 3.1, p. 58.
92 Hooker, *Laws*, Bk. I, 3.1, p. 58.
93 Hooker, *Laws*, Bk. I, 3.1, pp. 58–9.

So when Hooker goes on to discuss 'positive laws which men impose upon themselves' there is no ultimate tension for Hooker between the notion that these laws arise 'by vow unto God', or by 'contract with men'.[94] Societies have the gifted power of purposive self-limitation which imitates the divine, and which can be manifested – for instance – in the making of agreements among the people to place power in a prince or legislative body. In that this gift is the self-limitation of the society, power does not drop immediately from God to the Prince, but arises from the entire society who can invest it in the Prince. Political authority is from God, but mediated necessarily through the consent of society; in the act of purposive self-limitation we find an imitation of the divine made possible by grace not pride. God has given us the 'power of making laws whereby to govern'. This 'lawful power of making laws to command whole political societies of men belongeth so properly unto the same entire societies' that there is warning given that no 'Prince or potentate of what kind soever upon earth' should 'exercise the same of himself and not . . . by authority derived at the first from their consent upon whose persons they impose laws'.[95] For them to so do is 'no better than tyranny'.[96]

Like Burke later on, we have a pre-democratic principle of authority arising from the consent of the people, which consent is ultimately ordered to and derived from the divine. With Hooker, as with Burke later on, 'consent' is registered through a diffuse and implicit historical participation in a society and its institutions, to the point that just as a 'man's deed past is good as long as himself continueth: so the act of a public society of men done five hundred years since standeth as theirs, who presently are of the same societies'.[97]

'Contractual' arrangements will always be constructivist, but not necessarily the other way round (depending on how diffuse the notion of a 'contract' can be allowed to become). So for instance, Burke would be a constructivist, with the human construction being tested and authorized by the passing of time. The problem Burke has with contracterian models is less that they are constructed, or that the consent comes from the people, but rather the speed with which laws are framed. A contractarian thinker, such as Rawls, would be

---

[94] Hooker, *Laws*, Bk. I, 10.7, p. 92.
[95] Hooker, *Laws*, Bk. I, 10.8, p. 93.
[96] Hooker, *Laws*, Bk. I, 10.8, p. 93.
[97] Hooker, *Laws*, Bk. I, 10.8, p. 93.

comfortable with the hypothetical exercise of imagining the laws of a society being derived from a one-off and artificial rational reflection. The problem Burke has with contractarian models is not that they are constructed, or that the consent comes from the people; of much more concern to Burke is the one-off nature of the contractarian exercise, conceived of as happening in the fashion of a negotiating committee. A contractarian model conceives of it as possible that there could be – albeit hypothetically – a specific time when the complex and constructed self-determinations of society could be framed and sanctioned.

For Burke, even the parties necessary for a contract – such as the 'people' – only have an existence that can be discerned over a huge and complex swath of time. Some care is needed here in understanding the precise nuance of Burke's claim that in the state of nature there is 'no such thing as a people'.[98] The idea of a people is the idea of a 'corporation', 'it is wholly artificial; and made like all other legal fictions by common agreement':

> What the particular nature of that agreement was, is collected from the form into which the particular society has been cast. Any other is not *their* covenant. When men, therefore, break up the original compact or agreement which gives its corporate form and capacity to a state, they are no longer a people; they have no longer a corporate existence: they have no longer a legal, coactive force to bind within, nor a claim to be recognized abroad.[99]

There is, for Burke, no 'natural' appeal to democratic rights, if by 'natural' we strip away all of the artificial achievements of man's higher 'nature'. Outside of civil society, majority and minority are 'relations with no existence'.[100] The crucial subtlety to remember is that something being 'wholly artificial' for Burke just means that it is a higher part of nature, artifice being man's nature. So what is wrong with appeals to the 'people' that appeal only to raw nature ('the state of nature'), and which do not consider artifice, is that they fail to do justice to the true dignity and complexity of the 'natural' category 'the people'. Where there is 'a people' it is more than a natural animal category, and has connotations of order, beauty and harmony:

---

[98] Edmund Burke, 'Appeal from the New to the Old Whigs', in *Works and Correspondence*, Vol. IV, p. 462.

[99] Burke, 'Appeal', p. 463.

[100] Burke, 'Appeal', p. 465.

When great multitudes act together, under that discipline of nature,
I recognize the PEOPLE. I acknowledge something that perhaps
equals, and ought always to guide the sovereignty of convention. In
all things the voice of this grand chorus of national harmony ought
to have a mighty and decisive influence. But when you disturb this
harmony; when you break up this beautiful order, this array of
truth and nature, as well as of habit and prejudice; when you separate the common sort of men from their proper chieftains so as to
form them into an adverse army, I no longer know that venerable
object called the people in such a disbanded race of deserters and
vagabonds.[101]

There is a similar theological instinct here to that worked out in
Hooker. Where Burke talks of nature at its highest being artificial, we
are not so far removed from Hooker's understanding of human
beings, who in their (natural and created) freedom to construct
(artificial) political order imitate the purposive self-limitation of
God. For Burke, 'non-artificial' nature would not be complex and
rich enough to give birth to a people and its rights, any more than a
merely biological account of a person could describe the 'person'.

Both Hooker and Burke need to be approached with some caution
in relation to the notion of 'contract' : the more historically diffuse
the notion becomes the more it fits their positions, but the less there
is to be gained from calling it a 'contract', in that such careful
qualification is needed ('by "contract" we have in mind the historically diffuse incorporation within a society with consent being
shown by implicit and unreflective participation as much by explicit
assent'). The contrast here is well brought out by attending to Rawls'
notion, which is so clearly contracterian, with the original position
giving rise to explicit assent and articulation of a framework of
society. Of course, the contracterian original position in Rawls is
hypothetical, a device of representation; but there is, in Rawls, the
distinctive contracterian assumption that it is useful and possible to
conceive of the whole framework of society being worked out at one
synchronic moment, rather than there being a necessary diachronic
element involving time, trial and error.

Nonetheless, inasmuch as a theological anxiety about liberalism is
directed at the constructivist moment – the positing of the human as

---

[101] Burke, 'Appeal', pp. 466–7.

God not creature – thinkers such as Hooker, writing amid the (constructivist) origins of political liberalism, and later on Burke, are able to challenge the sense that there is only one theological story to be told about constructivism. In Hooker and Burke we have an account of human law-making which is to an extent constructivist, in that humans make arbitrary self-determinations on matters of government. Further, with both Hooker and Burke we have an understanding of law that opens the door to a certain relativism and particularism in political arrangements, in that what is binding for one society may not be for another. Alongside a commitment to the eternal law of God, there is also an acknowledgement that this eternal law can find legitimate expression in a finite number of different human laws. So Hooker makes no claims for the universality of the form of church government instituted in England, allowing that in France or Switzerland quite a different form of ecclesiastical polity might be appropriate. Although resisting Calvinist models of church government in England, Hooker concedes that Calvinist measures in Geneva were such that 'I see not how the wisest at that time living could have bettered, if we duly consider what the present estate of Geneva did then require'.[102]

The lesson we can draw from Hooker, and from Burke, is that constructivism and particularism need not be symptomatic of the human creation of order *ex nihilo*, but can be received by us as gift and possibility at the end of a long chain of ordered creation. Freedom, in the sense of purposive self-limitation, is the culmination of our createdness, one of our highest glories where we imitate the divine by fulfilling our created purposes, rather than by denying that we are creatures. Not only are we creatures, but we are created, and the creator is gracious and calls us to stewardship and responsibility.

A caveat: Anglicanism, invisibility and the national Church

There are parts of Hooker's *Laws of Ecclesiastical Polity* which shine out for us in terms of the theological engagement with pluralism and doctrinal conflict, alongside a commitment to peace and unity. In that political liberalism is an attempt to grapple with the same problems and aspirations, Hooker can help us to unearth a 'history of the present', the theologico-political origins of our predicament, and the

---

[102] Hooker, *Laws*, Preface, Ch. II.4, p. 6.

sources of hope and limitation therein. At the same time, it needs
to be faced that there are strands of *Laws of Ecclesiastical Polity*
where Hooker's strangeness to us comes to the fore, where we stand
cautioned if we are hoping simply to use him as a resource for framing a theological attitude to political liberalism. This needs to be
reckoned with, both for the sake of scholarly integrity, but also
because the difference between Hooker's situation and ours is
instructive for our understanding of the latter, as well as helping us
to unlock what is going on in some recent attempts – such as Radical
Orthodoxy – to return to a pre-modern polity.

Hooker regards the nation and the national Church of England to
be coextensive. For this reason Hooker can spend Book VIII of the
Laws of Ecclesiastical Polity arguing that the national sovereign
must also be head of the national Church. The assumption that a
citizen of the commonwealth will also be a member of the Church of
England, whose head will also be the civil governor, is clearly antithetical to the separation of powers, the diversity and the pluralism
prized by the political liberal. Although Hooker may establish theological grounds for reciprocity and toleration within the Church of
England, the Church stands for the whole nation in a way which
simply does not apply for us, and stands as a check to any 'liberal'
appropriation of Hooker.

To understand the full implications of Hooker's position, we need
to follow his argument very closely. The case he makes can be put
as follows. *When* the visible Church and the commonwealth are
identical it is 'expedient' as a matter of human law to have the King
as head of the Church. The reason for this is that the King, in both
civil and ecclesiastical matters, is bound by the law (in all the senses
discussed above): 'the *King* of himself cannot change the nature of
pleas nor courts . . . because the law is a bar unto him . . . the positive
laws of the realm have abridged therein and restrained the *King's*
power'.[103] So to have the King as the head of the visible Church is in
effect to have the ancient laws of the Church as supreme in the
visible Church, for '*Kings* have dominion to exercise in *Ecclesiastical*
causes but according to the laws of the *Church*'.[104] 'The received laws
and liberties of the *Church*' are such that 'the *King* hath supreme
authority and power but against them none'.[105]

---

[103] Hooker, *Laws*, Bk. VIII, 3.3, p. 150.
[104] Hooker, *Laws*, Bk. VIII, 3.3, p. 150.
[105] Hooker, *Laws*, Bk. VIII, 3.3, p. 150.

Ecclesiastical laws, like civil laws, are human laws which are ultimately answerable to eternal order, but mediately constructed by human communities practising their ability of purposive self-limitation. Recognizing the nature of the human laws of the visible Church – contingent, particular yet binding – helps us to realize that the visible Church is not the invisible Church. The danger of either Rome or Geneva, for Hooker, is that in different ways they obscure the human nature of the visible Church, by ambitiously conflating it with the invisible Church. Rome does this by having a Pope, not bound by ecclesiastical and civil laws in the same way as a King, whose ability as an *individual* to practise both spiritual and temporal power leads to tyranny. So Hooker complains that 'the yielding up of supreme power over all *Churches* into one only Pastor's hands' leads to 'woeful inconveniences whereunto the state of *Christendom* was subject heretofore through the tyranny and oppression of that one universal *Nimrod* who alone did all'.[106]

The pernicious influence from Geneva, as Hooker sees it, is towards smaller congregations who separate themselves from the commonwealth by forming communities of the saints, separated from their fallen brethren. If Rome tends to tyranny, Geneva tends to enthusiasm. Both allow undue influence to the arbitrary will of powerful individuals, rather than being ruled by the purposive self-limitation of generations, embodied within national laws. For Hooker at least, the role of the King as head of the national Church both flags and preserves its humble status as only the visible Church, always answerable to the invisible body of Christ which transcends visible boundaries. So because 'the *Headship* which we give unto *Kings* is altogether visibly exercised and ordereth only the external frame of the *Church's* affairs here amongst us . . . it plainly differeth from *Christ's* even in very nature and kind'.[107]

Hooker's argument contains both a theological instinct, which we endorse, and socio-political assumptions, from which we dissent. The theological instinct, which has been my concern throughout this chapter, is Hooker's refusal to conflate the visible and invisible Church, and the consequent call to charity, self-examination and reciprocity. The questionable socio-political assumptions are two-fold: first of all that the nation of England is co-extensive with the

---

[106] Hooker, *Laws*, Bk. VIII, 3.5, p. 157.
[107] Hooker, *Laws*, Bk. VIII, 4.5, p. 162.

Church of England, that there is a sort of corporate national body, bound together by generations of custom and law:

> . . . we hold that seeing there is not any man of the *Church of England*, but the same man is also a member of the *Commonwealth*, nor any man a member of the *Commonwealth* which is not also of the *Church of England* . . . that no person appertaining to the one can be denied to be also of the other.[108]

Even in Hooker's day this is a highly prescriptive claim rather than a neutral description. The unity Hooker assumes was indeed the purpose of the 1559 Acts of Supremacy and Uniformity, respectively establishing the King as the supreme head of the Church of England, and the forbidding of any public prayer than the second prayer-book of Edward VI; but it is precisely because of the pressure from Dissenters and the universality of the Roman Catholic claim that Hooker is motivated to write the *Laws of Ecclesiastical Polity*. In his stated assumption he denies what must be a *raison d'être* of his whole work. Hooker's crafted blindness here is related to his second socio-political assumption, that people outside the Church of England (those who gravitate either to Rome or Geneva) are not capable of the reciprocity, charity and respect for law and custom which is required to be a peaceful citizen of the commonwealth. Given these assumptions, Hooker's theological instinct leads him to identify the nation with the national Church, and guard against the dangers of Rome and Geneva by placing the law (in the form of the King) at the head of the visible Church.

Neither of Hooker's socio-political assumptions are at all tenable or acceptable today, if indeed they ever were. In Hooker's sense there is no Church of England, if by that we mean a corporate body which exclusively embodies the life, law and custom of the nation. Rather we have a vastly diverse range of traditions, both faith-based and secular. Neither is it at all plausible to suggest that Rome or Geneva are incapable of appreciating the importance of separating the visible from the invisible Church, as we have seen from the discussion above of von Balthasar and Karl Barth. All Churches – and perhaps all faiths – are capable of both insight and error here; particularly low points in the Church of England's career, I suggest later on, are the

---

[108] Hooker, *Laws*, Bk. VIII, 1.2, p. 130.

Stuart polity of Charles I, and aspects of the Radical Orthodoxy movement coming out of Cambridge in the late twentieth century.

The debate about the national Church in relation to the invisible Church is picked up in the nineteenth century by Samuel Taylor Coleridge's *Constitution of Church and State*. Coleridge, like Hooker, wishes to defend the notion of the national Church, which in some way is identified with the nation as a mystical corporate body, whilst also reckoning profoundly with the hiddeness of the invisible Church (in Coleridge's terms the 'Church of Christ'), and the need to negotiate pluralism and conflict.

Like Hooker, Coleridge has a powerful sense of the difference between any visible Church and the invisible Church, the Church of Christ. So Coleridge answers an imaginary interlocutor who asks '*In what relation then do you place Christianity to the National Church?*': 'In relation to the National Church, Christianity, of the Church of Christ, is a blessed accident, a providential boon, a grace of God . . .'[109] The Christian Church, the invisible Church of Christ, is 'no state, kingdom, of realm of this world; nor is it an Estate of any such realm, kingdom or state; but it is the appointed Opposite to them all *collectively* – the *sustaining, correcting, befriending* Opposite of the world . . .'.[110]

Coleridge does not make a complete identification of the Church and commonwealth, as Hooker does, but nonetheless sees an intrinsic interdependence between Church and state. Coleridge uses the word 'state' in two ways; in one usage 'state' denotes government, and indicates a sphere separate from 'Church', but in another sense 'state' can include within its scope 'Church' as one of the three estates of the realm. The three estates are the gentry, the merchant classes and the Church. The gentry provides, Coleridge considers, the necessary element of permanence ('law'), the merchants provide the counter-balancing progressivism ('liberty'), giving overall a balance of 'law and liberty'.

The proper end of the third estate, the national Church, is to form the character of the nation in such a way to combine freedom with civilization, 'to form and train up the people of the country to

---

[109] S. T. Coleridge, *On the Constitution of Church and State*, ed. J. Colmer (London: Routledge and Kegan Paul, 1976), p. 55. Vol. 10 of the Collected Works of Samuel Taylor Coleridge.

[110] Coleridge, *Constitution*, p. 114.

obedient, free, useful, organizable subjects, citizens, and patriots, living to the benefit of the state and prepared to die for its defence':

> The proper *object* and end of the National Church is civilization with freedom; and the duty of its ministers, could they be comprehended merely and exclusively as officiaries of the *National* Church, would be fulfilled in the communication of that degree and kind of knowledge to all, the possession of which is necessary for all in order to their CIVILITY. By civility I mean all the qualities essential to a citizen, and devoid of which no people or class of the people can be calculated on by the rulers and leaders of the state for the conservation or promotion of its essential interests.[111]

Here we have an intriguing interplay and tension with the issues surrounding civility, the invisible Church, Hooker and Rawls. On the one hand, we find Hooker and Coleridge addressing our situation powerfully. Motivating both is a resistance to any activist attempt to transform the visible Church into the invisible eschatological gathering in glory of the saints. I have identified this as the theological insight at the heart of political liberalism, that for *theological reasons* public power should not be used to save souls, or in Rawlsian terms, to assert a comprehensive conception of the good.

The virtues that the national Church is supposed to embody are virtues that the political liberal can learn from and endorse – toleration, charity, self-examination – all arising from a powerful sense that it is merely the visible Church, never to be confused with the invisible, the Church of Christ. On the other hand, with both Hooker and Coleridge, there is some sort of identification of the nation with the national Church, which fails both to address the pluralism of our time, and plausibly theirs also; there is also a conviction, which we cannot share, that other theological traditions must always tend towards an unhealthy identification of the visible and invisible, and so cannot be trusted to imbue the citizen with the civility required to live peacefully in society. Where Hooker was concerned about both Rome and Geneva, Coleridge's concern is focused more narrowly on Rome. *On the Constitution of Church and State* is provoked by the proposed Catholic Emancipation Bill of 1829, which promised effectively to undo the 1559 Acts of Supremacy and Uniformity, by

---

[111] Coleridge, *Constitution*, p. 54.

allowing Roman Catholic citizens to practise their Catholicism and to hold public office. Coleridge's overwhelming concern is not about Catholic doctrine, but the 'allegiance to a foreign power'[112] demanded of Catholics, in the form of obedience to the Pope. Coleridge regarded the Pope as a particularly pernicious foreign sovereign in that he conflated, by his office, the visible Church with the invisible Church of Christ, by his claim 'to temporal power and sovereignty, directly or as the pretended consequence of spiritual dominion'.[113] Coleridge's concern here is very close to Hooker's, with Coleridge commenting of the office of Pope that 'the erecting such an office for one man, which no one *man* in the world is able to perform, implies that to be possible which is indeed impossible . . . No one mortal can be a competent head for that Church which has a right to be *Catholic*, and to overspread the face of the whole earth.'[114] To erect such an office conflates the visible and the invisible, in that

> there can be no such head but Christ, who is not mere man, but God in the Divine humanity, and therefore present with every part of the church, and every member thereof, at what distance soever. But to set some one mortal bishop over the whole church, were to suppose that great bishop of our spirit absent from it, who has promised that he *will be with her to the end of the world.*[115]

We can understand the motivation behind the importance Hooker and Coleridge give to the national Church of England; both were motivated by the fear that attempts to improve on a broadly inclusive national Church would lead to various forms of tyranny and enthusiasm, arising from a tendency to conflate the visible and invisible. A resistance to such a conflation is at the heart of the case being made in this book, and is perhaps one of the insights with which Anglicanism is particularly – but not uniquely – gifted. Anglicanism's origins as a national Church – bound together by nation rather than a comprehensive conception of the good and unity in doctrine – is a source of both grace and limitation. Grace, in that Anglicanism has struggled profoundly and systematically – in figures such as Hooker – with the question of pluralism and diversity. There is a popular caricature

---

[112] Coleridge, *Constitution*, p. 78.
[113] Coleridge, *Constitution*, p. 137.
[114] Coleridge, *Constitution*, p. 126.
[115] Coleridge, *Constitution*, p. 126.

of Anglicanism that tends to revolve around its vagueness, its middle-of-the-road compromise between extremes and its attempt to make a rather bland *via media* between options which are all together more vigorous, interesting and full-blooded. By understanding the roots of the Anglican tradition such a caricature can be both explained, and yet exposed as a barely adequate pastiche. The Anglican endorsement of compromise, toleration and moderation is not based upon an indecisiveness, half-heartedness, lack of commitment or a politically apathetic acquiescence in the status quo. Rather it is based firmly on theologically mature doctrinal commitments that have arisen from a pragmatic and prayerful contemplation of historical complexity, tempered by a sense of the dangers of self-righteously conflating the visible and invisible. We are creatures, all of us under judgement and requiring mercy and generosity; we do well not to judge our neighbour, but to distrust ourselves and show charity towards others. All human understanding – including of scripture – is mediated through human reason, which is both created and fallen and mediated through complex historical factors. Human law and custom, accumulated and tested by time, in all its particular and diverse forms, has the potential to imitate, obscurely and imperfectly, the purposive self-limitation of God.

At the same time, Anglicanism's origins as a national Church are a source of limitation, which comes to the fore in considering Hooker and Coleridge. This element of Anglican identity relies on society being much less pluralistic and diverse than it is now. Even in Hooker's time, there was a degree of diversity and dissent that rendered the 'national' status of the Church of England problematic. The pain is felt both politically and ecclesiastically: politically in that even finely motivated thinkers such as Hooker and Coleridge end up recommending the exclusion of Dissenters and Catholics from the national life. Importantly, and precisely because of the distinction between the visible and the invisible, this exclusion from the national life is never conceived by Hooker or Coleridge as an exclusion from God's salvation history. So, in the context of intense anti-Catholic fervour, prejudice and fear of foreign (Catholic) invasion, Hooker was prepared to insist that even a Pope could be part of the invisible Church:

> I tell you, I would not be afraid to say unto a cardinal or a pope
> . . . 'Be of good comfort, ours in a merciful God'. Let me die if
> ever it be proved that simply an error would exclude a pope or a

cardinal from all hope of eternal life. I confess to you that if it be an error to think God may be merciful to save men when they err, then my greatest comfort is my error. Were it not for the love I bear this error, I would neither wish to speak nor to live.[116]

Such compassion, self-interrogation and generosity reflect the finest instincts of Anglicanism; nonetheless, exclusion from the national life is still exclusion, and is painful and unjust, however tempered with humanity and loving intentions. The painful limitations of Anglicanism's origins can be felt ecclesiastically also, in that it can be hard for the Anglican Church to know what to do when it is no longer the national Church, but is expected – by its own members and by wider society – to be more like a voluntary community united around a single conception of the good, which it never was, and where its not being such was in some respects its theological gift to the wider body of Christ.

Coleridge's nephew Henry Coleridge wrote a preface to the third edition of *On the Constitution of Church and State*. He ends his preface with an extraordinarily suggestive passage, commenting that 'when the Nation, fatigued with the weight of dear and glorious recollections, shall resolve to repudiate its corporate existence and character, and to resolve its mystic unity into the breathing atoms that crowd the surface of the land, – then the national and ancestral Church of England will have an end'.[117] It would require considerable bravado to declare that the Church of England today provides a 'mystic unity' to the English nation, constituting its 'corporate existence and character'. We live in an irreducibly pluralistic culture, with citizens holding a range of reasonable but incompatible conceptions of the good. There can be no doubt then that the 'national and ancestral' Church of England celebrated by Henry Coleridge is at an end. Far from being the end for Anglicanism, it may be a source of renewal, if we draw on the strongest traditions of Anglican thought which – alongside thinkers from other traditions – are motivated by a refusal, manifested in self-deprecation and moderation, to

---

[116] Sermon given in the Temple Church on 1 March 1586, quoted extensively in Philip B. Secor, *Richard Hooker: Prophet of Anglicanism* (Tunbridge Wells: Burns and Oates, 1999), p. 189. The Hooker reference is *A Learned Discourse of Justification, Works and How the Foundation of Faith is Overthrowne*, 1586, Trinity College Dublin, MS 118, *Folger V*.

[117] 'H. N. Coleridge's Preface to the Church and State (1839)', in Coleridge, *Constitution*, p. 200.

conflate the visible and invisible. As H. N. Coleridge put it, 'although the Church *of* England may fall, the Church of Christ *in* England will stand erect; and the distinction, lost now in a common splendour, will be better seen and more poignantly felt by that darkening World to which the Christian Church must become a more conspicuous opposite'.[118]

---

[118] Coleridge, *Constitution*, p. 200.

3

Overcoming Evil With Good –
The American Eschatology and
Crusading Liberalism

President George W. Bush's speeches in the months following the terrorist attack on the World Trade Center on 11 September 2001 espoused a world-view which can be characterized as having three theological moments. First of all there is a tendency to divide the world into good and evil, and to be confident that the two groups can be identified as such, and located in space and time. This division of the world into good and evil is given a dramatic history, stretching back through the ages, and pointing forward to future battles and climaxes. Evil is powerful in this story, and gathers its forces at particular cruxes in the world's history.[1] The second theological moment in Bush's speeches is the reassurance that the forces of good can know that the gathering of evil is just a prelude to its more dramatic defeat. Human action will inaugurate a new world-order of peace, liberty and justice. Third, the forces of good are aligned with a certain zeal for liberty and democracy. We will see that the fight for 'liberty' is closely aligned with a sense of God's purposes within history. In all three cases America has a uniquely responsible, privileged and pivotal role to play, as leader of the axis of good, as the agent for the destruction of evil through tumultuous military action and sacrifice, and as the leader of the free world, the beacon of liberty.[2]

Extracts from various speeches given by Bush are well crafted to convey all three themes in a compact and unambivalent form. So in

---

[1] See the Appendix for a critique of prominent commentaries on American eschatology from Robert Bellah and Clifford Longley.

[2] An earlier version of this chapter was presented to a conference 'Freedom's Threat: Faith, Terror and Global Capitalism' at Heythrop College, University of London, June 2002.

his 'Address to a Joint Session of Congress and the American People' on 21 November 2001 Bush announces the division of the world into good and evil, and locates it in a history of ancient warfare, and future struggle, with the assurance of God's victory, which is the victory of democratic freedom:

> The advance of human freedom – the great achievement of our time, and the great hope of every time – now depends on us. Our nation – this generation – will lift a dark threat of violence from our people and our future. We will rally the world to this cause by our efforts, and by our courage. We will not tire, we will not falter, we will not fail.
>
> The course of this conflict is not known, yet its outcome is certain. Freedom and fear, justice and cruelty, have always been at war, and we know that God is not neutral between them.[3]

By the time of the State of the Union Address on 29 January 2002, all these themes are more developed. Speaking of North Korea, Iran and Iraq, Bush comments: 'States like these, and their terrorist allies, constitute an axis of evil, aiming to threaten the peace of the world.' Having divided the world into good and evil, and located evil within certain times and spaces, Bush explains America's role in a history of the struggle against evil. In this speech we find the promise, after the tumultuous battle which is to take place, of an era of peace and freedom:

> History has called America and our allies to action, and it is both our responsibility and our privilege to fight freedom's fight.
>
> This time of adversity offers a unique moment of opportunity – a moment we must seize to change our culture. Through the gathering momentum of millions of acts of service and decency and kindness, I know we can overcome evil with greater good. And we have a great opportunity during this time of war to lead the world towards the values that will bring lasting peace . . . [4].

---

[3] President George W. Bush, 'Address to a Joint Session of Congress and the American People', United States Capitol, Washington D.C., 21 November 2001. Source: www.whitehouse.gov/news/releases/2001/09/20010920–8.html.

[4] President George W. Bush, 'President Delivers State of the Union Address' 29 January 2002, United States Capitol, Washington D.C., www.whitehouse. gov/news/releases/2002/01/20020129–11.html.

So, for Bush, America is called to the epoch defining defence of 'liberty':

> In a single instant, we realized that this will be a decisive decade in the history of liberty, that we've been called to a unique role in human events. Rarely has the world faced a choice more clear or consequential . . . Steadfast in our purpose, we now press on. We have known freedom's price. We have shown freedom's power. And in this great conflict, my fellow Americans, we will see freedom's victory . . . May God bless.[5]

America's battle, we know, is conceived by Bush as being one against evil. In the President's Easter message on 31 March 2002, we find that this is also Christ's fight, with an explicit link being drawn between the two:

> Easter Sunday commemorates . . . the joy and promise of Christ's triumph over evil . . . .Easter's message of renewal is especially meaningful now during this challenging time in our nation's history . . .
> . . . In the wake of great evil . . . America responded with strength, compassion, and generosity. As we fight to promote freedom around the world and to protect innocent lives in America, we remember the call of the Battle Hymn of the Republic: 'As he died to make men holy, let us live to make men free.'[6]

We have here what might be called Bush's eschatology, with its division of the world into the historical struggle between good and evil, combined with an activist account of how good will overcome evil, and inaugurate the aeon of peace and liberty. In this chapter I will suggest that this eschatology is deeply rooted in a strand of American culture and history. It is, in many of its broad structural features (although not of course its substantial details), the eschatology – that is, the understanding of history and human responsibilities in the light of the world's divinely appointed purpose and

---

[5] President George W. Bush, 'President Delivers State of the Union Address' 29 January 2002, United States Capitol, Washington D.C., www.whitehouse. gov/news/releases/2002/01/20020129–11.html.

[6] President George W. Bush, 'President's Easter Message' 31 March 2002, www.whitehouse.gov/news/releases/2002.

end – of the Puritan founding fathers of America in the seventeenth century.

The story here is a continuation of the discussion of Hooker and the Puritans. The frustration felt since the inauguration of the English Reformation by the 'righteous', the radical Protestants, continued to be fanned and excacerbated during the run up to the English Civil War. The growing influence of the Catholic sympathizer Archbishop Laud in Charles I's court, and the persecution of Puritans between 1629 and 1640, saw twenty thousand radical Protestants fleeing England. The intransigence of the old order led the 'faithful' to depart, giving rise to a profound pessimism about old England. 'I saw the Lord depart from England . . . and I saw the hearts of most of the godly set and bent that way (towards the new way)', wrote Thomas Shepard in his *Autobiography*, 'and I did think I should feel many miseries if I stayed behind . . . the Lord let me see the glory of those liberties in New England'.[7] So also John Winthrop – to become a founder of New England – wrote to his wife: 'all other churches of Europe are brought to desolation, and it cannot be but a like judgement is coming upon us'.[8]

This understanding of the mission and purity of New England was drawn out emphatically by descendants of the settlers in the eighteenth and nineteenth centuries. During this period the understanding of the mission and role of an independent and united America in the world was identified inextricably with a correct interpretation of the biblical drama of salvation history. We will find, at each stage in the history of America, a division of the world into good and evil, a sense of America's activist role in inaugurating the Kingdom, and a zeal for a notion of 'liberty' which arises not from a secular theory of human rights, but from a Calvinist theological tradition which draws a parallel between what it understands to be the proper form of covenantal church government amongst the 'elect', and a democratic form of political government. Democracy, in this tradition, is a symptom of true religion.

In the larger purpose of this book, this chapter shows the necessity of separating the political liberalism defended from theologically

---

[7] Thomas Shepard, *Autobiography* (Boston, 1832), pp. 42–3. Quoted in H. W. Schneider, *The Puritan Mind* (London: Constable, 1931), p. 79.

[8] Quoted in Michael Walzer, *The Revolution of the Saints: A Study in the Origins of Radical Politics* (London: Weidenfeld and Nicolson, 1966). Walzer is quoting from E. S. Morgan, *The Puritan Dilemma: The Story of John Winthrop* (Boston, 1958), p. 40.

over-zealous appropriations of the notion of 'liberty', that emanate, for instance, from some American presidents. We will see how the notion of 'liberty' employed in England, America and France can have some quite distinct theological lineages. So in America the passion for 'liberty' has some of its roots in the Calvinist notion of covenantal church government (liberty from Romish hierarchies) and Christian liberty from sin, guaranteed through the saint's pre-election, leading to activist projects to eliminate evil.

Hooker's thought casts something of a searchlight over this tradition, in that it is precisely the Puritan forebears of this tradition of talking about 'Christian liberty' that Hooker has in sight when writing the *Laws of Ecclesiastical Polity*. The warning Hooker delivers concerning a group of men with great 'zeal and forwardness' rings down into our contemporary situation, as we will observe when considering features of the presentation of American foreign policy, and the rhetoric of anti-globalization protestors. Hooker's complaint against the Puritan has a wider resonance against all those who would be judges, those who confidently divide good from evil and announce an eschatological confidence in the possibilities of human activism. Lying behind and arising from this hubristic judgement and self-righteousness is a conflation of the visible and invisible Church. Hooker's critique can be launched, almost without alteration, against a particular strand of crusading 'liberalism' espoused by certain American presidents which traces its political and theological roots back to the Elizabethan and Stuart period.

An Augustinian eschatology

We can get a grip on the distinctive and controversial nature of the eschatology of the Protestant founding fathers of America by comparing it with the account of history and salvation given by Augustine. Augustine[9] has a division between good and evil, in that he divides humanity into those who belong to the City of God, the communion of saints, the elect, and those who belong to the City of Man – the damned, the unregenerated. The communities are

---

[9] I have found the discussion by R. W. Dyson useful here: 'Introduction', *The City of God Against the Pagans*, ed. R. W. Dyson (Cambridge: Cambridge University Press, 1998), pp. x–xxix; Latin text, *The City of God Against the Pagans*, Loeb Classical Library (London: Heinemann, 1957), in seven volumes.

identified not by their race, history, form of government or language, but by the objects of their love. A people (*populus*) for Augustine is 'an assembled multitude of rational creatures bound together by a common agreement as to the objects of their love', from which 'if we are to discover the character of any people, we have only to examine what it loves'.[10]

The crucial difference between the Augustinian approach and the American eschatology, is that for Augustine the City of God is *not* co-extensive with any institution, historical movement, state or Church. It is a community that transcends space and time and that has little to do with history. So of the elect, those presently alive on earth form only a small part. Other members of this heavenly city are angels who remain loyal to God, and the souls of the elect who have died and are now in heaven. Also the City of Man is not straightforwardly any one empire (Babylon, Assyria, the Roman Empire), nor all of them together, but the souls of the reprobate who are living, the souls of the damned who have died, and its founder members (the apostate angels who fell away from God). In Augustine we have one of the first articulations of the dangers of identifying the visible and invisible Church.

Notably there is not – as there is in the American tradition of eschatology – a gradual historical elimination of one community by the other; there is no overcoming evil with good, no activist inauguration of the invisible Church. Only a small part of each city exists in historical linear time at all. The extent to which the two cities can do no work in history is exemplified by the way in which we cannot tell to which city anyone belongs. So of the saved and the damned, the good and the evil, Augustine comments that:

> When she is a pilgrim in this world, the City of God has with her, bound to her by the communion of the sacraments, some who will not be with her to share eternally in the bliss of the saints. Some of these are concealed. Some of them, however, join openly with our enemies, and do not hesitate to murmur against the God Whose sacrament they bear. Sometimes they crowd into the theatres with our enemies, and sometimes into the churches with us.[11]

---

[10] Augustine, *City of God*, Bk. xix. 24, pp. 960–1. 'Populus est coetus multitudinis rationalis rerum quas diligit concordi communione sociatus . . .', '. . . ut videtur qualis quisque populus sit, illa sunt intuendo quae diligit', Vol. vi (Loeb), pp. 230–2.

[11] Augustine, *City of God*, I, 35; '. . . sicut ex illorum numero etiam Dei

In this wicked world, and in these evil days . . . many reprobate are mingled in the Church with the good. Both are as it were collected in the net of the Gospel; and in this world, as in a sea, both swim together without separation, enclosed in the net until brought ashore.[12]

In this world, until the end of history, the two cities – the saved and the damned – are irreducibly mixed together, which makes a group identification with any one city impossible. Neither good nor evil can be located straightforwardly in any time or space. They will only be visibly divided at the end of history, after history, when Christ comes in judgement. The Kingdom, the end of salvation, is an entirely unworldly, supra-historical affair, characterized by a perfect enjoyment of God.

. . . God will be the end of our desires. He will be seen without end, loved without stint, praised without weariness. And this duty, this affection, this employment, will, like eternal life itself, be common to all.[13]

Then shall we be still, and know that He is God: that He is what we ourselves desired to be when we fell away from Him . . . But when we are restored by Him and perfected by His greater grace, we shall be still for all eternity, and know that He is God, being filled by Him when He shall be all in all.[14]

---

civitas habet secum, quamdiu peregrinatur in mundo, conexos communione sacramentorum, nec secum futuros in aeterna sorte sanctorum, qui partim in occulto, partim in aperto sunt, qui etiam cum ipsis inimias adversus Deum, cuius sacramentum gerunt, murmurare non dubitant, modo cum illis theatra, modo ecclesias nobiscum replentes', Vol. I (Loeb), pp. 136–8.

[12] Augustine, *City of God*, Bk. XVIII. 49, pp. 896–7; 'In hoc ergo saeculo maligno, in his diebus malis . . . multi reprobi miscentur bonis et utrique tamquam in sagenam evangelicum colliguntur et in hoc mundo tamquam in mari utrique inclusi retibus indiscrete natant, donec perveniatur ad litus.', Vol. VI (Loeb), p. 60.

[13] Augustine, *City of God*, XXII, 30; '. . . Ipse finis erit desideriorum nostrorum qui sine fine videbitur, sine fastidio amabitur, sine fatigatione laudabitur. Hoc munus, hic affectus, hic actus profecto erit omnibus, sicut ipsa vita aeterna, communis', Vol. VII (Loeb), p. 374.

[14] Augustine, *City of God*, XXII, 30; 'Ibi vacantes videbimus quoniam ipse est Deus; qoud nobis nos ipsi esse voluiumus quando ab ilto cecidimus . . . A quo refecti et gratia maiore perfecti vacabimus in aeturnum, videntes quia ipse est Deus, quo pleni erimus quando ipse erit omnia in omnibus', Vol. VII (Loeb), p. 374.

Overcoming the Antichrist and crusading liberalism

We can see clearly that Bush's eschatology is not on any reading Augustinian. There can be, for Augustine, no visible division of the world into good and evil, and there is no historical movement towards some sort of end or completion. The destiny of both the cities lies outside history. The City of God is destined to remain secret and hidden until the end, it 'lives like a captive and a stranger in the earthly city, though it has already received the promise of redemption, and the gift of the Spirit as a kind of pledge of it'.[15] There is a built-in limit to what activism of any nature can achieve. Society can never be thoroughly 'redeemed' by human action, because our wills are too intent upon their own egocentric ends.

We find a challenge to this historically non-activist eschatology from some Protestant interpreters of the Reformation,[16] who move away from the idea that the world will go on in the same way until judgement day breaks in. It is understandable that there might be something of a pressure on reformers to arrive at a different account of history, in that they must deal with the apparent scandal that God has allowed the Church to become so unregenerate. One possible explanation is to account for the power and corruption of the Catholic Church in terms of an historical progression God is making in overcoming evil, of which the Reformation is one particularly important victory.[17]

---

[15] Augustine, *City of God*, Bk. XIX. 17, pp. 945–61; '. . . dum apud terrenam civitatem velut captivam vitam suae peregrinationis agit, iam promissione redemptionis et dono spiritali tamquam pignore accepto . . .', Vol. VI (Loeb), p. 194.

[16] At this point I have found useful the discussion in Ernest Lee Tuveson, *Redeemer Nation: The Idea of America's Millennial Role* (Chicago: University of Chicago Press, 1968), Ch. 1.

[17] We can see something of this attitude in the young Milton, when writing *Of Reformation Touching Church Discipline in England: And the Causes that hitherto have hindered it* (London: Oulton and Gregory Dexter for Thomas Underhill, 1641), Bk. I, pp. 5–6: 'But to dwell no longer in characterizing the depravities of the church, and how they sprung, and how they took increase; when I recall to mind at last, after so many dark ages, wherein the huge overshadowing train of error had almost swept all the stars out of the firmament of the church, how the bright and blissful Reformation (by divine power) struck through the black and settled night of ignorance and antichristian tyranny, methinks a sovereign and reviving joy must needs rush into the bosom of him that reads or hears; and the sweet odor of the returning gospel imbathe his soul with the fragrency of heaven. Then was the sacred Bible sought out of the dusty

The Revelation of St John is highly appropriate for this sort of millennialism. The book accounts for history as the progressive overcoming of evil by good. This progress is not a gradual linear one, but involves a series of dramatic defeats of evil, with all means – spiritual, political, military and social – being used to overthrow the evil. The drama of the book of Revelation has seven 'vials' being opened upon the 'beast', the Antichrist, each vial being a stage in the defeat of the evil one. A key figure in the American context, who typifies this eschatological approach, is Jonathan Edwards, a president of Princeton, and a leading light in the evangelical revival of the 1740s known as the 'Great Awakening'. In his 'History of the Work of Redemption' Edwards lays out an historical progression which moves towards the earthly inauguration of the millennial Kingdom of God, which will be before the day of judgement. After describing the corruption into which the pre-Reformation church had fallen Edwards glories that with the Reformation, when 'the fifth angel poured out his vial on the seat of the beast',[18] 'God began gloriously to revive his church again, and to advance the kingdom of his Son'.[19]

The 'authority and dominion of the Pope'[20] (the Antichrist) is now severely diminished. But precisely because of the threat posed to it 'when the Reformation began, the beast with seven heads and ten horns began to rage in a dreadful manner'.[21] Edwards understands the seven heads as the seven hills of Rome, and the ten horns as the kingdoms into which the Roman Empire broke up. The raging of the beast is interpreted as being a reference to the persecution of

---

corners where profane falsehood and neglect had thrown it, the schools opened, divine and human learning raked out of the embers of forgotten tongues, the princes and cities trooping apace to the new erected banner of salvation; the martyrs, with the unresistable might of weakness, shaking the powers of darkness, and scorning the fiery rage of the old red dragon.'

[18] Edwards himself is quoting Revelation. The context of the quote is as follows: 'It is said, Rev. xvi. 10 that "the fifth angel poured out his vial on the seat of the beast;" in the original, it is *the throne of the beast*; "and his kingdom was full of darkness, and they gnawed their tongues for pain, and blasphemed the God of heaven because of their pains and sores and repented not of their deeds." He poured out his vial upon the throne of the beast, i.e. on the authority and dominion of the Pope . . .' In Jonathan Edwards, 'History of the Work of Redemption', pp. 11–303, in *The Works of President Edwards in Eight Volumes*, Vol. v (Leeds: Edward Baines, 1809), pp. 229–30.

[19] Edwards, 'History', p. 229.

[20] Edwards, 'History', pp. 229–30.

[21] Edwards, 'History', p. 233.

Protestants in Europe.[22] Given the continuing power of the beast in Europe, the bringing of the gospel into New England marks a crucial new development in the overthrow of Satan's power:

> ... yet I think we may well look upon the discovery of so great a part of the world, and bringing the gospel into it, as one thing by which divine providence is preparing the way for the future glorious times of the church; when Satan's kingdom shall be overthrown, throughout the whole habitable globe, on every side, and on all its continents.[23]

The bringing of the gospel to New England is a crucial victory, but by no means one to be complacent about. Just as with the pouring of the fifth vial (the Reformation), the 'powers of hell' became more desperate, so too now and in the future Edwards promises a 'violent and *mighty opposition* made' by 'Satan's visible kingdom'.[24] America will confront and overcome this resistance, ensuring that 'all countries and nations, even those which are now most ignorant, shall be full of light and knowledge':[25]

> ... this is most properly the time of the kingdom of *heaven upon earth*. Though the kingdom of heaven was in a degree set up soon after Christ's resurrection, and in a further degree in the time of Constantine; and though the Christian church in all ages of it is called the *kingdom of heaven*; yet this is the principal time of the kingdom of heaven upon the earth.[26]

This pattern for interpreting history becomes the dominant Evangelical model in the second half of the eighteenth century. It is certainly the framework within which Bush's predecessor, John Adams, the second president of the United States, is thinking in his *Dissertation on the Canon and Feudal Law* published in the *Boston Gazette* of August 1765.[27] Adam's *Dissertation* contains in abundance the three

---

[22] The list Edwards gives is as follows: Germany, Bohemia, Poland, Lithuania and Hungary, Italy, Spain, France under Louis XIV, and England under Mary. Edwards, 'History', pp. 234–5.

[23] Edwards, 'History', p. 238.

[24] Edwards, 'History', p. 258.

[25] Edwards, 'History', p. 270.

[26] Edwards, 'History', p. 269.

[27] John Adams, 'A Dissertation on the Canon and the Feudal Law', in *The True Sentiments of America* (London: I. Almon, 1768).

theological moments identified in Bush – judgement of who is good and evil, activism and an explicitly religious zeal for 'liberty'. Adams can give us a particular insight into the way in which a certain notion of liberty and democracy is aligned with a form of Calvinist ecclesiastical government, characterized by the rule of the elect (the saved) within a covenant. The proper form of ecclesiastical and political governance is set in contrast to the unholy alliance made between the Roman Empire ('feudal law') and the Roman Church ('canon law'). This alliance chained 'human nature' in a 'cruel, shameful, and deplorable servitude'[28] to Satan.

What we do not find here is a defence of liberty or democracy on the basis of a secular Enlightenment view of human rights. Neither is the defence made on the basis of the self-examination, caution, tolerance and self-restraint encouraged by Hooker, Burke, Acton and Rawls, if the argument of the last two chapters is correct. No more is the defence made on the basis of the ancient liberties of the subject. Rather the case for political liberty is made on the back of a conviction about the nature of true religion. Only the Reformation was able to lift this 'wicked confederacy between the two systems of tyranny' which was so 'calamitous to human liberty'.[29] Both political and ecclesiastical systems of 'ascendancy' or hierarchy are, for Adams, part of the armoury of Satan who wishes to prevent the gospel regenerating sinners by 'impressing on their minds a blind, implicit obedience' to both the 'priesthood' and 'civil magistracy'.[30]

Here we have a key, from a former president of the United States writing a theological tract, to understanding some of the differences between the theoretical origins of democracy in America, Britain and France (arguably the three countries where the modern democratic model was formulated). There is a narrative – which a figure like Adams challenges – about American democracy, which claims that it is a child of Enlightenment reason, of a secular experiment to eliminate traces of bigotry, superstition and religion from a rational Lockean contract made among the people. According to this account, the division in America between church and state is an example of the way in which the business of politics is kept hygienically clean of inappropriate religious enthusiasms and hopes. An implication of this myth is that it is others who have traces of strange

---

28 Adams, 'Dissertation', p. 126.
29 Adams, 'Dissertation', p. 116.
30 Adams, 'Dissertation', p. 116.

eschatologies and religious hopes, whether the 'others' are Communist idealogues or fundamentalist Muslims. Contrasting someone like Adams with an early theorist of democracy in a British or French context can help us to see that this story is problematic, in that the notion of 'liberty' in American religious and political history has consistently had a theological motivation and importance which has been explicitly disowned in a European context.

To take the example of Britain, we can see that an early theorist of democracy such as Hobbes was working in the context of a recent English Civil War in the 1640s. Hobbes perceived the conflict as largely caused by disputes about religious doctrine,[31] in general terms around the issue of how Calvinist the Church of England should be. In his work *Behemoth,* where Hobbes gives his account of the causes of the Civil War in England, he lists some theological 'mysteries' and disputes (such as the Trinity, the Incarnation and Free-will), and comments that 'these and like points are the study of the curious, and the cause of all our late mischiefs'.[32] Hobbes determined that reli-

---

[31] See Thomas Hobbes, *Behemoth: The History of the Civil Wars of England, From the Year 1640, to 1660* (London, 1680). Setting Hobbes and Adams against each other reaps rich rewards, when one considers how Hobbes makes explicit – from a diametrically opposed point of view – the link between the demands for political and religious liberty, along with the links between obedience to kings and to church government. Consider Hobbes' observations on the dangers of the Reformation conviction that the gospel regenerates the elect and brings them to a sense of their Christian liberty:

> ... for after the *Bible* was translated into English, every man, nay every boy and wench that could read English, thought they spoke with God Almighty, and understood what he said; when by a certain number of chapters a day, they had read the Scriptures once or twice over, the Reverence and Obedience due to the *Reformed Church* here, and to the *Bishops* . . . was cast off; and every man became a Judge of *Religion*, and an Interpreter of the *Scriptures* to himself . . . this licence of interpreting the *Scripture*, was the cause of so many several sects as have lain hid till the beginning of the late King's reign; and did then appear, to the Disturbance of the *Common-Wealth.* (*Behemoth*, pp. 28–9)

Remember the parallel Adams drew between canon and feudal law, and then consider how Hobbes claims that what the ministers 'did in the *Pulpit*' to 'draw people to their opinions, and to dislike the *Church-Government*, *Canons*, and *Common-Prayer-Book*; so did the other [Gentlemen] make them [the people] in love with *Democratie*, by their *Harangues* in the *Parliament* and by their discourse and communication with people in the country, continually extolling *Liberty*, and inveighing against *Tyranny*, leaving the people to collect of themselves, that this *Tyranny* was the present *Government* of the *State*' (p. 30).

[32] Hobbes, *Behemoth*, p. 73. The theological 'mysteries' Hobbes lists as:

> How it may be made out with wit, that there be Three that bear rule in Heaven, and those Three but One? How the Deity could be made flesh? How

gious opinion and dissension should not be allowed to disturb the peace of the realm again. His solution was two-fold. First of all, to find something upon which all people could agree. This something was fear of death. Everybody having a fear of death, there could be a contract made between the people to put over themselves an absolute ruler, whose absolute rule depends entirely upon his ability to protect the people from attack, both from a foreign power, and from each other. Therein lies Hobbes' democratic quality: although we have an absolute ruler, his power is secured only by the consent and contract of the people. It is not the role of the ruler to promote true religion, but simply to preserve the peace by preventing religious conflict.

The second part of the solution, seemingly paradoxical, was to insist upon an established church. It is quite explicit in Hobbes that the point of having an established Church of England is to make the ecclesiastical power entirely *subservient* to the civil authority, which he perceived as being the only way in which the absolute ruler (the Leviathan, who must crucially be the governor of the Church[33]) can

---

that flesh could be really present in many places at once? Where's the place, and what the torments of hell, and other metaphysical doctrines? Whether the will of man be free, or govern'd by the will of God? Whether sanctity comes by inspiration or education? By whom Christ now speaks to us? Whether by the *King*, or by the Bible to every man that reads it, and interprets it to himself; or by a private spirit to every man? (p. 73)

Hobbes also identifies republican theories from classical Greece and Rome as a contributing cause for the conflict, blaming the universities of Oxford and Cambridge for both the theological and republican subversions:

They (the ruler) must punish then the most of those that have had their breeding in the *Universities*, for such curious questions in *Divinity* are first started in the *Universities*; and so are all those Politick Questions concerning the Rights of Civil and *Ecclesiastical* Government; and there they are furnished with arguments for liberty, out of the works of *Aristotle*, *Plato*, *Cicero*, *Seneca*, and out of the histories of *Rome* and *Greece* . . . .therefore I despair of any lasting peace among our selves, till the *Universities* here shall bend and direct their studies to the . . . teaching of absolute obedience to the Laws of the *King* and to his publick edicts under the Great Seal of *England*. (p. 74)

[33] This message is strikingly represented on the title page illustration of Hobbes' *Leviathan*, which was drawn with close collaboration between the artist Hollar and Hobbes. On the lower right hand side of the title page there are panels depicting in ascending order a church council deciding a doctrinal dispute, a collection of two and three-pronged 'theological' weapons. These weapons, with various theological concepts engraved, upon them might represent 'the division between Catholics and Protestants and the schism within the English Church between Puritans, Presbyterians and Anglicans', Arnold A.

prevent religious conflict from dividing the realm. With John Adams it is explicit that having a separation between church and state is imperative, so as to preserve the necessary freedom for the spread and influence of true religion. With Hobbes, the point of the established church was not to promote true religion, but to prevent people (by force if need be) worrying and arguing about the truth, which would eventually prevent them killing each other (which is the sole end of Hobbesian political theory).[34] This was not overlooked by Hobbes' contemporaries, and there were plenty of Royalist Anglicans (with whom Hobbes was ostensibly on side) who were not pleased first of all to have the royal authority depend upon a contract made by the people,[35] and secondly to have doctrine in the Church of

---

Rogow, *Thomas Hobbes: Radical in the Service of Reaction* (London: W. W. Norton, 1986, p. 159). Above the weapons is a cloud emitting lightning bolts – God's wrath on warring factions. Above this is a mitre symbolizing religious authority and a church, the seat of religious power. Mirroring these panels on the left hand side we have the political corollary and consequence of these religious disputes 'the emergence of civil society from the state of nature and the "war of all against all" (the battlefield of the bottom panel) through the termination of fighting (the stacked weaponry and silent cannon of the next two panels), to the crown, symbolizing sovereignty . . . and the fortified castle or fortress representing the seat of power', Rogow, *Hobbes*, p. 159. At the top of both, commanding all, is Leviathan, holding in his right hand the sword of state, and in his left the staff of religion. Leviathan, whose body is constituted by a collection of people facing the monarch, is the 'State, which is but an Artificiall Man', and has complete authority over the religious and the civil, and must do in order to sustain the peace.

[34] Hobbes himself is clearly not worried about the truth. He summarizes the list of doctrinal disputes which caused the Civil War – featuring trivial issues such as the Trinity, the Incarnation and free-will versus determinism (see note 32 above) – as 'unnecessary doctrines' which do 'no good'. Hobbes' only concern is that where the absolute ruler sees it as necessary to proclaim on doctrine it is 'the duty of every subject not to speak against them inasmuch as 'tis every man's duty to obey him or them that have the sovereign power, and the wisdom of all that have such powers, to punish such as shall publish or teach their private interpretations when they are contrary to the law, and likely to lead men to sedition, or disputing against the law', *Behemoth*, pp. 73–4.

[35] So Lord Clarendon denounced Hobbes as knowing no more about the English constitution that 'every other man of *Malmesbury*'. Hobbes' ignorance in this case was exemplified by his not realizing that the sovereignty of the King did not depend upon any sort of contract, but 'from a descent of six hundred years', and that the king 'was alone called Soveraign, had the title of Majesty from every one of his subjects, and was unquestionably taken by them for their King'. Quoted in J. Bowle, *Hobbes and his Critics: A Study in Seventeenth Century Constitutionalism* (London: Frank Cass, 1969), pp. 56–7. Hobbes' position was also accused of political expediency in that it allowed previous supporters of the King to swear the oath of allegiance to Cromwell's republic on the

England entirely governed by this contracted ruler. John Whitehall, one such critic of Hobbes, pointed out that if the sovereign in 1651 had been a Catholic:

> we ought to have embraced Romish idolatry. If a Jew had been general of the Army, and would have bidden him [Hobbes] be circumcised, he would have done it. If a Turk had been turned up Trump and bidden Mr. Hobbes go to Mecca and worship at Mahomet's tomb, he would have done it; if a Persian had proved uppermost and bidden him worship at Haly's shrine and say Haly was a greater prophet than Christ, he would have done it.[36]

Although an exaggerated accusation (and accusation it is, the intention not being to compliment Mr. Hobbes' broad-minded attitude), it is clearly one that could never have been made to early American theorists of democracy, and the difference has striking implications. In figures such as Edwards and Adams the key generating motivations for their democratic ideals are not self-preservation and the avoidance of conflict at all costs, but the regeneration of the elect, an escape from the tyranny of sin and the purifying of the Church from Romish hierarchy by establishing a rival model of covenantal government. On top of this there is a belief in the providential and progressive expansion of this model of government, which is co-extensive with the spread of true religion, and the inauguration of the

NB

---

basis that the King had broken the supporting conditions of the contract: in that by not being in power he was not able to protect his subjects from alien powers and from each other: see A. P. Martinich, *Hobbes: A Biography* (Cambridge: Cambridge University Press, 1999), Ch. 8. The serviceable ambivalence of Hobbes' position is reflected by the fact that the figure of Leviathan on the title page of *Leviathan* was variously thought to have been Cromwell or Charles II: see Rogow, pp. 159ff.

[36] John Whitehall, quoted by Bowle, *Hobbes and his Critics*, p. 180. The element of truth in this quote is born out by the way in which Hobbes angered Anglican bishops, and the Catholic court of Queen Henrietta Maria, by recommending in 1651 that Charles II accept a compromise with the Presbyterians which would involve abolishing the episcopacy in the Church of England. That such a constitutive element of the divide between royalist Anglicans and parliamentary Presbyterian did not bother Hobbes at all is an indication of the extent to which all matters of doctrine and ecclesiastical governance were entirely subservient to his goal of having an established church under the control of the ruler. See Rogow, *Hobbes*, Ch. 8.

Kingdom of God.[37] The elect could be regenerated by unmediated exposure to the gospel. Certain of their election, the saints could then come together in communities, which through the notion of a covenant with God could be confident that they constituted a providentially gathered group of these regenerated saints, the elect. Given the double certainty of your own election, and that of the group of which you are a member, it is not hard to understand the momentum towards a heady political sense of activism and egalitarianism: a crusading form of liberalism.

This story is of course an over-simplification, and to some extent a distortion, of the original rather complex relationship between Puritanism and democracy and of the political implications of Calvinism. As is often the case with inaccurate appropriations, it is the imperfect interpretation that must concern us if we are to understand the complex and imperfect history of thought; in that it is the over-simplified story which many influential Evangelical preachers (presidents of Princeton such as Edwards) and politicians (presidents of America such as Adams) recited to themselves, and which came to constitute one popular strand of an American philosophy of history. Nonetheless some account of the nature of the distortions and adaptations should be attempted.

To take first of all the equation between Puritanism and democracy, it is clear that there were wide disagreements among early Puritans as to the extent to which the liberty conferred as a spiritual gift (from the shackles of the 'law', mediated often by 'Popish' hierarchies) had an application beyond the individual's religious

---

[37] Locke is a more complex figure in regard to such a British–American comparison. A strong textual case can certainly be made that Locke supports liberty, autonomy and toleration just because he considers that these are the preconditions for a person finding true religion. For an interpretation of Locke as a Calvinist natural theologian see John Dunn, *The Political Thought of John Locke* (Cambridge: Cambridge University Press, 1969). Of course, in that Locke is arguably a more important theorist for understanding American democracy than Hobbes, this does not cut against our thesis as to the link between democracy and religion in America. But what Locke does seem to lack is any notion of a progressive and dynamic eschatology. His vision of society, as with Hobbes, seems to regard the end of political authority to be a lack of conflict, which underpins people's self-preservation. Governmental interference in religion, as with Hobbes, is restricted to the purpose of keeping the peace. The relationship between liberty and true religion for Locke is a less political and historical affair than for someone like John Adams; one might venture the thought that, for Locke, liberty is the pre-condition for true religion, rather than being an expression of it.

experience. Puritan attitudes went from the politically conservative Presbyterians who sought to limit any inference drawn from 'Christian liberty' to political liberty. At the other extreme, parties such as the Levellers insisted on the full political application, to the unregenerate and regenerate, of Christian liberty; the predominant party 'the Independents', under Cromwell's leadership, adopted a variety of intermediate positions. A similar spectrum of positions was found in the early American Puritans, with a figure such as Roger Williams extending Christian liberty to a degree that more authoritarian figures such as John Winthrop found alarming.

Later attempts to proclaim democracy's Puritan roots are highly selective, in that plenty of actual Puritans were trenchantly anti-democratic.[38] Even within the congregation of the elect, there would be a spectrum of positions as to how democratic or authoritarian the covenant should be. So Perry Miller, describing the American situation in the seventeenth century comments that

> there certainly were in it democratic stirrings; there were undoubt-edly in it provisions that could effectively stifle those impulses. It was largely a question of where the emphasis was to be put; if upon the eldership, the result would be an aristocracy, an oligarchy, a theocracy; if upon the congregation, the result would be more democratic.[39]

On the issue of the appropriation of Calvinism, it is possible to trace at least two of the ways in which elements of Calvinism have been selectively augmented, minimalized or adapted to arrive at a highly activist creed. First of all, in a writer such as Jonathan Edwards, 'regeneration' becomes sentimentalized and associated with feelings, emotions and an affective personal transformation which leads to activism. Edwards in this regard shares a typical and pervasive eighteenth-century interest in the importance of sentiment and feeling. Edwards distinguishes the soul's 'perceiving faculty' and

---

[38] For original accounts of some of these differences, the Putney debates are a good read. See *Puritanism and Liberty: Being the Army Debates (1647–49) from the Clarke Manuscripts*, ed. A. S. P. Woodhouse (London: Everyman, 1986). For my brief discussion of Puritanism and democracy I am indebted to Woodhouse's Introduction to this text.

[39] Perry Miller, *Errand into the Wilderness* (Cambridge, Mass.: Harvard University Press, 1956), p. 23.

the will 'by which the soul chooses';[40] these two faculties are united in the 'heart'. Grace is characterized as a spirit entering 'the heart', the seat and centre of the entire personality, with the heart's predominance over both feeling and will taking clear precedence over the 'understanding' alone. Accordingly Edwards insists that holiness 'consists not only in contemplation, and a mere passive enjoyment, but very much in action'.[41]

The second way in which we find Calvinism adapted in a distinctly activist direction is in the increasing emphasis placed on the notion of the covenant alongside that of election.[42] According to some parts of Calvin's work, a person might never achieve a 'working conviction' that he was of the regenerate. So Calvin speaks of the inscrutable secrets of the divine will:

> Let them remember that when they inquire into predestination, they penetrate the inmost recesses of Divine wisdom, where the careless and confident intruder will obtain no satisfaction to his curiousity, but will enter a labyrinth from which he will find no way to depart. For it is unreasonable that man should scrutinize with impunity those things which the Lord has determined to be hidden in himself; and investigate, even from eternity, that sublimity of wisdom which God would have us to adore and not comprehend, to promote our admiration of his glory.[43]

---

[40] Jonathan Edwards, *Religious Affections*, ed. John E. Smith (New Haven: Yale University Press, 1959).

[41] Jonathan Edwards, 'True Saints, when Absent from the Body', *Works*, ed. E. Hickman (10th edn, 2. vols., London, 1865), II, 31. I am indebted here to Alan Heimart's *Religion and the American Mind: From the Great Awakening to the Revolution* (Cambridge, Mass.: Harvard University Press, 1968), pp. 109ff.

[42] I am indebted here to Perry Miller's 'The Marrow of Puritan Divinity', in *Errand into the Wilderness*.

[43] John Calvin, *Institutes of the Christian Religion* (London: SCM Press, 1960) Library of Christian Classics, Vol. XXI, Bk. III, xx ii, I, pp. 922–3; Jean Calvin, *Insitution de la Religion Chrestienne, Livre Troisième*, publiée par Jean-Daniel Benoit (Paris: Librarie Philosophique J. Vrin, 1960): '. . . qu'il leur souvienne que grand ils enquièrent de la prédestination ils entrent au sanctaire de la sagesse divine, auquel si quelcun se fourre et ingère en trop grande confiance et hardiesse, il n'atteindra iamais lá de pouvoir rassasier sa curiosité, et entreta en un labyrinthe où il ne trouvera nulle issue. Car ce n'est pas raison que les choses que Dieu a voulu estre cachées et dont il s'est retenu la cognoissance, soyent aimi espluchees des hommes, et que la hautesse de sa sapienne, laquelle il a voulu estre plustost adorée de nous qu'estre comprinse (afin de se rendre admirable en icelle) soit assuiettie au sens humain, pour la chercher iusques à son éternité', pp. 406–7.

The seventeenth-century theologian William Ames perceived that if God was held to behave in ways which defied all human logic or expectation, it could be to detriment of the 'consolation and peace which Christ hath left to believers'.[44] As Perry Miller puts it, God needed to be rendered 'understandable in human terms'[45] to bring God 'to time and reason, of justifying His ways to man in conceptions meaningful to the intellect, of caging and confining the transcendent Force, the inexpressible and unfathomable Being, by the law of ethics, and of doing this somehow without losing the sense of the hidden God'.[46] A way of achieving this was by being assured of God's self-elected faithfulness to a covenant among the elect, so that membership of the compact made among the elect was a guarantee of the individual's status. Morality and active works are enjoined by the compact made between the elect and God. Some theologians seemed even to go so far as to suggest – *contra* Calvin – that there could be an element of free will in responding to grace. For instance, Thomas Hooker of New England pushed Calvinism beyond its limits when he suggested that anyone who could force their soul to the point of readiness would certainly receive grace: 'If ever you thinke to share in the salvation that Christ hath purchased . . . prepare for him, or else never expect him . . . If the soule be broken and humbled he will come presently.'[47] The combination of Calvinist regeneration effecting the 'heart' and so enjoining action, and the regenerate being confident of their status as a group, is a potent recipe for a confident sense of boundaries between the elect and the damned (good and evil), and a sense of the responsibilities and possibilities of activism.

The equation between Calvinist religion and American democracy is also mirrored back to Americans by European commentators, such as Alexis de Tocqueville who commented in *Democracy in America* (first published in 1835) that:

The greatest part of British America was peopled by men who, after having shaken off the authority of the Pope, acknowledged no other religious supremacy: they brought with them into the New World a form of Christianity which I cannot better describe than by styling it a democratic and republican religion. This

---

44 William Ames, *Medulla Sacrae Theologiae* (London, 1643), p. 118.
45 Miller, 'Marrow', p. 55.
46 Miller, 'Marrow', p. 56.
47 Thomas Hooker, *Soules Preparation* (London, 1632), p. 155.

contributed powerfully to the establishment of a republic and a democracy in public affairs; and from the beginning, politics and religion contracted an alliance which has never been dissolved.⁴⁸

The moral to be drawn from this brief comparison of the intellectual history – and influential appropriations and interpretations of this history – of democracy in American and British contexts, is that although things can look the same, they can have alarmingly different pedigrees. So a typical difference in presentation between American and European leaders concerning notions of liberty and freedom, where an American leader is much more likely to invoke God, and a sense of mission and providence, may be more than just a superficial rhetorical flourish. It may point to a deeper pattern of variance in aspirations, fears and expectations which surround the ideals of 'freedom', with a lineage going back to sixteenth-century theological disputes.⁴⁹ We can also draw from the material a warning that things which appear to be different, may indeed be so, but not in the way they first appear. The separation in America of church and state, in its origins at least, was as much to preserve and protect the full scope, integrity and influence of true religion as it was to protect the state from religious interference; whereas in England, maintaining an established church was motivated by a desire to protect the state from religious enthusiasm and conflict.

Moving forward from 1765, when Adams wrote his dissertation, to 1801, the same themes emerge of good (synonymous with a form of Christian liberty) overcoming evil in a mission to which America is especially called. In a sermon entitled 'Overcoming Evil with Good', a phrase echoed by George W. Bush's 'overcoming evil with greater good' in his State of the Union Address (29 January 2002),

---

⁴⁸ Alexis de Tocqueville, *Democracy in America*, Vol. 1 (New York: Alfred A. Knopf, 1945), p. 300.

⁴⁹ It should be clear by this point how my thesis differs from Weber's attempt to trace the origins of capitalism to the Protestant 'work ethic' of communities in Northern Europe and America. My thesis makes no claims to have discovered the unique and exhaustive origins of capitalism. My claim is that the notions of 'liberty' employed in England, America and France have quite distinct lineages, and to access these distinctions we need to attend to the historical and theological roots of the concept in these different contexts. So in America the passion for 'liberty' has some of its roots in the Calvinist notion of covenantal church government (liberty from Romish hierarchies) and Christian liberty from sin, guaranteed through the saint's pre-election, leading to activist projects to eliminate evil.

the Calvinist preacher Stanley Griswold makes a clear equation between the political notion of democratic liberty, Christianity and American destiny. Speaking of 'our forefathers' Griswold tells us that it was 'the spirit of freedom' that 'drove them from their native land and brought them to this then howling wilderness'. Griswold goes on to extol their 'most distinguishing traits . . . Liberty and Religion. In both they were sincere, and prized them above all price. With beams extracted from these sources, their souls were illuminated and warmed.'[50] We then have a dig at the French, increasingly a feature of Evangelical American sermons at this time, following the French Revolution. American preachers noticed that the French passion for 'liberty' was strikingly different from the New England notion of liberty, in that it was hostile to all forms of Christianity, and certainly to 'true religion' as they understood it. So it would not have escaped notice that <u>Rousseau</u> considered Christianity to be incompatible with the social contract which forms a virtuous republic:

Christianity as a religion is entirely spiritual, occupied solely with heavenly things; the country of the Christian is not of this world . . . .Imagine your Christian republic face to face with Sparta or Rome: the pious Christians will be beaten, crushed and destroyed . . . But I am mistaken in speaking of a Christian republic; the terms are mutually exclusive. Christianity preaches only servitude and dependence. Its spirit is so favourable to tyranny that it always profits by such a regime. <u>True Christians</u> are made to be slaves, and they know it and do not much mind: this short life counts for too little in their eyes.[51]

---

[50] Stanley Griswold, *Overcoming Evil With Good. A Sermon Delivered at Wallingford, Connecticut, March 11, 1801* (Suffield: Edward Gray, 1801), pp. 25–6.

[51] Jean-Jacques Rousseau, *The Social Contract*, trans. Willmoore Kendall (Chicago, Ill.: Gateway, 1954), Bk. 4, Ch. 8, pp. 204–23. The original text reads as follows: 'Le christianisme est une religion toute spirituelle, occupée uniquement des choses du ciel; la patrie du chrétien n'est pas de ce monde . . . supposez votre république chrétienne vis-à-vis de Sparte ou de Rome: les pieux chrétiens seront battus, écrasés, détruits . . . Mais je me trompe en disant une république chrétienne; chacun de ces deux mots exclut l'autre. Le christianisme ne prêche que servitude et dépendence. Son esprit est trop favorable à la tyrannie pour qu'elle n'en profite pas toujours. Les vrais chrétiens sont faits pour être esclaves; ils le savent et n'en émeuvent guère; cette courte vie a trop peu de prix à leurs yeux'. *Du Contrat Social*, ed. R. Grimsley (Oxford: Clarendon Press, 1972), pp. 228–9.

At the same time Rousseau insists that citizens must – on pain of death – have a form of 'civil religion' (*la religion civile*), which perhaps resembles the 'American civil religion' for which we find Robert Bellah arguing in the 1970s, without the proposed incentive of the death-penalty to deter dissent (see the Appendix). The dogmas of the 'civil religion' were to be few and simple, and were dictated only by their relevance to the needs of the community. Positively they included the belief in God and providence, the immortality of the soul, the happiness of the just and the punishment of the wicked and 'the sacredness of the social contract and laws'; negatively there was the single dogma of the exclusion of intolerance.[52]

Even if Evangelical preachers had been aware of the qualified role for 'religion' in Rousseau, it is unlikely that it would – or should – have mitigated their accusation to any great extent. Rousseau is hostile to Christianity, and that is enough. In contrast, Griswold praises his New England forefathers in that 'they did not set up an out-cry about liberty with an insidious view to root out religion and overturn its institutions'.[53]

Griswold goes on to develop a militant and activist account of the responsibilities of Americans to crush opposition to God's democratic Kingdom:

> . . . uniting the principles of liberty with order, and crowning the whole with genuine religion, be *clear as the sun, fair as the moon, and terrible as an army of banners*. Amaze once more the tyrants of the earth when they look toward this land . . . .[54]

> . . . Let the American character be borne aloft. Let it soar like the Eagle of heaven, its emblem, bearing the scroll of our liberties through fields of azure light, unclouded by the low-bred vapours of faction; – and let it not be degraded into a detestable owl of night, to dabble in the pools of intrigue and party and delight itself in the filthy operations of darkness.[55]

Elsewhere in a sermon entitled 'The Good Land We live In' Griswold celebrates the 'political beatitude' which is America, free from the tyranny and torpitude of the old world:

---

[52] Rousseau, *Contrat*, p. 231, '. . . la sainteté du contrat social et des lois'.
[53] Griswold, *Overcoming Evil*, p. 31.
[54] Griswold, *Overcoming Evil*, p. 31.
[55] Griswold, *Overcoming Evil*, p. 32.

Thus Israel had a tyrannic and inexorable Pharaoh to deal with, and the Americans a British King. There is no portion of the civilized world but is, or has been, claimed and usurpation attempted to be set up by some one or more of these hereditary or self-made despots. Some nations have struggled to rid themselves of the pests, and have failed. Fortunate indeed is that people whose exertions are crowned with success, who can make themselves acknowledged by all the princes and nations of the earth to be a Free, Sovereign and Independent People.

O happy people, then AMERICANS! who can be compared to you? What other nation thro' the wide world enjoys such political beatitude? Long may you enjoy it, and resist every attempt to rob of you of it, under whatever specious name the attempt may be made.

In the gospel ANOTHER AMERICA is opened to our enraptured view, of which the one we now possess is but a faint type. It extends with infinite beauty over the everlasting hills on high, presenting pastures green with immortal verdure, and streams of endless pleasure. Pure is its light and mild its clime, *for the glory of God enlighteneth it and the Lamb is the light therof.*[56]

The Francophobia hinted at in Griswold flowers more dramatically in the work of Jonathan Edwards' grandson Timothy Dwight, a president of Yale. It pays us to attend to Dwight's dislike of the French for two reasons. First of all, it provides further evidence as to how things that look the same, in this case a passion for 'liberty', can have very different genealogies, and so different background expectations and aspirations which may still have a resonance in contemporary political discourse. Second, we can learn from Dwight how the structure of good versus evil can remain, with different contents being slotted into the role of the evil to be resisted. In 1801 Dwight wrote a piece entitled 'A Discourse on Some Events of the Last Century', where he explains the shifting form of the conflict between the Christian and the infidel. The enemy has taken the form of 'theism, natural religion, then mere unbelief, then Animalism, then Scepticism, and then partial and total Atheism'.[57] Dwight's particular targets in this discourse are the *philosophes* behind the French

---

[56] Stanley Griswold, *The Good Land We Live In: a Sermon Delivered at Suffield (Connecticut) on the Celebration of the Anniversary of American Independence, June 7th 1802* (Suffield: Edward Gray, 1802), p. 14

[57] Timothy Dwight, *A Discourse on Some Events of the Last Century* (New Haven: Thomas and Samuel Green, 1801), p. 33.

Revolution. Both the French and the New Englanders march to the clarion call of 'liberty', which is why it is so upsetting for Dwight to see that the French passion for 'liberty' is premised upon a rejection of true religion and scripture, based upon contractarian and Rousseauistic models of the 'general will', and supported by notorious atheists such as Voltaire. Dwight weighs in against this 'hollow Godless liberty' telling us that 'it was soon discovered, that *the liberty of Infidels was not the liberty of New England*; that France, instead of being free, merely changed through a series of tyrannies . . .'[58]

The enemy now is French philosophy, but the demand on Americans is the same to 'marshal yourselfs' and 'meet to face the bands of disorder, of falsehood, and of sin'. There must be a choice made, for Dwight asks *'what communion hath light with darkness? what concord hath Christ with Belial? of what part hath he that believeth with an Infidel?'* (original italics).[59] In an earlier discourse given by Dwight in 1798 – *The Duty of Americans at the Present Crisis*[60] – he describes 'another duty, to which we are eminently called', which is: '. . . an entire separation from our enemies. Among the moral duties of man none hold a higher rank than political ones, and among our political duties none is more plain, or more absolute, then that which I have now mentioned.'[61] The separation from evil is commanded by God: 'Come out, therefore, from among them, and be ye separate, saith the Lord, and touch not the unclean thing; and I will receive you, and will be a father to you: And ye shall be my sons and daughters, saith the Lord Almighty.'[62] Perhaps here we see a trace of another motivating tendency in American foreign policy, not towards activism but isolationism. Far from being a movement unrelated to and incompatible with the American eschatology as described here, it is to an extent accounted for by it. Being separate and pure – or as Griswold imaginatively puts it, not letting the American eagle transmography into a dirty (presumably French) owl – is a form of action and resistance in a world divided into good and evil. So isolationism can be interpreted as a phase in the struggle against evil.

---

[58] Dwight, *Discourse*, p. 33.
[59] Dwight, *Discourse*, p. 44.
[60] Timothy Dwight, *The Duty of Americans at the Present Crisis: Illustrated in a Discourse (on Rev. xvi.15) Preached on the 4th July, 1798* (New Haven: Thomas and Samuel Green, 1798), p19. The crisis referred to is the French Revolution, and its aftermath, the worst of which – for Dwight – seems to be atheistic French philosophy.
[61] Dwight, *Duty*, p. 19.
[62] Dwight, *Discourse*, p. 46.

Moving forward to Evangelical interpretations of the American Civil War, we find the same themes re-emerging. This time the evil to be burnt out takes the contingent form of the Federalists – the opponents of true democracy. When the evil is removed, America is again prepared for her millennial role. In 1864, in the context of likely victory against the Federalists, the Revd Marvin R. Vincent[63] gave a Thanksgiving sermon, 'The Lord of War and Righteousness':

> God has been striking, and trying to make us strike at elements unfavourable to the growth of a pure democracy; and these and other facts point to the conclusion that he is at work, preparing in this broad land a fit stage for the last act of the mighty drama, the consummation of human civilization.[64]

He interprets the Civil War as a burning off of the dross of lust, idolatry, vanity and brutality, giving rise to 'a national life crowned as with the glory of noonday; girt round with prayer, robed in purity, with love in its eyes and peace upon its lips, and in its hand the open charters of freedom'.[65]

America – Vincent declares – if she is true, will dominate the last act of the millennial drama:

> Who shall say that she (America) shall not only secure lasting peace to herself, but be, under God, the instrument of a millennial reign to all the nations? . . . In numerous respects democracy reveals itself as the natural ally and agent of Christianity . . . God's purpose in the present state of affairs is a moral and not a political one.[66]

Towards the end of the nineteenth century the same eschatological schema is intact, although apocalyptic references to Rome or the political corruption of Europe are replaced by other targets. In *The Presbyterian Review 1880* Edward D. Morris espouses a now familiar expectation of the Millennial Age inaugurated by human resistance to evil in history. More novel to our ears perhaps is the

---

[63] Marvin R. Vincent, *The Lord of War and Righteousness* (Troy, New York, 1864), p. 42. Preached in 1864 in the First Presbyterian Church of Troy.

[64] Quoted in Tuveson, *Redeemer Nation*, p. 203.

[65] Vincent, *Lord of War*, p. 40.

[66] Vincent, *Lord of War*, pp. 36, 41.

sociological note to the millennialism, with talk of the 'reconstruction of society' being equated with the 'renewal of the earth'.[67] This will become important in any evaluation of the American eschatology. Arguably the sense that one can perceive a complex situation in straightforward terms of the good to be supported and the evil to be overcome, and the conviction that activism is a crucial part of inaugurating the Kingdom – these are eschatological beliefs shared by the activist theological left. We will see increasingly that the eschatology behind the militaristic activism of a George Bush can be shared by theologians concerned with social justice and poverty. Before rushing to judgement it should be born in mind that the American eschatology is not just invoked by America at war, but by movements in America such as the social gospel movement of the 1920s, the Marshall plan, and the civil rights movement of the 1960s.

So Morris addresses the 'grand future for humanity on earth – a Millennial Age of truth, of righteousness, of purity and peace' which will involve 'the reconstruction of human society so that in all its elements and developments it shall become the very kingdom of heaven'.[68] The result will be – and here Morris alludes to Augustine whilst expressing a directly opposed eschatology – 'the *Civitas Dei* (the City of God) within whose sacred walls our race is at last to dwell'.[69] The vision is social reconstruction, but we still have the threat of the ancient enemy, as Morris promises that

> Even now, as in the days of John, are there many Antichrists: malevolent systems, philosophies, tempers, tendencies, which would trample Christianity out utterly, were they able. But other similar forces are yet to arise; the crown prince of evil has yet to receive his dark coronation . . . .There will be a downward as well as an upward movement in the moral career of mankind: Christ and Antichrist continuing their antithetical manifestations and activities even to the end.[70]

Writing in 1893, the theologian Josiah Strong in *The New Era* develops the equation of evils with social evils (including poverty and

---

[67] E. Morris, 'The Future of Humanity', *The Presbyterian Review 1880*, p. 426.
[68] Morris, 'Future', p. 426.
[69] Morris, 'Future', p. 426.
[70] Morris, 'Future', p. 444.

lack of housing). Strong makes the familiar case, *contra* Augustine, for the historical inauguration of the Kingdom of God on earth:

> We see, then, how comprehensive is the kingdom of God. It is of course as far-reaching as the laws of the King, though it is actually established only where those laws are obeyed, and in the Lord's prayer, 'Thy kingdom come: thy will be done in earth as it is in heaven,' we are taught to pray (and therefore to labour) for the complete establishment of that kingdom in all the earth, through perfect obedience to God's will as expressed in his laws.[71]

There is the characteristically militaristic call to activism:

> We call ourselves 'soldiers of the cross'. *Soldiers* indeed! Whose idea of 'service' is to 'sit and sing ourselves away to everlasting bliss', while there are vice and crime, moral and physical filth, ignorance and wretchedness, within hand-reach of every one ... In like manner, when a citizen of the Kingdom of God is at peace with any sin of society, becomes reconciled to any evil habits of the community or indifferent to anything inconsistent with the full coming of God's kingdom on the earth, he is disloyal to the kingdom.[72]

When dealing with evil Strong insists that:

> There must be no compromise, no truce, but a war of extermination. Wherever there is evil, it is the business of the church to smite it, and with the 'perseverance of the saints' to keep on smiting it even to the death. Every wrong on earth is a divine call to the Christian and to the church to right it.[73]

The list of projects required by this eschatological activism is strikingly different from anything we might have read in Edwards or Griswold: reconciling capital and labour, the purification of politics, tenement-house reform, improving drainage, ventilation and water-supply, the harnessing of commerce, manufactures and agriculture and the progress of science and art.[74]

---

[71] Josiah Strong, *The New Era* (London: Hodder and Stoughton, 1893), p. 231.

[72] Strong, *New Era*, pp. 242–3.

[73] Strong, *New Era*, p. 243.

[74] Strong, *New Era*, p. 250.

Over time we find that the content of the eschatological pattern varies (the 'evil' being variously Rome, Great Britain, the Federalists and French philosophers), but its structural features are the same: good overcoming evil by successive human action underpinned by a guarantee of America's unique mission and destiny in God's salvation history, with evil providing tumultuous but ultimately defeatable resistance.

This pattern does not change as we move into the twentieth century. The Manichean-activist eschatological structure emerges in twentieth-century presidential speeches at times of national crisis. President Wilson in 1919 described the role of American forces as being to 'make good their redemption of the world',[75] hailing the American soldiers 'as crusaders' whose 'transcendent achievement has made all the world believe in America as it believes in no other nation organised in the modern world'. Wilson concluded that 'America had the infinite privilege of fulfilling her destiny and saving the world'.[76]

On 6 January 1942 President Roosevelt put World War Two in the framework of the Manichean-activist eschatology: 'No compromise can end that conflict. There never has been – there never will be – successful compromise between good and evil. Only total victory can reward the champions of tolerance, and decency, and freedom, and faith.'[77] In 1949 President Truman proclaimed the providential protection America could hope for:

> I am confident that the Divine Power which has guided us to this time of fateful responsibility and glorious opportunity will not desert us now. With the help from Almighty God which we have humbly acknowledged in every turning point in our national life we shall be able to perform the great tasks which He now sets before us.[78]

Eisenhower, after working a long time in preparing his 1955 State of the Union Address, is reported to have concluded that: '. . . all he had

---

[75] Woodrow Wilson, at Oakland, 18 September 1919. In *Presidential Messages and Addresses, and Public Papers (1917–1924)*, ed. Ray S. Baker and William E. Dodd (New York and London, 1927), Vol. 2, *War and Peace*, p. 268.

[76] Wilson, *Presidential Messages*, p. 367.

[77] *Roosevelt Papers*, XIII, p. 507.

[78] Eighty-first Congress, 1st Session, House of Rep., document No. 1. Quoted in Seymour Fersch, *The View from the White House* (Washington, D.C.: Public Affairs Press, 1961), p. 125.

to recommend could be related to the basic issues of good and evil about which he was so much concerned'.[79] In 1958 Eisenhower described the Cold War as a struggle between the powers of darkness and light, concluding, 'with God's help, the future of mankind will be assured in a world of justice, harmony, and peace'.[80] The dualistic separation which Eisenhower saw was between the 'God-fearing peace-loving people' and the communist imperialists.[81]

Ronald Reagan's acceptance speech in 1980 to the Republican convention referred to America as 'This City on a Hill'. Reagan is quoting from the sermon of the founding father John Winthrop given on board the ship *Arbella*, on its way from Plymouth, England to the New World. Winthrop told his congregation: '. . . we must consider that we shall be as a city upon the hill with the eyes of all the world upon us . . .'[82] It is explicitly Reagan's intention to make reference to this founding myth, as he goes on to say:

> Three hundred and sixty years ago, in 1620, a group of families dared to cross a mighty ocean to build a future for themselves in a new world. When they arrived in Plymouth, Massachusetts, they formed what they called a 'compact': an agreement among themselves to build a community and abide by its laws . . .
> . . . Can we doubt that only a divine providence placed this land, this island of freedom, here as a refuge for all those people in the world who yearn to breathe freely?[83]

From Reagan then we have the same story as told by the likes of Edwards, Adams and Griswold concerning the religious origins of American democracy: a group of families brought by divine providence who formed a law-abiding community based upon a 'compact'.

---

[79] Merlo J. Pusey, *Eisenhower the President* (New York: Macmillan, 1956), p. 109.

[80] Pusey, *Eisenhower*, p. 51.

[81] Fersch, *The View From the White House*, p. 125.

[82] John Winthrop, 'A Modell of Christian Charity', in P. Miller and T. Johnson (eds.), *The Puritans: A Sourcebook of Their Writings*, Vol. 1 (New York: Harper & Row, 1963), pp. 195–9.

[83] Acceptance Speech, President Ronald Reagan, quoted in John Adair, *Puritans: Religion and Politics in Seventeenth Century England and America* (Stroud: Sutton Publishing, 1998), pp. 279–80.

Political implications and qualifications

Having surveyed the endurance and repetition of the American eschatology, and its role in defining America's sense of identity in the evangelical revival of the 1740s, the Revolution, the Civil War, two World Wars and the Cold War, we can hear again Bush's speeches with an ear more trained to the theological, political and historical harmonics that are being sounded. Bush's comments, if read blind, would not be out of place in a sermon by Edwards, Adams or Griswold. So we have the ancient battle between good and evil – 'freedom and fear have always been at war'. America plays a providential role in the progressive battle for freedom, with Bush announcing that 'the advance of human freedom . . . . – the great hope of every time – now depends on us'. 'We have been called to a unique role in human events', where 'liberty' and the evangelizing of the world in the name of freedom is hallowed by being God's purpose for humanity, with the President proclaiming that 'freedom and fear have always been at war, *and we know that God is not neutral between them . . .*'[84] '. . . in this great conflict, my fellow Americans, we will see freedom's victory . . . May God bless'.[85]

A statement of the importance of the American eschatology in contemporary American political discourse and public life needs to be framed in terms that are rigorously subtle. Of course, American political discourse is extremely porous to a number of vocabularies, sometimes quite removed from the eschatological: so there can be the language of prudential self-interest, of universal human rights and the respect of diversity, of international law and of classical republicanism (although this vocabulary, as we have seen, is invariably intermingled with covenantal models).[86] At the same time, it has not

---

[84] Bush, 'Address', 21 November 2001.

[85] Bush, 'State of the Union', 29 January 2002.

[86] A republic requires an active political community of participating citizens who practise a shared set of virtues. There is a long tradition in literature on America of associating the republican spirit with the religious, and with covenantal models of church government. We have already seen how de Tocqueville observes this relationship in his *Democracy in America*, p. 300: see p. 106 above. This thesis has been picked up more recently by Nathan Hatch in *The Sacred Cause of Liberty* (New Haven: Yale University Press, 1977), esp. Ch. 1, who argues that in the 1750s and 1760s religious solidarity was increasingly given a political interpretation, contributing to the republican ethos. Robert Bellah endorses this equation also in *The Broken Covenant* (Chicago and London: University of Chicago Press, 1992), pp. 176ff.

been necessary to speculate about the deep springs of the 'American mind' in order to see the pervasiveness of a Manichean and activist sense of America's mission to overcome evil with good. It must be said that this eschatological way of presenting problems, and expectations concerning solutions, is *at least* there – even where the explicit religious origin and hope is forgotten, and even where other vocabularies are there also. From the middle of the eighteenth century to the present day, with Bush, I have not resorted to obscure or extreme sources, or free-association in order to trace this strand: the majority of the quotations in this chapter have come from presidents of Princeton and Yale, or presidents of the United States.

So many manifestations of American 'religiosity', in the widest sense, including 'faith in the free-market' tend to share a substantial and controversial Manichean-activist eschatology, originating in – but no longer chained to – the Protestant America of the seventeenth and eighteenth centuries.[87] It is not hard to see how such an eschatology could lend itself to supporting an aggressive doctrine of world enlightenment through the spread of the ideals of the free

---

[87] Another example of the pervasive way in which the American eschatology is detectable behind apparent diversity, is the way in which the Catholic Church in America has historically been remarkable for its extrovert and activist nature. There are two clear examples of this. First of all consider how early Catholics in America attempted to establish a pattern of church government which was very similar to the ubiquitous Protestant model. In 1819 Catholic Irish settlers in Norfolk, Virginia sent a declaration to Rome announcing: '. . . in consequence of our inalienable right of patronage, our first bishop will be elected by us' (quoted in W. Herberg, *Protestant-Catholic-Jew*, London: Doubleday, 1960, p. 139). The crisis of 'trusteeism' spread from Norfolk, Virginia to Charleston in South Carolina and constituted 'the most serious crisis in the whole history of American Catholicism' , being an attempt to 'set up an Independent Catholic Church in America, free from all reference to Rome', in William L. Sperry, *Religion in America* (New York: Macmillan, 1946), p. 207. The second example of the moulding of American Catholicism to the American eschatology is to be found in the activist and extrovert nature of the American Catholic Church. For a discussion of this see Herberg, *Protestant-Catholic-Jew*, pp. 149ff. Herberg observes that the American church has frequently been suspected, by the Holy See, of the 'heresy of action', defined in 1950 by Pope Pius XII as the view that 'the world can be saved by . . . external activity' (Apostolic Adhortation, 'Menti Nostrae', 23 September 1950). So, for instance, in 1899 Leo XIII directed an apostolic letter, *Testem benevolentiae*, to Cardinal Gibbons, warning against activist tendencies which European theologians had claimed to detect as operative in the American church. The letter warns against over-emphasizing the active virtues 'at the expense of humility, charity and obedience; putting natural virtues above the supernatural; and employing untried methods of attracting non-Catholics to the faith' (Herberg, *Protestant-Catholic-Jew*, p. 149).

market, with those countries who resist being put into the familiar role of the evils to be overcome. All the ingredients are there: the division of the world into good and evil (those countries who accept free-market economics and those who resist); the activist mission of America in bringing the world to good (the free market) and over-coming resistance, and a religious zeal for a certain understanding of liberty and democracy. This suggestion would concord with John Gray's analysis that 'the market liberal philosophy that underpins globalisation' (along with Marxism) 'are essentially secular religions, in which the eschatological hopes and fantasies of Christianity are given an Enlightenment twist. In both, history is understood as the progress of the species, powered by growing knowledge and wealth, and culminating in a universal civilisation.'[88] Gray notes the crucial optimism about human activism, commenting that 'history's crimes and tragedies are not thought to have their roots in human nature: they are errors, mistakes that can be corrected by more education, better political institutions, higher living standards'.[89] The only qualification needed to Gray's account is to break down the reference to 'the eschatological hopes . . . of Christianity'; as we have seen, the Manichean-activist eschatology at work in the contemporary American context is a specific and locatable historical phenomenon, originating largely in eighteenth-century New England, and cannot be taken as the only eschatological hope that Christians can and have espoused. As we have seen, an Augustinian eschatology would be quite incompatible with such an historically activist account of inaugurating the Kingdom.

Nevertheless, it *is* important not be become too sensationalist about the influence of the tradition of American eschatology on American foreign policy, nor necessarily to suggest that the policy would be substantially different without this influence. No one could hope, least of all me, that this chapter is even remotely sufficient for accounting for American actions since 11 September 2001. It would be alarming in the extreme, both for America's interests and those of world stability, if Bush *really* thought that the entire reason for hostility towards America was, as he diagnosed it on the day of the attack, an extreme form of resentment 'because we're the brightest

---

[88] John Gray, 'The Era of Globalisation is Over', *New Statesman*, 24 September 2001.
[89] Gray, 'Globalisation'.

beacon of freedom . . . in the world',[90] unrelated to previous American interventions, historical tensions and instabilities in the Middle East. Whatever one's views on these issues – America's military intervention in Libya and Iraq, and its support of Israel – they are plainly more at the forefront of actual anti-American antagonism leading to violence, than a felt objection to something as abstract as 'freedom' or 'liberty'. For all these caveats, it is clear that the eschatological pattern does effect the presentation of policy, and the expectations, hopes and fears which surround action taken by America. Inasmuch as the conflict has a symbolic dimension also – something of which the terrorists were aware in the timing and location of their attack – presentation and expectation, and reaction to presentations, can become constitutive of events.

Being aware of the influence of this eschatology – certainly in presentation of policy, perhaps at some level in its formation – does not, I think, give us any theological short cuts through complex issues. Critiques of American foreign policy from, for instance, a theologically informed activist left – the same movement which often supports anti-globalization/anti-capitalism movements – frequently sound as if America is judged in principle and prior to any empirical considerations to be wrong, just for believing that a complex world can be divided into good and evil, with an activist and interventionist eschatology inaugurating a new world order. But is there not an identical eschatology underpinning the passion and energy of some direct action and anti-globalization protests? We find the same sense that a complex world can be divided into good and evil (global capitalists, and the anti-globalization lobby), with an activist and interventionist eschatology (bringing down an unjust system and inaugurating a just and equitable world order).

If Bush can sound like Edwards or Griswold, consider the way in which a publication from Church Action on Poverty can mirror the eschatological language of inaugurating the Kingdom which we found in Josiah Strong – coming out of the same Manichean-activist eschatological stable. In the document *Hearing the Cry of the Poor* there is an invocation to bring about a social order which 'mirrors, realises and incarnates the realities of the Kingdom'. In anti-globalization movements there can be a powerful tendency to describe something like a war between good and evil. So in an inter-

---

[90] Bush, 'Statement', 11 September 2001.

view in the *New Left Review* John Sellars[91] of the anti-capitalist movement 'The Ruckus Society' talks about 'building a truly global resistance to what is a completely global system of exploitation'. Implicated on this axis of evil are international corporations and organizations, as well as democratically mandated governments; a dichotomizing of the world which was reflected, for instance, in a presentation at a conference in Durham 2001 on 'Global Capitalism and the Gospel of Justice'. A plenary speaker described visiting a friend who had become a vicar living in a fairly comfortable four-bedroomed house, commenting: 'I question myself and wonder what has happened to the church *whose side they are on*, or are they the same as the political parties on the side of nothing but themselves and the Neo liberal system?'[92] The judgement and condemnation of specific American actions might have more integrity and ultimately more force if there was an awareness of the deep theological similarities between those who seem to share nothing. The situation might benefit also from an attempt not to mirror, and so escalate, the black and white dichotomizing of American foreign policy with similarly Manichean and blanket anti-Americanism.

Interestingly, it might be theologians on the activist left who are obliged to enter into the most detailed and empirical of debates with the American administration – concerning, for example, any military action – just because their activist eschatologies are so similar in many ways. This similarity in eschatological presupposition leads to a similar estimation of human responsibilities and capabilities in inaugurating the Kingdom, by building within history the invisible Church, the gathering in glory of the saints. The debate will involve a level of conceptual argument about whether lethal coercion can ever be legitimately used by a state in its foreign policy. To say that this can *never* be done is an extreme position, but not therefore an incoherent one. The extremism of the position should be underlined: military action would be ruled out even where it could be demonstrably shown that, over time, a much greater number of 'innocent' people (i.e. non-combatants) would be saved (not allowed to die) by resisting evil than by not resisting it, and where there would still be

---

[91] *New Left Review*, July/August 2001.

[92] Wayne Green, 'From Globalisation to Exclusion: Politics, Economics and the UK Churches'. The paper is forthcoming in a publication arising from the conference 'Global Capitalism and the Gospel of Justice', Ushaw College, Durham, July 2001 (emphasis added).

many more innocent people saved than would be killed in collateral damage in the event of action to resist evil.

The theologian Stanley Hauerwas[93] is thrillingly clear about accepting this implication. He asserts that God is in charge of history, and our worldly responsibilities are limited to a faithful and pure witness to the gospel, *irrespective of whether this produces greater good or evil*. So he argues that Christian pacifism is 'determined by the reality of Christ's cross' and insists that 'as followers of Christ we cannot be anything other than peaceful in a world inextricably at war'.[94] Immediately Hauerwas makes clear that just because war is 'incompatible with the teachings and example of Christ' it does not mean therefore that pacifism is a 'workable foreign policy'.[95] Hauerwas is explicit that his absolute pacifism is an eschatological commitment to God being in charge of history, and not based upon any assumption that it brings about a net good over evil, or that we have the means for achieving a warless or just world. John Howard Yoder,[96] pursues a similar line, arguing that non-resistance is right 'not because it works, but because it anticipates the lamb that was slain'.[97] Hauerwas is clear that in certain cases 'we must watch others die unjustly' commenting that this is 'surely harder than envisioning our own deaths'.[98] The striking thing about this eschatological commitment to pacifism is that it is based upon an extremely non-activist sense of the inauguration of the Kingdom, a lack of activism which could equally be transferred to social and humanitarian projects. God is in charge of history; our recognition of that involves accepting that our responsibilities and capabilities are limited. So Hauerwas writes, in regard to resisting evil: 'that such nonresistance may appear to let evil reign invites the charge of complicity with evil. Yet this attitude of leaving evil free to be evil is part of the nature of agape, as God's goodwill finally leaves sinners free to separate themselves from God.'[99] The Church on this account is a haven, rather than a place for the mobilization of the saints.

NB

---

[93] 'A Pacificist Response to the Bishop's Epilogue to Paul Ramsey's *Speak Up for Just War or Pacifism* (University Park and London: Pennsylvania State University Press, 1988).

[94] Hauerwas, 'Epilogue', p. 154.

[95] Hauerwas, 'Epilogue', p. 157.

[96] John Howard Yoder, in 'Peace Without Eschatology', in *The Original Revolution* (Scottdale, Penn.: Herald Press, 1971), p. 64.

[97] Yoder, 'Peace', p. 64.

[98] Hauerwas, 'Epilogue', p. 181.

[99] Hauerwas, 'Epilogue', p. 161.

In a sense Hauerwas's approach could be seen as a twist on the 'pure America' isolationist eschatology which we discussed above. Its ancestors are the close cousins but opponents of the revivalist Evangelicals who have dominated our discussion. So the New England separatists in the 1750s saw the role of the Church to live purely, and to gather the faithful for the Second Coming, which would in no way be instigated by human action.[100] From our point of view, the separatism of Hauerwas and Yoder is theologically from the same stable as the eschatological activism of the Elizabethan Puritan, and falls under the same accusation of conflating the visible and invisible Church. The separatist announces an enclave within the world, constituted by the saved, the already gathered saints who exist on the other side of history, purified and to an extent no longer involved in the complexities of a fallen world.

Self-righteousness can take the form of extreme activism or pacifism. A refusal to conflate the visible and the invisible Church is likely to turn one away from self-righteousness as such, and so also from the extremes of activism or pacifism, and towards cautious reform and constant vigilance (such as we find, for instance, in Burke). Always reckoning with the fallen distance between the visible and invisible leads us to a proper sense of the fallibility, frailty and complexity of human relations, and our consequent inability to separate good from evil, and the difficulties involved in humanly transforming the earthly before the Second Coming. Eschatologies that eschew extreme activism or pacificism are going to occupy a spectrum of positions about the role and scope of both military and social action, rarely ruling them out of court, but not engaging upon them with a messianic expectation that it will inaugurate the Kingdom. The debate will involve a complex consideration of empirical and contingent factors; the less activist will be uncomfortable with any excessive eschatological expectations around any action, the less

---

[100] Examples of this New England separatism can be found in the following: Ebenezer Frothingham, *The Articles of Faith and Practice, with the Covenant that is Confessed by the Separate Churches* (Newport, R.I., 1750); Solomon Paine, *A Short View of the Difference between the Church of Christ and the Established Churches of the Colony of Connecticut* (Newport, R.I., 1752), p. 60. John Rogers, *A Servant of Jesus Christ, to Many of the Flock of Christ that May be Scattered among the Churches of New-England, Greeting* (3rd edn, Newport, R.I., 1754). See Alan Heimart, *Religion and the American Mind* (Cambridge, Mass.: Harvard University Press, 1968, pp. 138ff.) for a discussion of Jonathan Edwards' condemnation of the separatists.

pacifist will not be content to be simply an anticipatory enclave within a darkening world.

Presented with something radically and unambiguously bad – and we can all agree that thousands dying in the World Trade Center, and three quarters of the world's population living in poverty are radically bad – we should be distrustful of the conviction, shared by American presidents and some anti-capitalist protestors, that because something is radically and unambiguously bad, there must *of necessity* be a radical, unambiguous and instant solution. Rather, because we are not gods, but creatures – and so involved in complex, frail and fallen structures – it is at least possible that in any instance the something radical and instant might just make things worse, requiring instead a more subtle, negotiated, time-consuming and less-expectant approach. That the situation is complex and fallen in precisely such a way is indicated by the way in which anti-globalization movements can present, as John Lloyd (of the think-tank *Demos*) puts it in *The Protest Ethic*: 'the critique without the antidote – an advantage for global movements. They are not forced to recognise the failings of any actually existing model of society that they are promoting.'[101]

In concrete terms, an eschatology with a greater sense of our complexity and frailty would be compatible not with revolutionary attempts to eliminate and overcome evil in a fell swoop of military or direct action, but rather with a negotiated, time-consuming and politically fraught process of reform. A reform which might include the steady building and support of global political and financial architectures to deal with the challenges posed by both anti-globalization movements and global terrorism: for instance, international courts and the rule of international law, global financial regulators and global bankruptcy courts.[102]

Having called on others to be aware of the uncomfortable allegiances that they implicitly hold, I should be as rigorous on myself. I should confess to a fear that my resistance to extreme activism or pacifism could be an illusory comfort, a justification for a lack of courage and insight in a world that demands decision and sacrifice. Knowing that I lack courage and insight, I find nevertheless that this is where I stand. Looking on at American presidents and anti-globalization protestors alike, I find a growing sense of bewilderment,

---

[101] John Lloyd, *The Protest Ethic* (London: Demos, 2001), p. 25.
[102] Cf. Lloyd, *Protest Ethic*, p. 14.

a dis-ease, a mixture of fear, envy and admiration, that people can be so sure of what to do in a world which seems too complex, precious and dangerous for either action or inaction.

4

Against Radical Orthodoxy:
The Dangers of Overcoming Political Liberalism

Let us mistrust . . . this admiration for certain ancient memories.[1]

Benjamin Constant
The Liberty of the Ancients Compared to that of the Moderns

The Radical Orthodoxy movement, taking in its leading thinkers John Milbank, Graham Ward and Catherine Pickstock, is about a lot more than a critique of political liberalism. My treatment here certainly has no pretensions to exhaustiveness or comprehensiveness.[2] I am concerned only with their critique of political liberalism, and aspects of their proposed solution. I understand this solution to be a strong form of communitarianism, vastly extended in ontological scope, invoking participatory and transformative communities and structures at every level of a hierarchical, teleological and analogically interrelated cosmos. I take a position to be strongly 'communitarian' if it subscribes to two positions: (1) that the individual is constituted largely or entirely by the range of self-interpretations available within the communities in which they find themselves, and (2) that our thought about ethics, politics and morality should always seek to further rather than restrict the natural priority of the community over the individual.

Political liberalism, in the form I have defended it, tends to endorse (1), and on the basis of this to reject (2), precisely because of the

---

[1] Benjamin Constant, 'The Liberty of the Ancients Compared to that of the Moderns', in *Political Writings*, ed. and trans. Biancamaria Fontana (Cambridge: Cambridge University Press, 1988), p. 323; 'Défions-nous . . . de cette admiration pour certaines reminiscences antiques', 'De la Liberté des Anciens comparée a celle des Modernes', in *De la Liberté chez les modernes: Écrits politiques*, texts selected and annotated by Marcel Gauchet (Paris: Pluriel, 1980), p. 509. All Constant references in this chapter are to these texts.

[2] An adapted version of this chapter, under the same title, has been published in *Modern Theology* (April 2004).

dangers implicit in (1). Political liberalism can tolerate a range of attitudes about the importance of participatory communities within society, but what it can in principle never tolerate is the notion of society itself as a participatory community, if – as Rawls puts it – 'by such a community we mean a political society united in affirming the same comprehensive doctrine. This possibility is excluded by the fact of reasonable pluralism together with the rejection of the oppressive use of the state power to overcome it.'[3] In less strident approaches to political philosophy[4] there will be different degrees of emphasis on the importance and correctness of both (1) and (2), such that with a more subtle position it is probably not even helpful to ask, without swathes of nuanced qualification, if it is communitarian or liberal; but in the strong form set out above communitarianism is quite distinct from political liberalism, and it is a strong form that is at work in Radical Orthodoxy.

Placing the Radical Orthodoxy movement into a wider communitarian movement seems justified in the light of John Milbank's own statement that his work can be seen as a 'temeritous attempt to radicalize the thought of MacIntyre'.[5] In view here is Alisdair MacIntyre's attempt in *After Virtue*[6] and *Whose Justice? Which Rationality?*[7] to break through modern nihilism (characterized by emotivism, instrumentalism, relativism and subjectivism) by the retrieval of virtuous teleological communities (the focus of *After Virtue*) and Christian moral philosophy (the focus of *Whose Justice? Which Rationality?*).

The methodology of this book, and my work as a whole, is in some ways closely aligned with one of Milbank's central claims in *Theology and Social Theory*, picked out perceptively by Fergus Kerr when he comments that 'Milbank's thesis is simplicity itself' amounting to the insight that:

---

[3] John Rawls, *Political Liberalism* (New York: Columbia University Press, 1995), p. 146.

[4] Such as we find, for instance, in Alisdair MacIntyre, who specifically rejects the notion of the whole of society as a participatory community, endorsing instead a range of participatory communities within society. Milbank's self-characterization as a radicalized take on MacIntyre is revealing.

[5] John Milbank, *Theology and Social Theory: Beyond Secular Reason* (Oxford: Blackwell, 2000), p. 327.

[6] Alisdair MacIntyre, *After Virtue: A Study in Moral Theory* (London: Duckworth, 1990).

[7] Alisdair MacIntyre, *Whose Justice? Which Rationality?* (London: Duckworth, 1988).

There is no need to bring theology and social theory together, theology is *already* social theory, and social theory is *already* theology. The task is to lay bare the theology, and anti-theology, at work in supposedly non-theological disciplines like sociology, and, analogously, to uncover the social theory inscribed in theology . . .[8]

Nor would I for an instant deny that there are many moments of electric insight, startling wisdom and sometimes ravishing beauty in the writings of Milbank, Ward and Pickstock, all of whom can combine a gift for literary reverie and conceptual lateralness with a prose style which can be evocatively, necessarily and painfully difficult.

Nevertheless, whatever else there is to the Radical Orthodoxy movement, there is at least a critique of political liberalism with some broadly communitarian-theological solutions. The political ambitions of the Radical Orthodoxy movement are perhaps gaining momentum in recent efforts to centralize information relating to Radical Orthodoxy on a web-site,[9] where the movement (shortened to 'RO') is described at one point as 'the organisation', with the promise of forthcoming information on the leading authors of the movement, and on 'workshops, classes and conferences generated by the organisation itself'. This seems to be consonant with sentiments expressed at a conference held in Oxford[10] by 'the organisation', where one of the leading authors of the movement talked of the progress made by the Radical Orthodoxy 'project', with it being envisaged that small cell-like groups might begin forming around the country, inspired by the Radically Orthodox vision. It is the political critique and the desire to mobilize Church and society towards a certain sort of solution, that is my concern in this chapter.

The Radical Orthodoxy critique of political liberalism is that it is symptomatic of an ontological nihilism; this amounts to a sense that the fundamental reality of the universe is a violent competitive struggle between opposing wills, bent upon their own self-assertion. Ontological nihilism breeds an environment of atomistic loneliness and violence. We find ourselves living in a disenchanted and flattened

---

[8] Fergus Kerr, 'Simplicity Itself: Milbank's Thesis', *New Blackfriars*, Vol. 73, no. 861, June 1992, pp. 305–11, p. 307.

[9] See www.radicalorthodoxy.com

[10] The conference which was, in fact, very well organized and conceived, was entitled 'Illuminations', and was held at St Stephen's House, Oxford, in July 2002.

universe, where order and beauty is a construction or projection, engineered all too often for a purpose other than the sheer contemplation of the good, the true, the beautiful. Radical Orthodoxy has a rival story to tell about the cosmos and our role in it: that we belong to participatory and analogical bodies (physically and socially) which are part of a hierarchical, teleological and analogically interrelated universe, and that there are ways of living – socially, politically and liturgically – which can bring us out of our forgetfulness about this peaceful and harmonious reality. It can feel unpleasant and bad-tempered to object to such a genuinely delightful and desirable vision. A little like the undergraduate who discovers that an objection to utilitarianism entails denying that we should seek the greatest possible happiness; it can feel as if we would rather there was misery, in that we recommend being sanguine about there being less happiness than possible. But as with utilitarianism, our dissent is based upon a theological and humane concern that the vision and the method invoked will ultimately be destructive to that which motivates both. In broad terms this chapter will flesh out this concern.

The chapter is structured around two fairly self-contained sections. The first part deals with the claim that the underlying framework for the 'secular' human condition – which would include political liberalism – is ontological violence and ethical nihilism. This claim is made forcefully in John Milbank's magnificent *Theology and Social Theory: Beyond Secular Reason*, and the focus here will be entirely on Milbank's argument. First, I will suggest that Milbank's positive solution is entirely imitative of the problem (as he sees it), and shares all its drawbacks. Second, I will challenge the characterization of our natural/secular condition as being marked by ontological violence and ethical nihilism, arguing for a more nuanced and mixed report on the 'secular' human condition.

The second part of the chapter will deal with the charge that liberalism leads to a social atomism and individualism that can be overcome with the help of a participatory-analogical theology. I consider the invocation to unity, participation and transformation to be theologically incautious,[11] politically naive and so dangerous, and

---

[11] Although my approach is quite different, I find myself in broad agreement with the instincts articulated by Gerard Loughlin in 'Christianity at the End of the Story', *Modern Theology* 8:4, October 1992, pp. 365–84, where he expresses a desire to 'resist any theological totalization – any advancement of theologico-philosophical metanarratives seeking mastery' (p. 375). I am also sympathetic in this regard to Romand Coles' anxiety that Milbank seems to

ultimately destructive to the fine and admirable motivations of the protagonists of the Radical Orthodoxy movement. My focus here will widen, looking at the sweep of the critique of liberalism and the radicalized communitarian solution offered in *Theology and Social Theory* by John Milbank, and in *Cities of God*[12] by Graham Ward. I will consider the way the political attitudes expressed in these works have been augmented, qualified or radicalized in other works such as *Being Reconciled: Ontology and Pardon*[13] (Milbank), *Truth in Aquinas*[14] (Milbank and Pickstock), and *After Writing*[15] (Pickstock). What we find in the latter two works is a moving emphasis on the Eucharist as the temporal expression of – responding to, invoking and enacting – the deepest ontological ambitions and yearning of the Radical Orthodoxy movement. I will suggest that the way in which the Eucharist is used here brings into focus the utopian-transformative nature of the Radical Orthodoxy movement. Further, I will argue that the type of eucharistic practice so valued, by Catherine Pickstock especially, is only possible within a structure such as political liberalism, thus subverting the Radically Orthodox critique of the same.

I have found it necessary to divide the argument into these two sections. Milbank's claim is that secularism, of which liberalism is an aspect, arises from an ontological nihilism and violence. His argument for this conclusion is not straightforward. He does not look for any empirical evidence as such; neither does he draw on any detailed social or political consideration concerning the problems and possibilities of participatory politics, for example. In the second part of the chapter I discuss such issues, but this discussion could not really come into its own until the rather nuclear threat offered by Milbank

---

'condemn all other stories – ultimately, insofar as they do not inadvertently contain the wisdom of the one true meta-narrative – to the waste bin of nihilism and subjugation' (p. 332), 'Milbank and Neo-Nitzschean Ethics', *Modern Theology* 8:4, October 1992, pp. 331–51. Neither Loughlin nor Coles share my enthusiasm for political liberalism, although one way of appreciating my argument is to see that their concerns about plurality in the face of the mastery of single metanarratives are well met by political liberalism.

[12] Graham Ward, *Cities of God* (London: Routledge, 2000).

[13] John Milbank, *Being Reconciled: Ontology and Pardon* (London: Routledge, 2003).

[14] John Milbank and Catherine Pickstock, *Truth in Aquinas* (London: Routledge, 2001).

[15] Catherine Pickstock, *After Writing: On the Liturgical Consummation of Philosophy* (Oxford: Blackwell, 1998).

over the whole terrain had been diffused. So although the first section does not specifically consider political liberalism, the claim I attempt to refute has devastating consequences for a wide raft of approaches, of which political liberalism is one prominent example.

The liberal subject and the will-to-power

The judgement on 'liberalism' emerging from Radical Orthodoxy is that it is symptomatic of the lonely human subject facing an entirely flattened universe, with order (such as there is) being a projection of the subject's will-to-power, in rivalry with other subjects. Milbank's view, developed by others, is that this world-view can be overcome by being exposed as itself a violent projection, which the theologian is at liberty to resist and replace with a rival ontology of peace. This rival ontology envisages participation and analogical interrelatedness between all levels of a hierarchical and teleological universe. I will suggest that there is a problem with both the characterization of the problem, and with the proposed solution, which seems exactly to imitate the very position it is so keen to resist. In brief, the problem with Milbank's solution is that the subject ends up constructing and asserting the meaningful, participatory universe in which they then may live; but the motivation for asserting this universe is to escape the condition whereby the only order facing the subject is that created by the subject. In order to escape this condition the Radically Orthodox theologian – in this case Milbank – asserts that there is a non-asserted universe.

To find a way into Milbank's daring and brilliant piece of theological panache we need to state his position in more detail, summarizing it in four main moves:

1 *Characterization of the problem*

Milbank offers the following characterization of 'postmodernism':

1 An absolute historicism, where every concept and claim must be understood not in terms of the claim it makes for itself, but in terms of its 'genealogy'. Following Foucault, 'genealogy' is not simply the intellectual history of an idea. Rather, a 'genealogy' always exposes how any truth claim is implicated in a network of power struggles, and mutually incompatible claims to dominance. If this exposure is

not made, we do not have a 'genealogy' in the quite specific sense involved here but a truth claim which must itself be further analysed in terms of its use as a means of assertion and violence amongst mutually incompatible power struggles. We note already a certain circular criterion for something counting as a genealogy: it will only do so, if it feeds the 'post-modern' characterization of the human world as marked by 'the ontology of difference' and 'ethical nihilism'.

2 This genealogical work exposes a persistent 'ontology of difference', 'the spectre of a human world inevitably dominated by violence'.[16]

3 The realization of the implication of all truth claims in power struggles, and the subsequent insight into the condition of 'ontological difference' leads to an 'ethical nihilism', where no truth claims or emancipatory movements can ground themselves, being implicated as they are in corrupt genealogies which constitute the space of the human condition, the ontology of difference.

2 False proposed solutions

Kant's 'liberalism' is an attempt to overcome the movement towards nihilism. In fact, it manages to be no more than 'the great delayer', for

> once it has been conceded, as by Kant, that ethics is to be grounded in the fact of the will and of human freedom, then quite quickly it is realized that freedom is not an ahistorical fact about an essential human subject, but is constantly distilled from the complex strategies of power within which subjects are interpellated as unequal, mutually dependent persons.[17]

Here we see Milbank endorsing a genealogical reduction of a Kantian claim about freedom and the will. Claims about 'freedom' are really always moves in a power struggle:

> If freedom effaces itself in favour of power, then how can one ever talk of there being more of less freedom in one society rather than another? Every society will exhibit both freedom and unfreedom,

---

[16] Milbank, *Theology and Social Theory*, pp. 278–9.
[17] Milbank, *Theology and Social Theory*, p. 279.

and a post-humanist, genealogical discourse must confine itself to the deconstruction of regimes of power, and not present this task as also a 'philosophy of history with a practical intent', or an emancipatory potential.[18]

Repeatedly, after Kant, there is a legitimate desire to make philosophy emancipatory, to give it a prophetic and political edge. Of course, it may not have this edge if all it can ever do is to offer genealogical reductions of truth claims, with its own genealogical reductions presumably joining the temporal flux of truth claims which need in turn to be reduced. This emancipatory space remains an impossible place, a utopia, in that it seems always necessary to 'smuggle back into' the philosophy 'an ahistorical Kantian subject who is the bearer of freedom', so that every 'new disguised, or semi-overt version of a Kantian practical reason . . . always succumbs to reapplication of the Nietzschian reduction of liberty to power'.[19]

3 The demand on thinking

Nevertheless, there remains a legitimate demand on our thought that it be emancipatory. Milbank quickly dismisses the alternative – the admission that philosophy cannot help politically and is irredeemably our Cassandra, singing her lethal genealogies – as 'mystical despair'.[20]

4 The only possible response

Milbank declares his own heroic response, which he claims is the 'only resort':

> One's only resort at this juncture, other than mystical despair, is to return to the demonstration that nihilism, as an ontology, is also no more than a *mythos*. To counter it, one cannot resuscitate liberal humanism, but one can try to put forward an alternative *mythos*, equally unfounded, but nonetheless embodying an 'ontology of peace', which conceives differences as analogically related, rather than equivocally at variance.[21]

---

[18] Milbank, *Theology and Social Theory*, p. 279.
[19] Milbank, *Theology and Social Theory*, p. 279.
[20] Milbank, *Theology and Social Theory*, p. 279.
[21] Milbank, *Theology and Social Theory*, p. 279.

The problem here is that Milbank's conclusion is complicit at every stage with the picture he critiques. The assertion of ontological violence is simply met – violently – by the assertion of ontological peace. Rather the question-mark needs to be put *over the assertive space* that is opened up by this picture, rather than contesting which meta-narrative will be slotted into it, and given the role of dominant metaphor (the nice peaceful one or the nasty violent one). The 'post-modernist', we were told by Milbank, is only in this space at all because he has smuggled back in the will to power, the ahistorical, non-spatial and non-temporal Kantian subject, who is placed outside the world (where 'freedom' must be reduced to the more or less deterministic and amoral play of power), and whose only decision is what attitude to take towards the whole world so understood. The post-modernist asserts a neo-pagan ontology of violence. Milbank asserts peace. We have an all-round levelling, in that Milbank founds the edifice of his theology on the basis that he is no *less* entitled to it than the post-modernist. A major factor in arriving at his conclusion is Milbank's demand that emancipatory philosophy and genealogy *will* be reconciled (see stage 3 of Milbank's argument above). Because there is this need, there must be a solution. So 'ontological peace' is justified as a means to an end in a pragmatic and secular way: the end is emancipatory genealogical philosophy, the means a declared ontological preference for peace.

I am troubled by the constant reappearance in Milbank of phrases such as 'equally unfounded' to describe both the 'ontology of peace' and the 'ontology of difference'. So, for instance, he comments that the 'alternative *mythos*' he proposes is 'equally unfounded', but that this is acceptable in that it 'conceives differences as analogically related, rather than equivocally at variance'.[22]

Note again the general levelling. Milbank is countering Nietzsche's will-to-power which he argues is sustainable only if 'one has transcendentally understood all differences as negatively related, if – in other words – one has allowed a dialectical element to intrude into one's differential philosophy'.[23] He does this by setting against Nietzsche the 'as possible' Christian perspective, which is 'to argue that the natural act might be the Christian, (supernatural) charitable act, and not the will-to-power', and so that 'an "analogical relation"

---

[22] Milbank, *Theology and Social Theory*, p. 279.
[23] Milbank, *Theology and Social Theory*, p. 289.

is as possible' a 'transcedental conception' as 'the positing of an *a priori* warfare'.[24]

Again, one has at play one of Milbank's favourite moves: to condemn the 'transcendental conception', yet to occupy it when proclaiming the ontology of peace. What can possibly be going on when Milbank says that an 'analogical relation' is *as possible* a transcendental conception as *a priori* warfare? Was not the problem the very possibility and violence of *any* transcendental conception? We are told that the post-modernist is not entitled to this conception, neither am I entitled – but by force one of us must claim it, and it will be me who wins. But of course it is the nihilist who has won (even if I am the nihilist), because the only thing the nihilist needs for victory is for truth claims to be equally illegitimate, and for there to be a victor rather than a prophet.

It is striking to note that Milbank uses a pattern of vocabulary which evokes an imaginative labour to re-invoke Augustinian universes. If genealogies can betray things, I would suggest that Milbank's emphasis on the work carried out by the imagination (the 'analogizing process',[25] as Milbank puts it) makes a chilling sort of sense if understood in the Lockean sense of the mind working on the 'scarce to be reckon'd' with matter of raw nature to create (in the mental realm) the coloured, aromatic and textured experience of our life-world, and in the material realm, to work on untoiled nature to create objects of use and value. The mind's 'working' is a richer affair than it was in Locke – involving writing, rhetoric, seduction and invocation – but the philosophical mechanism is the same.

Consider that for Locke the imaginative construction of our world out of the impoverished raw material of nature is present at every level:

> *Ideas* thus made up of several simple ones (ideas) put together, I call *complex*, such as are *beauty, gratitude, a man, an army, the universe*; which, though complicated as various simple *ideas*, or *complex ideas* made up of simple ones, yet are, **when the mind pleases**, considered each by itself as one entire thing, and signified by one name.[26]

---

[24] Milbank, *Theology and Social Theory*, p. 289.
[25] Milbank, *Theology and Social Theory*, p. 279.
[26] John Locke, *An Essay Concerning Human Understanding*, Bk. II, Ch. XII, sec. 1, (London: Everyman, 1961), p. 77 (italics original, bold mine).

Now hear Milbank, and ask if there is not something of the Lockean intellectual toil on the impoverished wasteland of raw nature: '. . . what we do or *make* is not prescribed by a preceding idea; on the contrary, we have to discover the content of the infinite through labour, and creative effort'.[27] With Locke, the mind constructs its world by organizing the raw empirical content it initially receives. Its constructions start with its own body and build up the ideas such as 'the universe'. Consider this, and then hear Milbank exploring the implications of his claim that 'analogy . . . [enters] into all unities, relations and disjunctions':

> . . . the likenesses 'discovered' are also constructed likenesses (whether by natural or cultural processes) which can be re-fashioned and re-shaped. And if certain things and qualities are 'like God', then it must also be true that the analogizing capacity *itself* is 'like God' . . . an analogizing process appears to organize *schematically* the empirical content.[28]

It is extraordinary to see such a bold statement of the constructive capacities and responsibilities – God-like even – of the subject. We can tend to read Locke through the hygienic lens of Kant and British-American analytical philosophy. The only part of the 'organizing activity' of Locke that we hear are Kantian-type categories which frame the possibility of a world, rather than providing the substantial content of that world: preconditions of experience such as substance and causation. When we come across descriptions of the mind organizing 'sense impressions' or empirical content, we remember only the ontological parsimony of Russell, with a fashionably hygienic world of atoms in motion. Listening again to Locke, and just Locke, prior to Kant and Russell, we might be shocked at the Byzantine carnival of things the mind constructs, and has a form of ownership over: bodies, beauty, gratitude, armies, universes and governments being but some explicitly named by Locke.[29] It is this Locke to which the Radical Orthodoxy movement has some striking conceptual similarities. This relationship to Locke would concern them perhaps more than it would me, for whom a debt to Locke is not necessarily a grave error. But the particular nature of the link to Locke is concerning: a

---

27 Milbank, *Theology and Social Theory*, p. 305.
28 Milbank, *Theology and Social Theory*, p. 305.
29 Locke, *Essay*, Bk. II, Ch. XII, sec. I, p. 77.

thoroughgoing constructivism about truth, which then allows theology to create world-views in the interests of political agendas. Such a politically serviceable construction seems to be at work in passages such as the following: 'Only, therefore, if we can reinvoke, like Augustine, another city, another history, another mode of being, can we discover for ourselves a social space that is not the space of the *pagus* crossed with the *dominium* of an arbitrary, Scotist God.'[30] Augustine was not 'reinvoking' the city of God, like some Middle Earth mage, but was delineating the contours of something which humbled all human invocation just because it did not require invoking. The City of God existed, exists, will exist in parallel to the City of Man; but the history of the latter is not changed or manipulated a jot because of the hidden as-yet pilgrim splendour of the latter. The City of God, in Augustine, is not a means to the construction of a 'social space'. We perhaps need to be cautious of this secular justification of theological world-views: we need a social space, therefore we will invoke an Augustinian city. Paradoxically, it is such a secular-instrumental attitude to theology that Milbank is so keen to resist.

To take stock of our position, we remember that the perceived problem was that the lonely (liberal) subject found herself in a nihilistic universe, without any given order, with any order there is being constructed, escalating the subject's sense of anxiety and dis-ease. Radical Orthodoxy here seems to reside entirely within the nihilistic universe, and to exacerbate this condition by asserting and constructing Augustinian world-views.

The diagnosis of the problem

Recalling the four-point summary of Milbank's argument above, we should turn our attention to the first move, where Milbank expounds the post-modernist claim that all truth claims can be subjected to a genealogical reduction, resting finally in an ontology of difference and an ethical nihilism. Milbank then goes on to review some attempts to occupy a transcendental assertoric space among this nihilism and judged them 'unfounded'. On the basis of these positions being unfounded, Milbank bases his claim to be able to found his own vision of Radical Orthodoxy. We have seen that this is illegitimate, in that the problem is with the assertoric space, rather

---

[30] Milbank, *Theology and Social Theory*, p. 321.

than the content that is asserted. It seems that Milbank's solution, as it stands, imitates the errors of that which it attempts to replace. Rather than sanctioning the search for 'other' solutions which do not do this, I would suggest that the problem lies deeper, and is to be found in the 'nihilistic' diagnosis of the problem. It lies in the notion of pervasive and slippery work done by the concept of 'power'.

Some care is needed here in separating out what Milbank presumes and what he denies. Ultimately Milbank wants to insists on two theses: first of all, that there is no need for Christian theology to engage rationally or apologetically with 'secular' reason, just because there is no neutral, foundational, rational space in which such a dialogue can really appear. We are simply called to out-narrate other stories, all of which are equally (un)founded. This thesis is justified because of a broad acceptance of the Foucaultian notion of geneaology, where truth claims are identified with power claims; hence Milbank's comment that 'one's only resort' is 'to put forward an alternative *mythos*, equally unfounded, but nonetheless embodying an "ontology of peace".[31] Which brings us to the second thesis Milbank wants to endorse, which is almost the opposite of the first, because indeed 'Christianity is the precise opposite of nihilism'.[32] The second thesis is that the Foucaultian conflation of power and truth, the assertion of ontological violence, is *wrong* when and only when it comes to describing the alternative *mythos* which is Christianity. In a wonderful conjuring trick Milbank *uses* Foucault as his ladder to climb high enough above apology and dialogue in order to be in the right space to assert his meta-narrative 'that-Foucault-is-wrong' (the 'ontology of peace'); but we can only claim that 'Foucault-is-wrong', in this case and in this way, if Foucault is right. There are two problems here: first of all, and this is the claim elaborated above, the position is self-referentially incoherent. Using genealogy, in Foucault's sense, is a dangerous game to play, and one cannot scratch out the trace of violence by shouting that one has always been peaceful (now that everyone else is defeated). Secondly, as I will now demonstrate, Foucault is not right anyway concerning the ubiquity of power, and so the 'last resort' for Christianity – simply to assert itself in a radically secular world – is a premature and alarmist judgement.

The problem with Foucault's genealogical approach, as appropriated by Milbank – prior to his Foucaultian assertion that Foucault is

---

[31] Milbank, *Theology and Social Theory*, p. 279.
[32] Milbank, *Theology and Social Theory*, p. 293.

wrong – is the sliding work done by the notion of 'power'.[33] Everything is described as a power struggle: even a charity or a minority justice-based resistance group is understood in terms of this social physics. Inasmuch as everything is accounted for as 'power' it seems to be simply a descriptive term, with no more sinister moral connotations than a notion such as 'gravity'. This descriptive notion of power is used to get the thesis off the ground that 'power' operates everywhere. But then there is a movement which associates 'power' with oppression and violence, and the term carries strong prescriptive undertones, which seem to make emancipation and peace impossible. The impossibility is not something discerned in the world, but is rather smuggled in at the very beginning prior to any observations. We get something like the following movement of thought, using equivocal understandings of the concept 'power':

'Power 1': is just that which is involved in any human action (including speech acts). 'Power' seems to include within its scope *any* attempt to communicate or influence, for to communicate or influence is to go out of oneself towards another and so be involved in persuasion and a 'power' dynamic. There is nothing particularly sinister, evaluative or prescriptive about such a notion.

'Power 2': involves a sub-section of human actions that are violent and oppressive. Such characterizations are possible in that we can make contrasts with other forms of human action. So an action being 'violent' or 'oppressive' is recognizable in the context of the linguistic possibility of calling other actions 'peaceful' or

---

[33] I am in agreement on this point with Nicholas Lash, who comments that 'Milbank himself too easily adopts Nietzsche's habit of confining the sense of 'power' (*Macht*) to domination and the violence which it entails. But surely an (Augustinian) Christian rejection of the myth of primal violence entails, in turn, rejection of the view that power, as such, is tainted and to be eschewed' (p. 358), in 'Not Exactly Politics or Power?', *Modern Theology* 8:4, October 1992, pp. 354–64. A similar concern is perceptively raised by Laurence Paul Hemming, who talks of the reinforcing of the '"power of power" found in Radical Orthodoxy, which would concede everything to Nietzsche and nihilism, even affirming that power in the Church is an effect of *der Wille zur Macht* . . . Indeed, radical orthodoxy's own articulation of nihilism recognizes that the question of power is sharply posed in postmodernity, but has lacked the ability to resolve it', 'Introduction', *Radical Orthodoxy? – A Catholic Enquiry*, ed. Laurence Paul Hemming (Aldershot: Ashgate Press, 2000), p. 17.

'emancipatory'. 'Power' in this sense carries strong evaluative implications, and if it were present everywhere would lead to ethical nihilism.

Then the movement of thought goes as follows:

1 'Power 1' is operative everywhere.
2 Wherever there is 'power 1' there is 'power 2'.
3 Therefore there is violence and oppression everywhere.

The difficult move here is of course (2). What sort of claim is this? Either it is a necessary conceptual claim (no counter-example will in principle be admitted), or it is a contingent empirical claim about human nature (where working from induction, we conclude that as no human act ever has been free of 'power 2', it never will be, although in principle a counter-example could topple the claim). In either case, the argument does not look a happy one.

If the claim is considered conceptually necessary, then the argument is won by a rather bloodless linguistic fiat that normal distinctions between 'altruistic', 'compassionate', 'ambivalent' and 'wicked' will be overridden, and *all* actions considered in some sense violent and oppressive. Such a fiat leads in the end to a conceptual breakdown and the need to reinvent language. Concepts such as 'violence' and 'oppression' get their significance from belonging to a complex weave of meaningful and possible contrasts, such as 'peace' and 'emancipation'. If we insist that every human action is 'violent and oppressive', then we will simply have to start inventing new concepts to capture the need to make everyday moral contrasts, where we want to be able to distinguish the 'violence and oppression' carried out by Oxfam and that carried out by the Nazi regime. So the former type of 'violence and oppression' will be characterized by concepts which circle around our present notions of compassion, justice and humanity, and the latter type will be characterized by concepts occupying the linguistic space which carves out the notions of cruelty, hate and sadism. In the end the characterization of actions as 'violent and oppressive' can simply drop out altogether, being implicitly understood as applying universally, and so as useless in making communicative moral distinctions. In a way curiously parallel to Milbank's critique of the Scotist-univocal notion of 'Being', we can say that a concept that describes absolutely everything, ceases to pick out anything in particular.

Language needs to be shaped around the human condition, rather than hypostasized in such a way that by linguistic fiat we can claim to discover something completely shocking about that condition. When the language is removed from the warp and weave of the human condition, we find that new concepts must simply be invented to take the place of the previous concepts that made distinctions crucial in our everyday life. This is very clear with a concept such as 'intelligence'. I could decide that the criteria for intelligence is a God-like omniscience. I would then 'discover' that no person had ever been intelligent, leading to potentially apocalyptic and nihilistic theories that 'everyone was stupid'. Such a theory would be able to feed on some cases of genuine or surprising stupidity, even where people apparently are clever, just as the 'post-modernist' genealogical reduction of truth to power can find instances where 'truth' has been so manipulated. We could then infer from this that we have an 'intellectual nihilism', an 'ontological ignorance'. But this would be a manifestly silly argument, resting on my idiosyncratic and over-rigorous notion of 'intelligence' which had nothing to do with the actual meaning of the concept, which arises from distinctions we wish to make *as humans* about the range of *human-type intelligence*. The genealogical reduction of all human interactions to power 2, and so to violence and oppression, works in a structurally similar way – by linguistic fiat – and is ultimately no less silly.

Now, of course, the argument could be an empirical one. On this reading the argument would be that some humanly possible actions would count as non-violent and oppressive, it just so happens that we never experience any. I assume there is no need to say much as to why such an empirical thesis would be 1. impossible to establish with the force needed to produce 'ethical nihilism', and 2. manifestly untrue anyway, in that there are countless acts of kindness, altruism and love, if these concepts are not defined so over-rigorously as to make them uninstantiable (which on the empirical approach they are not, this being what defines the empirical approach as such).

So there is really no need for Milbank to shove his way into the assertive transcendental space, which is in turn only opened up and made necessary because of the erroneous 'description' of our condition, which description arises from an inhuman and over-rigorous setting of the criteria for using concepts. We could say that a per-fectibilism about concepts leads to an unwarranted scepticism about human nature. We just need to challenge the initial genealogical reduction, in the way shown above. If the genealogical reduction leading to nihilism is really erroneous then we can do better than simply shout it down on the basis that our optimism is 'no less unfounded'. We can just show it to be wrong, and offer instead a more nuanced interpretation of the natural human condition, complete with all its hope, frailty, complexity, tragedy and immortal longings.

What we are then left with is neither nihilism, nor the full glory of a participatory city of God, but rather a broken middle, where the wheat and the chaff are thoroughly mixed until the coming of the Son of Man – a complex, graced but fallen inter-mingling of good and evil, of hope and despair.

Liberalism, participation and atomism

Having disposed of the global ontological complaint against the 'secular' condition, of which political liberalism would be one manifestation, it is time to attend to the more particular critique of elements of life under political liberalism, along with proposed solutions.

In *Cities of God* Graham Ward presents what he calls the 'burden for the rest of the book'; this consists of an analysis of 'social atomism' brought about by 'contemporary cyberspace, global cities, and new forms of mobile short-term "employment" (which erodes notions of society, family, and even nation) . . .'.[34] It is clear that Ward sees his project as aimed against the 'liberal, humanist approach' which he understands as based upon a 'social atomism, founded upon the rampant individualism of the I am, I want, and I will'.[35] Talking about earlier theological treatments of the city, Ward complains that 'they failed to grasp, in their liberal optimism, how deep the roots of secularism penetrate nihilism; the secular city is a radically unfoundational, virtual city'.[36]

The rival vision of the city that Ward propounds is a 'constructive theological project which maps our physical bodies on to our social and civic bodies, on to our Eucharistic and ecclesial bodies, on to the Body of Christ'.[37] Ward sees Christian theology as having a political

---

[34] Graham Ward, *Cities of God* (London: Routledge, 2000), p. 75.
[35] Ward, *Cities*, p. 70.
[36] Ward, *Cities*, p. 70.
[37] Ward, *Cities*, p. 70.

opportunity and responsibility 'to counter this advanced atomism' with a 'strong doctrine of participation' which requires a 'doctrine of analogical relationships networking the several bodies – physical, social, political, ecclesial, eucharistic, Christic and divine'.[38]

Milbank presents a similar yearning for a more participatory and unitary society when writing that: 'True society implies absolute consensus, agreement in desire, and entire harmony amongst its members, and this is exactly (as Augustine reiterates again and again) what the Church provides, and that in which salvation, the restoration of being, consists.'[39] For Milbank, the first conceptual battle against the atomistic society is to assert the harmonious ontology of peace against the nihilistic ontology of violence which he perceives as being behind political liberalism (among other things). This diagnosis of our situation, and the constructive solution, as we saw, are in not in any sense empirical, or even interpretative of something empirical, and require the special handling given in the first part of this chapter. Having refuted Milbank's distinctive critique and solution, we are still left with Ward and Milbank's shared sense of the atomism of liberal culture, the vacuity and destructiveness of the 'freedom' offered, and the need for a response at the theological level, re-envisaging our fundamental ontological frameworks.

There are two questions I want to put to this broad consensus between Ward and Milbank: the first concerning the accuracy of their cultural commentary, and the second pointing to a danger with their proposed solutions.

With regard to the accuracy of the cultural commentary, it is worth asking from whence comes the sense of 'social atomism'?[40] I suspect that it is not an 'impartial' assessment gleaned from studying the output of the Office of National Statistics; such an approach would smack too much of precisely the technological-instrumental approach to society that is to be overcome. It is much more likely that this critique comes from a sort of prophetic wisdom, imbibed from the theologian's own experience of the world, informed by a theological framework and the reading of fine cultural commentaries from the likes of Zygmunt Bauman and Jean-Luc Nancy.[41] It is the

---

[38] Ward, *Cities*, p. 75.

[39] Milbank, *Theology and Social Theory*, p. 402.

[40] Ward, *Cities*, p. 75.

[41] Both referred to deferentially by Ward. Jean-Luc Nancy, *The Inoperative Community*, tr. Peter Connor *et al.* (Mineapolis: University of Mineapolis Press, 1991) and Z. Bauman, *In Search of Politics* (Cambridge: Polity Press, 1992).

liberal who is accused of assuming a stand from nowhere, while projecting on to the human condition the fairly narrow and privileged confines and opportunities of their own situation. Perhaps the same suspicion could be raised against the prophets of Radical Orthodoxy, experiencing the occupational loneliness, marginality and political impotence of being academic theologians, living in large urban centres. Full participation (consoling and challenging) within a community of interest and understanding tends only to come about after several hours on an aeroplane, which takes one to the international conference where the handful of people who might have read you really attentively can be expected to gather. In between such meetings the 'community' has a diaspora existence through e-mail correspondence, with intellectual friends being identified with distant cities rather like the characters in a Shakespeare history play ('Exeter', 'Warwick', enter 'Canterbury' and so forth). Physical dislocation becomes the obstacle to participation in the flesh, with cyberspace making at times a painfully inadequate substitute.

So we can understand why Ward so enjoys the description of the 'inoperative (*desoeuvrée*) community' given by Jean-Luc Nancy, who in talking of cyberspatial communication writes that 'these "places of communication" are no longer places of fusion, even though in them one *passes* from one to the other; they are defined and exposed by their dislocation. Thus, the communication of sharing would be this very dislocation.'[42] Such a description applies with an acuity which is moving for the urban academic theologian, but perhaps of limited use as a global pronouncement of how a whole range of people live and suffer in the wider city, let alone in the suburbs, the provinces and the countryside (which are treated, if at all, as a construction within the city of the city's 'other', as if rural communities do not have their own narratives, and their own constructions of the 'urban' as other).

This may seem a strange way to conduct an argument. But when a cultural commentary is presented not on statistical but interpretative-prophetic lines, its efficacy and existential compulsion has to be challenged and assessed by each hearer. Ward and Milbank are professional theologians, with an Oxbridge background, writing from within an Anglican tradition. Exactly the same descriptions apply to me. The promise, but also the disappointment of the cultural

---

[42] Nancy, *Inoperative Community*, p. 75.

commentary that emerges from Radical Orthodoxy, is that it seems to describe perfectly a strand in my life (*qua* being an academic theologian), but not the whole, and not even a part of the whole of many of those I know and love the best.

A large number of close relatives, friends and acquaintances live not in a world of chrome-covered austerity and cyberspatial relationships, but in more participatory communities, based in the suburbs, provinces or in rural communities. There can be a sense of belonging, of participation, of being known, needed and loved from many directions. This can bring many blessings, but also its own sort of misery, not possible in the more lonely and ephemeral city existence. Living in thick or thin communities engenders its own possibilities and limitations; the human condition – with its frailty, complexity and fallenness – has a way of reasserting itself in either.

We might say that there are two sorts of 'liberty', which are incompatible, and that each bring their attendant problems. There is the liberty of the 'city'. Around such 'liberty' we can gather such experiences, limitations and possibilities as loneliness, lightness, unpredictability, choice, anxiety and mobility. The 'liberty' involved in more cohesive and participatory communities – more provincial, traditional or rural – tends to gather around it notions such as participation, heaviness, belonging, predictability, routine, duty, surveillance, care, judgement, attention and immobility. Both modes of life have their own glories and own problems, but it is vital to acknowledge that one is not in any straightforward sense the cure for the other, although both can look like it when one is immersed unhappily in either extreme. The problems are attendant upon the possibilities, and one removes the former only by eliminating the latter. So more cohesive communities have a strong sense of belonging and participation, which is engendered by a powerful mutual imitation, common ideals and an exclusive sense of the 'outside' and the strangeness of outsiders; so such a community will be less tolerant of certain forms of dissent, plurality, withdrawal and diversity, and will tend to construct its own coherence by building uncharitable models of non-conforming individuals or 'outsiders'. Remove this cohesive imitation and these common ideals and one has a society which is more tolerant of the dissident and the outsider, but only because it cares less, and the sense of belonging and unity has depleted.

In the early stages of researching the issues dealt with in this chapter, I spent some time with the Iona Community on the West Coast of Scotland. One of the most memorable workshops was led by the leader of the Corrymeela Community from Northern Ireland, a retreat house which brings together people from both sides of the sectarian divide who have been hurt in various ways by the conflict. It was during the course of this workshop that it became clear to me that there was something awry with the way in which the word 'community' is supposed to be a sort of panacea in theological discourse, with the word 'individual' always emanating connotations of hubristic self-sufficiency. Coming from the English-urban-academic background described above, my conviction then – being lonely – was that theology should tell to political philosophy of the need for more participatory communities. But from Trevor Williams, the leader of the Corrymeela Community, and other participants in the workshop from Northern Ireland and the West Coast of Scotland, I was hearing about theologically saturated communities where the sense of unity and belonging could not be stronger. At the same time in these communities there was also a strong experience of judgementalism, surveillance and immobility, with the cohesiveness of the participatory communities maintained by powerful internal imitation, common ideals and a violent construction of the other. Part of the job of the Corrymeela community was to help people remove their community-saturated identities and speak a more universal language of individual pain: this woman of the pain of being ostracized for loving a Catholic man, this man of the childhood terror of a father shot on the doorstep.

Now of course the response to this is obvious. Some communities are debased by their scapegoating and violent construction of the other. This would especially not surprise Milbank, with his interest in Girard, and the emphasis on the ontological violence which he sees underlying secular nihilism. The goal must be to create communities – such as, for instance, the Iona Community and the Corrymeela Community – where the ontological priority of peace can be remembered. This is correct, but it is not a response to my objection to 'participatory' theologies. My point was never that communities are always 'worse' than individuals, or irredeemable, or never sites of grace; rather that they are just as prone to sin, frailty and pain as individuals, and are not in themselves salvific of our individual frailties and vices. Further, my claim is that, given the pervasive – albeit contingent – human condition, there are certain tendencies that can be mapped conceptually and *a priori*. So where a community is more cohesive certain dimensions of life are enhanced, such as a sense of belonging and unity, while certain dangers become more pronounced, such as the tendency to scapegoating, judgement and immobility; where a community is more anonymous and atomistic, the possibilities of choice, autonomy and mobility are strong, but carry with them the burden of loneliness and anxiety.

It is worth reflecting in this regard that communities such as Iona and Corrymeela are not 'natural' communities, but formed artificially by *removing individuals* from the communities to which they belong (in which they participate) for a consciously limited period of time, allowing people to stand out in their individuality in a way that they could not do in their 'native' environment. A sense of the artificiality and transience of the formed community is valued and institutionally preserved by the Iona Community, for instance, who stipulate three years as a maximum residency for volunteers. In other words, such communities can work so well, and be such sites for grace, just because they balance the possibilities available to both more anonymous and more participatory communities. My anxiety about the participatory solutions called for by Milbank and Ward is not that what they hope for is always impossible, but that there are non-accidental attendant dangers in seeking to build participation and unity, and that these dangers remain when the 'building' is symbolic and theologically literate. It is never politically advisable to work towards solutions whose prerequisite or goal is a radical transformation of the human condition, whether conceived individually or collectively.

I would maintain that there is a strand in the liberal tradition – too rarely acknowledged – that is profoundly aware of all the dangers, limitations and possibilities discussed above. The wisdom, if we would look, is already set out in the eighteenth/nineteenth-century French liberal Benjamin Constant.[43] Constant is distinguishing the liberty of the ancients from the liberty of the moderns; broadly speaking, his types fit our 'liberty' within participatory communities ('the ancients') and within more atomistic communities ('the moderns'). The historical or geographical locating of these types is of little importance. I suggested that – in my experience – the 'liberty' of thicker communities can tend to coincide with non-urban environments; Constant's 'type' of the cohesive and participatory community is the

---

[43] Although Swiss by birth, Constant became a prominent figure in French political life following the revolution of 1789. He was a leading member of the liberal opposition to Napoleon and, following that, to the Bourbon monarchy.

ancient city states. In neither case need the connection be necessary or exhaustive. Of vital importance is the conceptual relationship Constant demonstrates between participation and certain limitations and dangers on the one hand, and 'modern' autonomy, loneliness and anxiety on the other. Constant adds a nuance to our analysis in addressing the nostalgia for the liberty of the ancients that moderns will inevitably undergo, but should be cautious of.

Speaking in 1819 of the 'liberty of the ancients' Constant paints a picture of participation and unity, with the people 'exercising collectively, but directly, several parts of the complete sovereignty', with deliberation in all matters being carried out in 'the public square'.[44] The attendant limitation of this 'collective freedom' is, as we would expect 'the complete subjection of the individual to the authority of the community':[45]

> You find among them almost none of the enjoyments which we have just seen form part of the liberty of the moderns. All private actions were submitted to a severe surveillance. No importance was given to individual independence, neither in relation to opinions, nor to labour, nor, above all, to religion. The right to choose one's own religious affiliation, a right which we regard as one of the most precious, would have seemed to the ancients a crime and a sacrilege. *In the domains which seem to us the most useful, the authority of the social body interposed itself and obstructed the will of individuals.*[46]

Thus among the ancients the individual, almost always sovereign in public affairs, was a slave in all his private relations. As a citizen,

---

[44] Constant, *Liberty*, p. 311; '. . . à exercer collectivement, mais directement, plusieurs parties de la souveraineté tout entière', '. . . la place publique . . .', Constant, *Liberté*, p. 495.

[45] Constant, *Liberty*, p. 311; 'l'assujettissement complet de l'individu à l'autorité de l'ensemble', *Liberté*, p. 495.

[46] Constant, *Liberty*, p. 311; 'Vous ne trouverez pas chez eux presque aucune des jouissances que nous venons de voir faisant partie de la liberté chez les modernes. Toutes les actions privées sont soumises à une surveillance sévère. Rien n'est accordé à l'indépendance individuelle, ni sous le rapport des opinions, ni sous celui de l'industrie, ni surtout sous le rapport de la religion. La faculté de choisir son culte, faculté que nous regardons comme l'un de nos droits les plus précieux, aurait paru aux anciens un crime et un sacrilège. Dans les choses qui nous semblent les plus futiles, l'autorité du corps social s'interpose et gêne la volonté des individus', *Liberté*, p. 498.

he decided on peace and war; as a private individual, he was constrained, watched and repressed in all his movements; as a member of the collective body, he interrogated, dismissed, condemned, beggared, exiled, or sentenced to death his magistrates and superiors; as a subject of the collective body he could himself be deprived of his status, stripped of his privileges, banished, put to death, by the discretionary will of the whole to which he belonged.[47]

In contrast, among 'the moderns', 'the individual, independent in his private life, is, even in the freest of states, sovereign only in appearance. His sovereignty is restricted and almost always suspended. If, at fixed and rare intervals, in which he is again surrounded by precautions and obstacles, he exercises this sovereignty, it is always only to renounce it.'[48] Although impotent at the level of the polis, the modern individual enjoys the benefits and suffers the anxieties of 'liberty' within a thin community:

> ... the right to be subjected to the laws, and to be neither arrested, detained, put to death or maltreated in any way by the arbitrary will of one or more individuals. It is the right of everyone to express their opinion, choose a profession and practise it, to dispose of property, and even to abuse it; to come and go without permission, and without having to account for their motives or undertakings. It is everyone's right to associate with other individuals, either to discuss their interests, or to profess the religion which they and their associates prefer, or even simply to occupy

---

[47] Constant, *Liberty*, p. 311; 'Ainsi chez les anciens, l'individu, souverain presque habituellement dans les affaires publiques, est esclave dans tout ses rapports privés. Comme citoyen, il décide de la paix et de la guerre; comme particulier, il est circonscrit, observé, réprimé dans tous ses mouvements; comme portion du corps collectif, il interoge, destitue, condamne, dépouiller, exile, frappe de mort des magistrats ou ses supérieurs, comme soumis au corps collectif, il peut à son tour être privés de son état, dépouillé de ses dignités, banni, mis à mort, par la volonté discrétionnaire de l'ensemble dont il fait partie', *Liberté*, p. 496.

[48] Constant, *Liberty*, p. 312; 'chez les modernes, au contraire, l'individu, indépendent dans la vie privée, n'est, même dans les Etats les plus libres, souverain qu'en apparence. Sa souveraineté est restreinte, presque toujours suspendue; et si à époques fixes, mais rares, durant lesquelles il est encore encore entouré de précautions et d'entraves, il exerce cette souveraineté, ce n'est jamais que pour l'abdiquer', *Liberté*, p. 496.

their days or hours in a way which is most compatible with their inclinations or whims.[49]

The price for such liberty is impotence and loneliness, for at the level of the polis 'we can no longer enjoy the liberty of the ancients, which consisted in an active and constant participation in collective power':

> Our freedom must consist of peaceful enjoyment and private independence. The share which in antiquity everyone held in national sovereignty was by no means an abstract presumption as it is in our own day. The will of each individual had real influence: the exercise of this will was a vivid and repeated pleasure . . . This compensation no longer exists for us today. Lost in the multitude, the individual can almost never perceive the influence he exercises. Never does his will impose itself upon the whole; nothing confirms in his eyes his own co-operation.[50]

Constant has an acute sense of the difficulties of imposing a participatory 'liberty' on any significant scale, 'for the ancients when they sacrificed that independence to their political rights, sacrificed less to obtain more; while in making the same sacrifice, we would give more to obtain less'.[51] In his comments about the 'excusable'

---

[49] Constant, *Liberty*, p. 311; '. . . le droit de n'être soumis qu'aux lois, de ne pouvoir ni être arrêté, ni détenu, ni mis à mort, ni maltraité, par l'effet de la volanté arbitraire d'un ou de plusieurs individus. C'est pour chacun le droit de dire son opinion, de choisir son industrie et de l'exercer; de disposer de sa propriété, d'en abuser même; d'aller, de venir, sans en obtenir la permission, et sans rendre compte de ses motifs ou ses démarches. C'est, pour chacun, le droit de se réunir à d'autres individus, soit le soit pour conférer sur les intérêts, soit pour professer le culte que lui et ses associés préfèrent, soit simplement pour remplir ses jours et ses heures d'une manière plus conforme à ses inclinations, à ses fantaisies.' *Liberté*, p. 495.

[50] Constant, *Liberty*, p. 316; '. . . nous ne pouvons plus jouir de la liberté des anciens, qui se composer de la participation active et constante au pouvoir collectif. Notre liberté, à nous, doit se composer de la jouissance paisible de l'indépendance priveé. La part que, dans l'antiquité, chacun prenait à la souveraineté nationale, n'était point, comme do nos jours, une supposition abstraite. La volonté de chacun avait une influence réelle; l'exercice de cette volonté était un plaisir vif et répété . . . Ce dédommagement n'existe plus aujourd'hui pour nouns. Perdu dans la multitude, l'individu n'aperçoit presque jamais e'empreint sur l'ensemble; rien ne constate à ses propres yeux sa coopération.' *Liberté*, p. 501.

[51] Constant, *Liberty*, p. 317; 'Car les anciens, lorsqu'ils sacrifiaient cette indépendance aux droits politiques, sacrifiaent moins pour obtenir plus; tandis qu'en faisent le même sacrifice nous donnerions plus pour obtenir moins.' *Liberté*, p. 502.

yearning for ancient forms of liberty which caused 'infinite evils during our long and stormy revolution'[52] (the French Revolution), we can perhaps also hear something that would touch, gently but subversively, the Radical Orthodoxy movement:

> Their error itself was excusable. One could not read the beautiful pages of antiquity, one could not recall the actions of its great men, without feeling an indefinable and special emotion, which nothing modern can possibly arouse. The old elements of a nature, one could almost say, earlier than our own, seem to awaken us in the face of these memories. It is difficult not to regret the time when the faculties of man developed along an already trodden path, but in so wide a career, so strong in their own powers, with such a feeling of energy and dignity. Once we abandon ourselves to this regret, it is impossible not to wish to imitate what we regret.[53]

Remember the most politically alarming of Milbank's sentences in *Theology and Social Theory*: 'True society implies absolute consensus, agreement in desire, and entire harmony amongst its members, and this is exactly (as Augustine reiterates again and again) what the Church provides, and that in which salvation, the restoration of being, consists.'[54] Now hear what Constant has to say about the post-revolutionary political theologian the Abbé de Mably – who passionately desired theologically informed unity and participation – and ask if there is not a whiff of Milbank in the air:

> ... to him any means seemed good if it extended his area of authority over that recalcitrant part of human existence whose independence he deplored. The regret he expresses everywhere in his works

---

[52] Constant, *Liberty*, p. 317; '. . . des maux infinis durant notre longue et orageuse révolution'. *Liberté*, p. 502.

[53] Constant, *Liberty*, p. 317; '. . . leur erreur même était excusable. On ne saurait lire les belles pages de l'antiquité, l'on ne se retrace point les actions de ces grands hommes, sans ressentir je ne sais quelle émotion d'un genre particulier, que ne fait éprouver rien de ce qui est moderne. Les vieux éléments d'une nature, antérieure pour ainsi dire à la nôtre, semblent se réveiller en nous à ces souvenirs. Il est difficile de ne pas regretter ces temps où les facultés de l'homme se développaient dans une direction tracée d'avance, mais dans une carrière si veste, tellement forte de leur propre force, et avec un tel sentiment d'énergie et de dignité; et lorsqu'on se livre à ces regrets, il est impossible de ne pas vouloir imiter ce qu'on regrette', *Liberté*, p. 502.

[54] Milbank, *Theology and Social Theory*, p. 402.

is that the law can only cover actions. He would have liked it to cover the most fleeting thoughts and impressions; to pursue man relentlessly, leaving him no refuge in which he might escape from its power.[55]

The Eucharist and political transformation

The transformation, as conceived by Milbank, Ward and Pickstock is to be brought about by the Church, or more precisely by the liturgical consummation available in the Eucharist. Initially, this seems a promising qualification. A worry about Milbank's position must be that it smacks of theocracy,[56] and too smooth an identification of the visible with the invisible Church (that is to say, the actual visible institutions of the Church, with the invisible eschatological Church, the not-yet gathering in glory of all the saved).[57] Milbank seems to soothe these anxieties in a response to criticism of *Theology and Social Theory* where he comments that it was not his purpose to 'imagine the Church as Utopia. For this would have been to envisage the Church in spatial terms – as another place, which we might arrive at, or *as this* identifiable site'.[58]

If our anxiety is that the Radical Orthodoxy movement can too closely identify the visible with the invisible Church, overlooking the rupture and brokeness of our created and fallen state, then there is

---

[55] Constant, *Liberty*, p. 318; '. . . tous les moyens lui paraissent bons pour étendre l'action de cette autorité sur cette partie récalitrante de l'existence humaine, dont il déplorait l'indépendance. Le regret qu'il exprime partout dans ses ouvrages, c'est que la loi ne puisse atteindre que les actions. Il aurait voulu qu'elle atteignît les pensées, les impressions sans relâches et sans lui laisser un asile où il pût échapper à son pouvoir', *Liberté*, p. 504.

[56] A criticism made by Aidan Nichols OP in ' "Non tali auxilio": John Milbank's Suasion to Orthodoxy', *New Blackfriars*, Vol. 73, no. 861, June 1992, pp. 326–32.

[57] Nicholas Lash expresses a similar concern, suggesting that Milbank mistakes the Church for the Kingdom. Replying to Milbank's claim that 'all "political" theory, in the antique sense, is relocated by Christianity as thought about the Church' (John Milbank, 'Enclaves, or Where is the Church?' *New Blackfriars*, Vol. 73, no. 861 June 1992, p. 341), Lash writes: 'Might it not be more prudent to say: is relocated as thought about the *Kingdom*? That would remind us that, though Christ has come, although salvation has occurred, the classic Christian grammar of these things require us also to say: salvation is occurring now and is still awaited eagerly in hope', Nicholas Lash in 'Not Exactly Politics or Power?', *Modern Theology* 8:4, October 1992, p. 362.

[58] Milbank, 'Enclaves', pp. 341–52.

comfort to be taken from the passage in *Truth in Aquinas* where Pickstock and Milbank write: 'For in a fallen world, we do not infallibly experience the unknown depth as a participated unknown which partially discloses its truth in the manifest; to the contrary, we experience it also as a rupture from God and ultimate truth or meaningfulness.'[59] Reading further, one begins to suspect that this 'rupture' does not remain as a structural feature of our fallen createdness, but rather is something that is removed by our participation in the Eucharist. So the rupture described above causes a 'hesitation' (even the understatement is telling) which 'is *overcome*' (italics mine)

> when we encounter, with the eyes of faith, the divine bridging of this rupture so that (here in the Eucharist) we see and taste a material surface as immediately conjoined to the infinite depth. Participation is, in this case, so entire that God as the participated truth is fully present, without lack, in the material bread and wine which participate.[60]

When and where is this full participation given? In the Church, which is to be found 'on the site of the Eucharist'.[61] But this site, we are told, is not a discrete moment in time, the present moment when contact is made between the tongue and bread, for 'the Eucharist is not a site, since it suspends presence in favour of memory and expectation'.[62] So the full participation of the Eucharist spills out into both memory and expectation, with the present only ever being the invisible interweaving of the two. The full participation of the Eucharist does in truth 'overcome' the rupture spoken of above, occupying for us, time as such.

It begins to seem that what preaching is for the Calvinist, the Eucharist is for the Radically Orthodox, performing a not dissimilar function. For the Calvinist our wretched natural condition is overcome by our conversion on hearing the scriptures, which unlocks our predetermined and elected status as saved, enabling us to gather with the righteous to transform the visible Church and wider society in the model of the eschatological Kingdom. For the Radically Orthodox, our wretched natural condition is immersion in secular nihilism, with

---

[59] Milbank and Pickstock, *Truth in Aquinas*, p. 94.
[60] Milbank and Pickstock, *Truth in Aquinas*, p. 94.
[61] Milbank, 'Enclaves', p. 342.
[62] Milbank, 'Enclaves', p. 342.

the transformation and perfection of our nature being brought about by our participation in the Eucharist, which enables the 'participants' (the righteous) to transform the visible Church and wider society according to the model of the participatory-analogical universe.

My suggestion to both the Calvinist and the Radically Orthodox is that our natural condition (sinfulness/secular nihilism) is not as wretched as presented, and that the redemption from our (less bleakly conceived) natural condition is not as complete, dramatic and politically instrumental as both seem to imply. It is worth remembering that the Eucharist is a re-enactment of a meal marked by real presence fully given within the reality – among the 'visible Church' of the disciples – of fear, anxiety, uncertainty and immanent betrayal. As then, so today. The Eucharist is not the generating centre of political transformation, or the site of 'full participation', if by that we mean the elimination – from expectation and memory – of all confusion, frailty, complexity and fallenness. It does not authorize and sanctify the actions or political vision of the communicants; for which of us knows who is Judas and who Peter, and who can be certain that, for them, the cock will not crow a second time?

The transferral of utopian political ambitions from the Church onto the Eucharist (and so back to the Church, which is the site of the Eucharist) is very clear in Catherine Pickstock's *After Writing*. Pickstock seems to regret the passing of the pre-Vatican II Roman Rite, in that it stood for a more holistic interweaving between the secular and the religious. The gradual elimination of the role of the state in the religious life of the people, and vice versa, is seen almost entirely in terms of loss with 'the rise of a soteriology of the State as guarantor of social peace and justice' leading Pickstock to ask wistfully 'to what dimension was the religious relegated?'[63] Pickstock traces the beginning of this process of 'privatization of religion' – which culminates in the rise of political liberalism in the seventeenth century – back to figures such as Marsilius of Padua (*c.*1275 – *c.*1342), 'an . . . opponent of papal claims to comprehensive power, [who] already argued that the natural process of earthly politics had a self-sufficiency which not only needed no completion or rectification from higher sources, but could be represented as endangered by such interference'.[64] There can be no doubt, from the tone or

---

[63] Catherine Pickstock, *After Writing: On the Liturgical Consummation of Philosophy* (Oxford: Blackwell, 1998), p. 152.

[64] Pickstock, *After Writing*, p. 153.

substance of Pickstock's writing, that this imagined 'self-sufficiency' of politics is conceived to be hubristic and destructive. The effect on religion is to 'privatize its relevance and segregate it from the ecclesial sphere of bodily practice', with the nadir of this tendency being reached in 1576 when Jean Bodin 'brought it (the privatization of religion) to its most explicitly realized expression: people should be free in conscience to choose whatever religion they wished'.[65] This has the result that 'religion no longer comprises bodily practices within the sphere of the *Corpus Mysticum*, but becomes limited to the realm of the "soul"'.[66] In contrast, Pickstock argues, 'the complex rituals and institutions of charity in the early and high Middle Ages made possible a fusion of love and power upon a liturgical basis'.[67]

At this point the nostalgia about a more enchanted, pre-liberal church polity needs to be checked, and some serious questions asked about what exactly Pickstock is recommending. *After Writing* is a beautiful and suggestive appreciation of the pre-Vatican II Roman Catholic Rite. At the same time, we have a critique of state neutrality, and a nostalgia for the fusion of 'love and power' which is only possible prior to the liberal separation of church and state. But of course, where the state is not theologically neutral, public power can be used to save souls, by more or less direct forms of coercion, privileging and exclusion. The very rite Pickstock is recommending, the pre-Vatican II Catholic Rite, could not have been publically practised, without heavy censure, by any British subject after the Reformation – specifically the 1559 Acts of Supremacy and Uniformity, respectively establishing the King as the supreme head of the Church of England, and the forbidding of any public prayer than the second prayer-book of Edward VI – and prior to the Catholic Emancipation Act of 1829. The Emancipation Act was a crucial milestone in the emergence of a theologically neutral state setting out as it did to remove 'restraints and disabilities . . . imposed on the Roman Catholic Subjects of His Majesty',[68] so as to allow 'the Invocation of the Saints and the Sacrifice of the Mass, as practised in

---

[65] Pickstock, *After Writing*, p. 154.

[66] Pickstock, *After Writing*, p. 154.

[67] Pickstock, *After Writing*, p. 157.

[68] 'Catholic Emancipation Act 1829', in Samuel Taylor Coleridge, *On the Constitution of Church and State*, ed. J. Colmer (London: Routledge and Kegan Paul, 1976), Vol. 10 of the Collected Works of Samuel Taylor Coleridge, p. 203.

the Church of *Rome*', alongside the 'sitting and voting in Parliament' and the 'Exercise of Enjoyment of any Office, Franchise, or Civil Right'.[69]

The implications of this Act were feared by contemporaries such as Samuel Taylor Coleridge, who opposed it on grounds with which Pickstock could have some sympathy. So Coleridge was concerned about the fracture which would emerge between the corporate identity of church and state, the national Church and the nation. So strong was this identity, in Coleridge's view, that in the 'highest sense of the word STATE', 'it is equivalent to the nation', which 'considered as one body politic . . . therefore includes the National Church' where that Church is 'the especial and constitutional organ and means' of the 'primary ends of' the state, 'the hope, the chance' of the spiritual welfare of all citizens.[70] The Catholic Emancipation Act is very much in the spirit of precisely the political liberalism that Coleridge fears and Pickstock critiques. Yet without the state neutrality legislated for in the Act – a neutrality which political liberalism so prizes – Pickstock's endorsement of the pre-Vatican II Rite would be heavily censured, and incompatible with – as the Act puts it – her 'Exercise of Enjoyment of any Office, Franchise, or Civil Right'.[71]

Where the state withdraws from questions of religious truth and personal salvation, we actually find that a greater degree of participation in the national life becomes possible for those religious groups which have been previously marginalized, or alternately marginalized and privileged, depending on the nature of the regime. We also find that certain forms of theological creativity, such as we find in Radical Orthodoxy when it endorses the pre-Vatican II Roman Rite, are only guaranteed protection from persecution and made possible because of the way the liberal state no longer uses public power to save souls. Critique should be tempered with awareness of indebtedness, if not gratitude.

The force of my argument has been that a principled neutrality on theological matters need not arise from an indifference to religious truth, but out of a sense of humility, of being chastened by the pain of religious conflict, the need for self-restraint, and a charitable commitment to the importance of tolerating difference. The indi-

---

[69] Coleridge, 'Catholic Emancipation', p. 203.
[70] Coleridge, *Constitution*, Ch. VIII, p. 73.
[71] Coleridge, 'Catholic Emancipation', p. 203.

vidual is made the ultimate political unit not necessarily because of
a confidence in the hubristic self-sufficiency of the individual, but
because of a sense of the frailty of individuals who need to be protected from the enthusiasms of others, whether those others are
acting individually or collectively. To characterize all this as the
'relegation' of religion to a privatized sphere is only to give part of the
story. For the state to remain silent on religious truth, but to preserve
freedom of conscience, toleration and the right of free association, is
actually to facilitate a greater diversity of public spaces.

There is something regrettably shrill and unscholarly about the
broadside given by Milbank in his recent *Being Reconciled:*
Ontology and Pardon, where he comments that 'political liberalism
. . . engenders today an increasingly joyless and puritanical world'
marked by a 'totalitarian drift . . . its [political liberalism's] empty
heart . . . besieged by an irrational cult or race, class, science, style or
belief'.[72] This is just wrong. Any careful attention to political liberalism – on the conceptual or historical level – makes it evident that the
finest instinct of a political liberal is not to empty their hearts, and in
a slide towards 'totality' to 'confirm that . . . free-will as such' be
'identified with the good';[73] it is rather to make room in their hearts
– out of love, humility and charity – and in the heart of society, for a
diverse range of incompatible but humanely possible identifications
of the good. Something that it is not always clear that Radical
Orthodoxy has room for, in its more extravagant flourishes at least.
Milbank's allusion here to the 'puritanical' becomes ironic in the
light of my – admittedly heuristic – characterization in Chapter 2 of
the 'Puritan' type as one who identifies the visible and invisible
Church, insists on giving irreducibly and exclusively religious
reasons, and who wishes to use public power to save souls. Arguably
these are all features of Radical Orthodoxy at its most bombastic and
rhetorical.

It is better for *every* individual and group to feel some degree of
discontent and alienation, because the state remains silent on religious truth, than for some individuals within one group to be completely satisfied at the cost of all the others. What begins to emerge is
that while political liberalism is not sufficient for supplying our
theological commitments and religious needs – and in that sense we

---

[72] John Milbank, *Being Reconciled: Ontology and Pardon* (London:
Routledge, 2003), p. 25.
[73] Milbank, *Being Reconciled*, p. 25.

must go beyond it – it can be seen to be *necessary* for certain forms of religious and theological creativity, such as, for instance, Radical Orthodoxy. It is one of the oldest text-book errors to mistake non-sufficiency for non-necessity.

We should avoid blaming pervasive and structural problems in the human condition on specific doctrines such as political liberalism. We can feel the loneliness, excitement and anxiety which comes with 'choice' in a liberal culture, or we can feel the oppression, surveillance and belonging of more participatory communities; sometimes we can feel both in parallel in different dimensions of our life. Radical Orthodoxy can present a moving if partial account of some of our misery, but when we hear Milbank's dreams of true society as 'absolute consensus, agreement in desire, and entire harmony',[74] or Pickstock's vision of the liturgical fusion 'of love and power'[75] in the Middle Ages, we would do well to heed Constant's caution: 'Let us mistrust . . . this admiration for certain ancient memories.'[76]

---

[74] Milbank, *Theology and Social Theory*, p. 402.
[75] Pickstock, *After Writing*, p. 157.
[76] Constant, *Liberty*, p. 323; 'Défions-nous . . . de cette admiration pour certaines reminiscences antiques', *Liberté*, p. 509.

5

Radical Orthodoxy and the
Stuart Polity:
A Lesson from History on the
Dangers of Analogy

There are certain features of the universe invoked by Royalist theologians during the period 1603–1640 that share striking resemblances to the world-view eulogized by the Radical Orthodoxy movement. They express a communitarian vision, where the individual is subsumed into the wider, organically interrelated society, which is organized in a teleological and hierarchical manner. According to this vision, each level of creation desires and participates in the higher level, with the physical king representing the invisible King. The Royalists who develop this vision make extensive use of analogies between our physical bodies, social bodies and the Christic body, in a way that the Radical Orthodoxy movement could find most attractive. Such Royalists tend to share to some extent Hooker's neo-Platonic vision of order, and his sense that reason can discern laws governing this order. To some extent they share his temperamental distrust of radical innovation based upon a confident separation of good and evil and the elimination of evil. But they tend to be so exultant and confident of the healthy manifestation of the divine in the body politic that they effect an identification of the visible and invisible which is not dissimilar to that of the Puritans.

For the Royalists, the Kingdom of Heaven is not so much to be inaugurated by human activism, but already mirrored in the rule of God 'visible to man', the king. There is none of Hooker's subtlety, the self-reflexive sense of common human moral implication and complicity. There is certainly none of Hooker's insistence on the eschatological distance between the visible and invisible Church. For this reason I find Aidan Nichols' suggestion that when Milbank speaks about the Church, he is really talking about 'Anglicanism –

which is to say, in effect, the Church of England',[1] so nearly right, except in one important detail. Nichols finds that 'what Milbank desires indeed [is] "theocracy" . . . the restoration of the Tudor polity in England, shorn of those monarchical, aristocratic and proto-bourgeois features which militate against its (as it were) 'socialist' character'. Milbank's ideal, according to Nichols, is 'Richard Hooker's *respublica christiana* . . . the English people in their twin offices as temporality and spirituality . . .'[2] If I have done anything in this book, I hope I have demonstrated that Hooker's aversion to separating the world into good and evil, his reluctance to allow public power to save souls, and his sense of the complexity and frailty of the human condition, push him away from the Radical Orthodoxy movement. Replace 'Tudor polity' with 'Stuart', and I think Nichols may be closer to the mark.

I do not claim that the Radical Orthodoxy movement is at all aware of these Royalist thinkers, or that there is any intellectual debt. Nevertheless, they are of interest to us in that both the Radical Orthodoxy movement and the Royalist theologians discussed here are High-Church Anglicans who share some very similar world-views. It might pay us to investigate the parallel to see if we might learn anything. By putting the Royalist sermons and tracts in an historical context, it will emerge that there are indeed grave dangers of approaches that hanker after order and harmony, and believe confidently that human reason and political action can deliver them by reason discerning the 'common good'. Royalists speak incessantly of the common good, using ample analogies from natural law and the natural world. Such passages are often affecting and moving, but a little historical background shows the lurking dangers. We will see how the notion of the common good was used to violate ancient liberties of the subject, leading to imprisonment without trial, forced taxation without parliamentary consent and confiscation of property.

---

[1] Aidan Nichols OP in ' "Non tali auxilio": John Milbank's Suasion to Orthodoxy', *New Blackfriars*, Vol. 73, no. 861, June 1992, p. 331.
[2] Nichols, 'Non tali auxilio', p. 331.

The king, the common good and the violation of ancient liberties

In 1606 the Royalist layman Edward Forset wrote *A Comparative Discourse of the Bodies Natural and Politique.* Forset describes a world shot through with order at every level, with each level resembling by analogy the higher, and all participating in all. The result is highly communitarian, in the sense that the individual is constituted by and subsumed within the organic whole. Forset is in raptures concerning the 'commonwealth', '. . . with all her parts, orders, qualities, and requisites . . . set forth by sundry fit resemblances, as by the architecture of an house, by the swarming and cohabiting of bees in a hive'.[3] Forset calls man the 'lesser world', 'the diminuitive and modell of that wide extending universe', and so extols us to 'observe the good correspondence between every particular parts or faculties in man, and the other distinct parts, powers, and operations of that bigger bulke . . .'[4]

Lay this passage alongside the contemporary Anglican clergyman Graham Ward, and the continuity is striking: 'Since creation issued from the Word of God, then, seen from the perspective of God's glory, all creation bears the watermark of Christ. The material orders participate in theological orders such that they are rendered both physical and symbolic.'[5] Where Ward speaks of 'the mutability of the body' of Christ such that there is both 'identification with and participation within it',[6] Forset talks of the divine participation in creation in terms of 'God's own imitating of himself in the likeness of the less with the greater', such that: '. . . the incomprehensible wisdom of God, in the composing and ordering of his works in nature, hath so dignified them with all perfection, as that they be left unto us as eminent and exemplary pattern as well for the consolidating, as for the beautifying of that wee worke by art or policy . . .'[7] Forset is always afraid of the destructive tendencies of prevalent readings of the universe which threaten 'to disjoin the well coupled from their lovely analogy of each to other' leading to 'a violent divorce and

---

[3] E. Forset, *A Comparative Discourse of the Bodies Natural and Politique* (London: John Bill, 1606), p. iii.

[4] Forset, *Discourse*, p. iii.

[5] Graham Ward, *Cities of God* (London: Routledge, 2000), p. 99.

[6] Ward, *Cities*, p. 102.

[7] Forset, *Discourse*, p. iv.

distraction'.[8] Forset's concern here would be well met by Milbank's complaint of post-modernity's assertion of an atomistic and violent ontological nihilism. Some of Ward's observations could be grafted into Forset's text here with little difficulty, where for instance Ward calls for a 'strong doctrine of participation' requiring a 'doctrine of analogical relationships networking the several bodies – physical, social, political ecclesial, eucharistic, Christic and divine'.[9]

For Forset, the common good is secured by the correspondences which exist at every level between the micro and the macro. Just as in man the soul is active and the body passive, so in the state, the sovereign is the active soul and the people the passive body. There is a symbiotic relationship, leading to life and delight: 'As the coupling of the soul and body, tendeth not only to give life, but also to the attaining of a perfect and happy life: So the right temper of sovereignty and obedience, intendeth and effecteth not only the being, but also the flourishing and felicity of a commonwealth.'[10] Because the created order is shot through with this perfection it makes sense to order 'the affairs of state . . . by marking and matching of the works of the finger of God, either in the larger volume of the universal, or in the abridgement therof, the body of man'.[11] It is precisely the 'well agreeing semblances' of different levels of creation, 'the lovely analogy of each to other' which makes it possible to read the political and prescriptive from the 'natural' and descriptive. It is this which enables Forset to proclaim that 'in every particular person, there is both the seed and similitude of a state incorporat'[12] just because '. . . in the very composure of man, there is manifestly discovered a summary abstract of absolute perfection by the which as by an excellent Idea, or an exact rule, we may examine and exemplify all other things'.[13]

Royalist sermons lure us into security as we are reassured that we belong to an harmonious organic whole, with desire and love drawing the lower orders towards the higher, and beneficence and bounty emanating from the higher. Such reassurance reaches shrill intensity in the sermon of a Royalist Anglican, Henry Valentine. The sermon

---

[8] Forset, *Discourse*, p. vii.
[9] Ward, *Cities*, p. 75.
[10] Forset, *Discourse*, p. 4.
[11] Forset, *Discourse*, pp. iv–v.
[12] Forset, *Discourse*, p. viii.
[13] Forset, *Discourse*, p. 1.

– delivered in St Paul's Cathedral – is unambiguously titled *God Save the King*, delivered on the brink of war between the King and Parliament in 1639. Valentine speaks out of the same – albeit now cracking and fragmenting – universe as Forset. The violence of the times demand that he makes violently and quickly explicit the political implications of such an organic and hierarchical view of a body politic which is in lovely analogy to the natural body:

> For the King is the fountain of government, government of order, and order of beauty; so that a King governing his people with good and just laws, makes the commonwealth [an] . . . excellence of beauty, which otherwise would be but . . . [a] . . . *monstrous informe*; A mass of confusion, an ugly and deformed monster.[14]

The passage has such urgency and momentum, one idea smashing into the other – king–government, government–order, order–beauty, if no king, no order, no beauty and so chaos and monstrous informity. It is as if Valentine is trying by the muscle of argument, by the speed of his words, to hold the great chain in place, against enormous pressures and strains.

If we are worried by the Puritan identification of the visible and invisible, the earthly kingdom with the Kingdom of God, the same hackles should be raised when we hear Valentine stating that as God is our 'invisible King' so the king is our 'visible God'.[15] On the basis of this identification of the king and God, the earthly and heavenly kingdoms, Valentine is able to describe the king as a source of joy and common bounty: 'Fit it was that an universal benefit should be entertained with an universal joy. A King is *commune bonum*, a common good; and good the more common it is, the better it is; and the better it is the more joy it occasions.'[16] The king is the sun, is the 'beauty of Israel';[17] kings are 'fountains and common blessings, the streams of whole government' which gladden the 'City of God': 'When the King watches we may all sleep, when he labours we may

---

[14] Henry Valentine, *God Save the King: A Sermon Preached in St. Paul's Church on the 27th March 1639, Being the Day of His Majesties Most happy Inauguration, and of His Northern Expedition* (London: John Mariott, 1639), p. 5.

[15] Valentine, *God Save the King*, p. 6.

[16] Valentine, *God Save the King*, p. 17.

[17] Valentine, *God Save the King*, p. 18.

all rest, his term is our vacation, and when he works every man may keep holy day.'[18]

Graham Ward's description of the image of Adam in paradise could be transposed without difficulty onto Valentine's description of the body of the king, an 'incarnation of divine beauty and goodness . . . [possessing] the power to attract, to invoke a desire which draws us towards an embrace, a promise of grace'.[19]

Royal power and the liberties of the subject: natural law and common law

These sermons and tracts, although expressive of a sometimes beautiful longing for a certain type of order and harmony, are complexly involved in the politics of seventeenth-century England. Johann Sommerville[20] has shown how there was an escalating ideological conflict between 1603 and 1640 concerning the nature and limitations of royal power in relation to the liberty of the subject.

To get a grip on the issues at stake here, we need to draw out the distinction between natural law approaches, commonly used by Royalist supporters of absolute royal power, and common law approaches, used by those concerned about the royal violation of the liberties of individuals. The tradition of natural law, derived from Aristotle, saw it as the duty and ability of reason to discern the purposes of every part of creation within an ordered cosmos. The actual nature of this order, within which things have a purpose, arguably owes a great deal to neo-Platonic Augustinian themes, with all things desiring and participating in the higher, leading to desire for God.[21]

---

[18] Valentine, *God Save the King*, p. 18.

[19] Ward, *Cities*, p. 100.

[20] Johann P. Sommerville, *Royalists and Patriots: Politics and Ideology in England 1603–1640* (London and New York: Longman, 1999). The following discussion is indebted to Sommerville's excellent book.

[21] Johann Sommerville seems to overlook the Platonic element in some natural law thinking, and consequently neglects a source of theological conflict in the seventeenth century. So Sommerville concludes that 'the existence of the law of nature was not at issue in the controversies between predestinarian Calvinists and their opponents . . . Nor was the fact that since the Fall human nature was corrupt, so that the law of nature could not now be fully obeyed or perceived' (p. 18). This overlooks the way in which a broadly 'natural law' schema could be employed in very different ways by Calvinists and Anglican conformists. Both sides resort to the created purposes of God for humanity. The crucial difference lies in the *nature* of the creation that these sides thought they were

The whole industry of drawing analogies and correspondences, in seventeenth-century Royalist literature as well as Radically Orthodox writing, is made possible by this vision of the outward creativity of God – a true self-imitation in all God's works – and the nostalgia-like longing for return in all of creation. Such natural law approaches tend to be communitarian and philosophically ambitious; which is to say that individuals are always constituted primarily by their role within a grand theological vision of the participatory whole.

Natural law could be understood by anyone employing right reason who discerned the patterns and order of nature correctly. The common law, on the other hand, was the repository of the laws of England which had been accumulated since 'time immemorial'. It was not based upon any grand philosophical vision of the universe, but was intended to be pragmatic, flexible and slowly evolving, built up case by case using the wisdom that only time and experience could bestow. Its goal was understood to be to protect the ancient liberties of the subject. Principles of common law upon which there was broad agreement were that one could not be a judge in one's own case, that one should not be imprisoned without trial, and that one could not have property confiscated. The latter principle, that one should not have one's property confiscated was construed as entailing that a subject could not be taxed by a sovereign without giving their consent, which consent could only be registered by the House of Commons. Common lawyers, of whom there were many in Parliament, did not need any particularly ambitious theological or theoretical vision over-arching the principles they supported; indeed, it was supposed to be part of the virtue of the common law that it was pragmatic rather than theoretical. Because there was no particular conception of the cosmos over-arching the application of common law, it was not possible, as with natural law, to read off truths about the world simply by applying reason to discern patterns of order. Where natural law approaches tended to be communitarian and philosophically ambitious, common law approaches were much

---

describing. This could be conceived in violently divergent ways, either through explicit argument or a starkly contrasting use of metaphors and imagery. Although there are Renaissance traces of order and harmony in some of Calvin's work, these are set in agonizing contrast to his anxieties about chaos and contingency in a nature which is controlled only by the sovereign but contingent will of God; such an anxiety would have been completely impossible for a thinker such as Richard Hooker, and the difference in their conceptions of order, beauty and desire has striking political corollaries.

more concerned with the liberties of the individual, regardless of one's overarching theological vision, justifying Sommerville's comment that modern liberalism 'owes much to the English common law'.[22]

Although the common law *need* not have a theological motive or theory behind it, in the work of Hooker, and later on of Burke, I would argue that there is a distinct theological impulse at work. We have seen that Hooker employs motifs which belong both to natural law and common law: discerning order and patterns within a neo-Platonic universe, but at the same time talking of the need for custom, experience and tradition. In Burke's case also we saw a natural law basis (order and purpose in nature) overlaid with a subtle understanding of sin, loss and complexity, leading to an acknowledgement of the need for custom, slow and patient experience and the wisdom that transcends not only individuals but generations. The individual can only be protected by understanding the nature and limitations of individuals. These limitations are to do with our fallenness, the frailty of even our best intentions – 'the best of what we do is painful' (Hooker) – and the complexity of our motives and affairs.

Putting individuals *en masse* and forming communities does not eliminate or redeem any of these features of the human condition, but if anything makes their ramifications and dangers more enormous and unpredictable. Consequently, there is a way of invoking the need for custom to protect the individual that is motivated by a powerful sense of the limitations of individuals, acting individually or – even worse – collectively. The caution about human nature is so emphatic that it is not thought enough to preserve the individual from the enthusiasms of another individual, or of a collectivity within society; rather individuals must be protected from whole generations, by having their liberties secured in an ancient constitution. The laws protecting these liberties were subject to the consent of the people, but consent measured by the test of time, memory and patient experience. So we find the common lawyer Sir John Davies, Attorney-General for Ireland in 1615, writing that 'the common law of England is nothing else but the Common Custome of the Realm',[23]

---

[22] Sommerville, *Royalists and Patriots*, p. 102.
[23] Sir John Davies, *Le primer report des cases & matters en lay* (Dublin, 1615) preface, sig. *2a; in David Wootton (ed.), *Divine Right and Democracy: An Anthology of Political Writing in Stuart England* (Harmondsworth: Penguin, 1986), pp. 131–43, p. 131. Quoted in Sommerville, *Royalists and Patriots*, p. 84.

such that when a people found a practice to be 'good and beneficial' it would become a custom, and that 'being continued time out of mind, it obtaineth the force of law'. So Davies comments that 'a custome doth never become Law to bind the people, untill it hath been tried and approved time out of mind, during all which time there did thereby arise no inconvenience'.[24] Another common lawyer, Thomas Hedley, writes of 'time' that it is 'the trier of truth, author of all human wisdom, learning and knowledge', and that from time 'all human laws receive their chiefest strength, honour, and estimation'.[25]

There is a view of human nature behind such an attitude to time that again could be described under the heading 'obscured order'. People can create order and laws under which they may live and flourish; but our capacity for doing this is so limited and obscured, that we must take a great deal of time and patience in the process. If people were hopelessly fallen, beyond any capacity to discern and create order, one could take all the time in the world and still fail to construct anything which permitted human flourishing in society. Likewise, if people were not disordered by sin, and our human condition not so complex, there would be no need to be so emphatically cautious about lawmaking and the discerning and creation of order. So although the common law does not appear to rest upon the back of an *ambitious* theological vision, we can see that the attitude towards time and experience that it relies on reflects a broad theological instinct about obscured order. The instinct is towards modesty and humility, hence the qualification that I have consistently used that common law thinking does not rest upon an *ambitious* theological vision; it does rest upon a theological vision, but a modest one, which hopes to discern order, but is humble about our ability to do so, and certainly cautious to the point of allergy concerning the spontaneous and enthusiastic human construction of order.

The common law preserves the life, liberty and property of the subject, and is held by its supporters to be the ultimate arbiter of justice in England. So Sir Edward Coke writes that the common law is 'the most ancient and best inheritance that the subjects of this

---

[24] Davies, in Sommerville, *Royalists and Patriots*, p. 84.
[25] E. R. Foster (ed.), *Proceedings in Parliament 1610*, 2 vols. (1966), Vol. II, p. 175. Quoted in Sommerville, *Royalists and Patriots*, p. 85.

realm have',[26] with Nicholas Fuller remarking that is was 'the high inheritance of the Realme, by which both the King and the subjects are directed'.[27]

Rather than being directed by the common law, we find that Charles I would frequently violate the liberties of the subject, protected by the common law, in the interests of the 'common good', understood by confidently reading 'the natural law' and the lovely correspondences between all levels of creation. So when Valentine tells us that the king, as the fountain government, secures the 'common good', does he have in mind the king's power to confiscate property, levy punitive taxes without Parliamentary consent and imprison without trial? These were all actions taken by Charles I, with the forced loan of 1627, 'widely regarded' as the prominent historian Sommerville tells us, 'as a violation of the most fundamental principles of the English constitution':

> The arrest (without cause shown) of refusers of the Loan dramatic-ally raised the question of the king's power to imprison his subjects. Charles' obvious reluctance to allow the legality of the Loan to be tested in court suggested that he was prepared to subjugate the law to his own convenience. The billeting of troops, the enforcement of martial law, the purging of dissidents in the universities, and the introduction of religious policies which flouted the spirit if not the letter of statute law, confirmed the conclusion that Charles was, in fact, subverting the constitution and introducing absolute government.[28]

These consequences are regrettably all too compatible with the unobscured continuity which Royalists like Forset and Valentine see between the visible and the invisible, the Kingdom of Heaven ruled by God, and the Kingdom of England ruled by Charles I. The identification of the invisible with the visible, and the uncomplicated reading of order, purpose and analogy in support of a political regime or programme, make it possible to slide from an emphasis on

---

[26] Coke, *The Reports of Sir Edward Coke*, in 13 parts, ed. J. Fraser (London: Butterworth, 1827), 5 preface, f. iiia, in *The Reports*, ed. G. Wilson (1776). Quoted in Sommerville, *Royalists and Patriots*, p. 99.

[27] 'The Argument of Master Nicholas Fuller', *Proceedings in Parliament* 1610, Vol. II, p. 152. Quoted in Sommerville, *Royalists and Patriots*, p. 99.

[28] Sommerville, *Royalists and Patriots*, pp. 108–9.

the common good into an endorsement of the authority of the community over individuals, which authority is enacted by the fountain of the common good, in this case the king. In the interests of the public, and on the basis of a confident discerning of natural order, harmony and beauty, the king can imprison, tax and confiscate, and all for the common good. Anglican clergymen, with their too confident identification of the Kingdoms of England and Heaven, became notorious among common lawyers. So in 1610 we find Richard Martin warning the House of Commons that the 'Kings wants may drive him to extremities', particularly if he listened to clerical advice. Martin complains that absolutist ideas are rife amongst clergymen because 'the highway to get into a double benefice or to a higher dignity is to tread upon the neck of the common law', with sermons being 'made everyday to rail upon the fundamental laws of the kingdom'.[29]

This correlation between communitarian approaches that are confident of their reading of natural and cosmic order and a tendency to violate the liberties of individuals, is no accident. As the political liberal Friedrich Hayek comments about the communitarian tendencies of a very different beast, National Socialism in Germany during the 1930s and 40s, *any* notion of the common good is bound to be one person's or one group's conception which, if it is to be socially effective, must in some way impose upon individuals who are marginal or opposed to the great project. So Hayek complains that any talk of the 'social good', the 'common purpose', the 'common good', involves the commitment that we can 'direct all our activities according to a single plan' which

> presupposes that every one of our needs is given its rank in an order of values which must be complete enough to make it possible to decide between all the different courses between which the planner has to choose. It presupposes, in short, the existence of a complete ethical code in which all the different human values are allotted their due place.[30]

A very complete sort of ethical code, but by no means the only one, is the analogical universe paraded by Royalist preachers in

---

[29] *Proceedings in Parliament* 1610, Vol. II, pp. 328–9. Quoted in Sommerville, *Royalists and Patriots*, p. 111.
[30] Friedrich Hayek, *The Road to Serfdom* (London: Routledge, 1944), p. 43.

seventeenth-century England, or the analogical visions celebrated by the group of Anglican theologians in our own time who are at the heart of the explicitly anti-liberal Radical Orthodoxy movement.

We should beware of nostalgia and theological reconstructions of enchanted spaces, in case anti-liberalism cashes out as a tendency which is anti- the liberties of individuals. Even if this imposition is manifested as a pious desire for unity and transformation, is it a unity at the expense of diversity and complexity, and transformation by subtly violent – if seductive – means? The Anglican theologian John Milbank has no Charles I to encourage, but we should be cautious of his insistence on the common good, ontological peace, the analogical universe, and participatory structures in 'true society' where Milbank tells us there is 'absolute consensus, agreement in desire, and entire harmony amongst its members'.[31] Perhaps there are disturbing resonances with seventeenth-century 'analogical' approaches that fail properly to register the fallen distance separating the visible from the invisible, the body of Christ from our broken social, ecclesiastical and political bodies, the Kingdom of Heaven from the Kingdom of England.

---

[31] John Milbank, *Theology and Social Theory* (Oxford: Blackwell, 2000), p. 402.

6

The Church in the World

The position I have been circling around in this book is that there is order, meaning and participation, but that it comes to us in ways that are fragmented, graced, unbidden and hidden. I have argued that a refusal to conflate the visible and invisible Church leads us to endorse some strands of political liberalism, while cultivating an aversion towards global invocations of new (or ancient) world-views and divinely sanctioned political activism. On the other hand, the Church – because of the specific and theological nature of its endorsement of political liberalism – is always called to resist liberal triumphalism and global revolutions and wars in the name of 'liberty', when these campaigns ride roughshod over the fallenness and complexity of our shared human condition.

There are dangers contained within the politically liberal approach I broadly endorse. A preference for judicious reform over revolution, a caution about globally activist projects, and a sense of the frailty of human agency – personal, social and political – can become so refined as to lead one into a subtly principled, but nonetheless trenchant, inertia – which to all the world might look like an unthinking acceptance of the *status quo* and complacency. It is no accident that a thinker such as Burke is perceived as socially conservative, supportive of the *status quo* and extremely wary to the point of complacency about social and political activism. It may not be thought enough to point out, as I did in Chapter 1, that Burke was an active political reformer.

The deep complaint against my position, and it would be well made, is that my account comes from a position of relative comfort and privilege, where it is unsurprising that I should defend political liberalism, seeing as I enjoy its protections so bountifully. The charge would be that I am too silent concerning the suffering, the brokenness, the poverty and the anger of those who are outside such charmed circles, and exploited and oppressed by international markets, global superpowers and catastrophic social, climatic or political conditions. As I have been so keen on Edmund Burke, it may be worth hearing Tom Paine's response to Burke's *Reflections on the Revolution in France*, and seeing if they are not pertinent to me also. Paine complains that when describing the violence of the revolutionaries it 'suits his [Burke's] purpose to exhibit consequences without their causes': 'It is one of the arts of drama to do so. If the crimes of men were exhibited with their suffering, the stage effect would sometimes be lost, and the audience would be inclined to approve where it was intended they should commiserate.'[1]

The charge that my condemnation of transformative projects and endorsement of political liberalism lead me to overlook the suffering of humanity demands a serious response. First, I do not intend to set up a certain tradition of political liberalism as the global solution. The case I have been making must be seen in the context of the prevailing wind, as I feel it blowing, in the theological academy, which is to dismiss liberalism as a product of sinful Enlightenment attempts at self-sufficiency and self-determination. From this critique of liberalism there can then be an attempt to leap beyond or behind liberalism to a more enchanted and less 'secular' space. In this context, there was a timely word to be said against the caricature of liberalism, and in caution against, what seemed to me, the naivety and danger of the proposed transformative projects. This is certainly not the last word on the subject, but it was perhaps not irresponsible to raise the concerns, if only it leads those with a more visionary bent to consider the better aspirations of liberalism and the possible dangers of its replacement. They may still wish to critique the former and further the latter, but it will hopefully be a more nuanced approach if this process of reconsideration has taken place.

Second, I would suggest that my concerns about global transformative projects are motivated by a horror at the human suffering that comes about when people are used as manipulable tools in the interest of a greater vision of the common good, the Kingdom of Heaven or the destiny of a people. Vast swathes of suffering can be associated with totalitarian or totalizing projects of social transformation: from Fascism and Communism in the twentieth century, to our contemporary world bearing the wounds of global capitalism

---

[1] Tom Paine, 'The Rights of Man: Part I', in *Political Writings*, ed. Bruce Kuklick (Cambridge: Cambridge University Press, 1989), pp. 71–2.

and a return to religiously inflamed warfare, with calls to slaughter the infidel being echoed with calls to eliminate the axis of evil. My theological concern throughout has been to challenge the easy and rigid bracketing of the world into good and evil. Political liberalism is precisely endorsed in as much as it mitigates against this hubristic human judgementalism, and in as much as it joins the 'great melody', as Yeats calls it, which can be heard underlying Burke's consistent struggle against the abuse of power in America, Ireland, India and France.[2]

An aversion to political liberalism, one suspects, is frequently motivated by a profound discomfort at the ravages of late global capitalism; such a discomfort I would suggest is the driving force behind Milbank's self-styling as a Christian socialist. If nothing else, this book should show that there is a tradition of political liberalism that is much older than global capitalism, and that is conceptually quite distinct from it. Political liberalism is motivated by the desire to preserve the liberties of the individual within a framework of law and fair institutions. A sense of the frailty of human individuals and their vulnerability to the enthusiasms of other individuals leads the political liberal to adopt a cautious attitude when presented with attempts to plan society on the model of a unifying common good, a 'political community'.

Political liberalism, so outlined, is compatible with a range of views about the market: from fairly strong commitments to welfare protections and restrictions on excessive wealth disparities (Hobhouse, Keynes, Rawls) to a much more emphatic insistence on unregulated market freedom (Hayek). Where we do have the latter, there can be a humanizing effect on the debate when it is realized by those on the left that even a notorious figure such as Hayek, appropriated as he was by Keith Joseph and Margaret Thatcher in the 1980s, can be seen to have fine motivations behind his free-market economics. So Hayek was emphatically not of the view that free-market competition was the only possible model because of the essential greed or egotism of individuals. Hayek states that individualism, and the preservation of the liberties of the individual within a

---

[2] I am indebted to Conor Cruise O'Brien's *Edmund Burke* (London: Vintage, 2002), p. 3 for this quote. O'Brien is quoting from Yeat's 'The Seven Sages':

American colonies, Ireland, France and India
Harried, and Burke's great melody against it.

Yeats' 'it' refers to the abuse of power.

legal and economic framework 'does not assume, as is often asserted, that man is egoistic or selfish, or ought to be':

> It merely starts from the indisputable fact that the limits of our powers of imagination make it impossible to include in our scale of values more than a sector of the needs of the whole society, and that, since, strictly speaking, scales of value can exist only in individual minds, nothing but partial scales of values exist, scales which are inevitably different and often inconsistent with each other. From this the individualism concludes that the individuals should be allowed, within defined limits, to follow their own values and preferences rather than somebody else's, that within these spheres the individual's system of ends should be supreme and not subject to any dictation by others.[3]

Hayek's endorsement of the free market was the result of his extreme anxiety about planning, arising from his concern about the way in which the frailty of individuals is trammelled upon when a group tries to impose its plan for the common good on a diverse collection of individuals with many legitimate conceptions of the good. The twentieth-century context of Hayek's work, between two totalitarian attempts to plan society, makes this anxiety more comprehensible. So for Hayek, the free-market, and so 'competition', was the only way to acknowledge the complexity and frailty of human affairs; any attempt to regulate, where competition was possible, would risk placing one frail and limited individual or group of individuals over others. Even with Hayek, there is something we can agree on in terms of what he is most afraid of, although we can differ in our convictions as to what must be done to avoid that which we both fear.

It is beyond the scope of this book, and my competence, to present a favoured economic model. Nevertheless, one suspects that attempts such as we saw in Thatcher's Britain, to instantiate the awareness of human complexity and frailty by means of the free market fail precisely and paradoxically because it takes a large amount of central planning and interference, according to a global vision of social transformation, to impose free-market competitive values on professions, communities, practices and institutions where it has no natural

---

[3] Hayek, *Road to Serfdom*, p. 44.

place.[4] In this regard Michael Oakeshott's comment on Hayek is extremely apposite, where he notes that 'the main significance of Hayek's *Road to Serfdom*' is not the 'cogency of his doctrine, but the fact that it is a doctrine'. Oakeshott uses the term 'Rationalism' to describe any attempt to organize society to promote human perfection. He goes on to say of Hayek:

> A plan to resist all planning may be better than its opposite, but it belongs to the same style of politics. And only in a society already deeply infected with Rationalism will the conversion of the traditional resources of resistance to the tyranny of Rationalism into a self-conscious ideology be considered a strengthening of those resources.[5]

A respect for frailty and an acknowledgement of our created embeddedness and limitations, which feeds into political liberalism, might give stronger resources than would be imagined for a critique of the ravages of global capitalism. Burke – no enemy to indigenous (Smithian) capitalist market models, as we saw in Chapter 1 – launched an extraordinary attack on the economic and cultural exploitation of India by the British. It is worth at this point rereading some of the passages from Burke's early speeches on India, to see how they would not embarrass the most principled of anti-globalization critics. Incensed by Warren Hasting's directorship of the East India Company, Burke raged at the way that the British violated the native traditions and history of Indian society:

> But God forbid we should pass judgement upon people [India] who framed their laws and institutions prior to our insect origins of yesterday. With all the faults of their nature, and errors of their institutions, the institutions, which act so powerfully on their natures, have two material characteristics which entitle them to respect: – first, great force and stability; next, excellent moral and civil effects . . . They have stood firm on their ancient base – they have cast their roots deep in their native soil.[6]

---

[4] See John Gray, 'The Strange Death of Tory England' in *Endgames: Questions in Late Modern Political Thought* (Cambridge: Polity Press, 1997), Ch. 6.

[5] Michael Oakeshott, *Rationalism in Politics and Other Essays* (Indianapolis: Liberty Press, 1991), p. 26.

[6] E. Burke, 'Speech on the Impeachment of Warren Hastings' (3rd Day, 18

Burke had no hesitation in identifying capitalism's demand for profit as the root of the exploitation. So Hastings and his agents showed 'the avarice of English dominion' with an 'unbounded license to plunder'. Burke complained to Parliament that they built no schools, no hospitals, no bridges, but were merely out for 'profit' and the 'transmission of great wealth to this country'.[7]

We can see that there is a range of attitudes toward the market compatible with political liberalism. Nevertheless, there is a certain sort of economic dream of social transformation that is incompatible, precisely in that it embodies the sort of universalizing and global pretensions to which we have learnt to be so allergic. As John Gray points out, just as the Communist totalitarian utopia had its own 'ubiquitous corruption and apocalyptic environmental degradation',[8] so global capitalism 'in time may come to rival it [Communism] in the suffering it inflicts':[9]

Already it has resulted in over a hundred million peasants becoming migrant labourers in China, the exclusion from work and society of tens of millions in the advanced societies, a condition of near-anarchy and rule by organized crime in parts of the post-communist world, and further devastation of the environment.[10]

In Chapter 3 I expressed some reservations about the equally globalizing, judgemental and messianic language of anti-globalization protestors. The reader could be forgiven for feeling some frustration in that there is little sense of an overall, positive and constructive solution. But that is precisely the point. If we are serious about human imperfectibility and frailty, global constructive solutions (and perhaps global critiques) are dangerous; and I could not be asked to be taken seriously if I meant all global constructive solutions except mine. In political liberalism we have a tradition that acknowledges the dangers and limitations of human projects of self-perfection. But this does not tell us for all particular times and places what our

---

February 1788) in *Works* (Boston, 1869), Vol. 7, pp. 43–5. Quoted in Isaac Kramnick, *The Rage of Edmund Burke: Portrait of An Ambivalent Conservative* (New York: Basic Books, 1977), p. 128.

[7] Burke, 'Warren Hastings', p. 128.
[8] John Gray, *False Dawn: the Illusions of Global Capitalism* (London: Granta Books, 1998), p. 3.
[9] Gray, *False Dawn*, p. 3.
[10] Gray, *False Dawn*, p. 3.

approach should be to an economy, an institution or a proposed course of action (such as a war); except to say that always our approach should be moulded to the particular in all its contextual intricacies and complexities, rather than the particular being moulded to fit an *a priori* and universalizing template.

A caution about radical social transformation must always be cautious most of all about itself. Precisely because this caution is motivated by a self-reflexive sense of common human moral implication and complexity, there must be a never-ceasing vigilance to ensure that this wariness of transformation is not born out of self-interest and cowardice, and that the preference for judicious and ample reform over revolution is never mistaken for acquiescence with greed and injustice. Again, Burke states with gravity and precision the tensions we face; when commenting on the importance of both preservation and reform, Burke sees the need for 'a vigorous mind, steady, perservering attention, various powers of comparison and combination, and the resources of an understanding fruitful in expedients'. All of these 'are to be exercised in a continued conflict with the combined force of opposite vices, with the obstinacy that rejects all improvement, and the levity that is fatigued and disgusted with every thing of which it is in possession'.[11]

An allergy to global reconstructive activist projects cuts all ways politically, depending on whether it is the right or the left who are marching with raised fists. In *The Unbearable Lightness of Being* Milan Kundera has one of his creations, Sabina, frame the thought: '. . . behind Communism, Fascism, behind all occupations and invasions lurks a more basic, pervasive evil and . . . the image of that evil was a parade of people marching by with raised fists and shouting identical syllables in unison'.[12] The Church is not called to officiate at such parades, but prayfully to discern, amidst our fallen freedom, the hidden flowerings of participation, unity, prophetic protest or grace – the 'already but not yet' intimations of the Kingdom.

The call here to the 'Church' is to the visible Church. I can anticipate an anxiety about my position which goes as follows: the strong distinction insisted upon between the visible and invisible Church tends to render redundant the notion of the invisible Church; if the relationship between the visible and invisible is so impossible to rely

---

[11] Edmund Burke, 'Reflections on the Revolution in France', p. 289.
[12] Milan Kundera, *The Unbearable Lightness of Being* (London: Faber & Faber, 1995), pp. 96–7.

on or to build up, then the Church of Christ becomes a sort of idle-wheel in our thought and practice, apparently spinning away somewhere, but having no friction or momentum in our lives. In the spirit of self-examination I have extolled in this book, I should concede that this is the danger of my ecclesiology, the extreme towards which it tends, but should not go. Political liberalism suffers from a similar tendency. It can become too acquiescent in relation to the world, and – albeit from principled and sophisticated motivations – it can fail to resist evil.

Nonetheless, these are dangerous tendencies into which my position *can* fall, and so needs to be vigilant about, but I cannot see that it is intrinsically in trouble in the way I have described. The visible Church is called always to approach the invisible, not by self-righteously declaring its having arrived, but by witnessing constantly to the already-but-not-yet reality of the Kingdom, manifested by an awareness of both our frailty and fallenness alongside our calling to perfection and redemption. The visible Church witnesses to the power and dominion of the invisible by humbling herself in its shadow, and confessing to the world that she is not yet what she will be. Rather than facing down the world with its own sin and fallenness, the self-humbling visible Church can really be the Church in the world, and the Church for the world, standing before God with the people on her heart, in solidarity, compassion and humility. By confessing her own frailty and promise, she can hope to bring the darkening world to repentance and hope; when she announces her own glory and triumph, she must stand chastened and responsible when the world imitates.

In practical terms such a vision involves patient and rigorous self-examination and criticism, and a determination to resist simplifying slogans which attempt to effect political change by demonizing movements, countries or people. Specifically in relation to political liberalism, the Church and the theologian should beware of seeking precarious forms of political re-enchantment, and reckon instead with the call to an active and vigorous custodianship of the highest ideals of political liberalism. In this way, our institutions might be called back to their origins and purposes where they become neglectful, and cautioned where they become presumptiously ambitious, replacing the Church when they should only facilitate. This at any rate would be better than an ill-informed caricature of our political traditions, alongside utopian invocations of pre-modern world-views.

Appendix

Robert Bellah and Clifford Longley: Religion in America

There is something of a tradition of commenting on the religious dimension of American politics and public life. I use the word 'religious' here advisedly, in that the commentary often seems to lack a *theological* dimension, relying rather on sociological instincts about 'religiosity' or 'Protestantism'. In this appendix I develop this claim by discussing two highly influential approaches to religion in American public life: Robert Bellah's 'civil religion' thesis and Clifford Longley's recent 'big idea' concerning the religious dimension to American and English identity. Although both approaches have their virtues, I will concentrate on the flaws in their work which arise from a lack of theological depth.

Robert Bellah's 'Civil religion in America' thesis

Robert Bellah's claim, which has generated much debate since the 1970s, is that there exists in America 'alongside of and rather clearly differentiated from the churches an elaborate and well-institutionalized civil religion in America' which, he claims, ' has its own seriousness and integrity and requires the same care in understanding that any other religion does'.[1] There are instructive differences between my thesis and Bellah's.

Bellah uses Kennedy's Inaugural Speech to conclude that there is a public civil religion in America which makes a broad reference to God and an afterlife, but is neutral on more specific and substantial doctrines. This suggests that the civil religion becomes a sort of lowest theistic common denominator between what are sometimes called the three religions of American democracy: Protestantism,

---

[1] Ch. 9 'Civil Religion in America' in *Beyond Belief: Essays on Religion in a Post-Traditional World* (New York: Harper and Row, 1976), p. 168.

Catholicism and Judaism.[2] Bellah invokes in his support Eisenhower's comment that 'our government makes no sense unless it is founded in a deeply felt religious faith – and I don't care what it is'.

The extract from Kennedy's speech which Bellah uses is as follows:

> We observe today not a victory of party but a celebration of freedom – symbolizing an end as well as a beginning – signifying renewal as well as change. For I have sworn before you and Almighty God the same solemn oath our forebears prescribed nearly a century and three quarters ago.
>
> Now the trumpet summons us again – not as a call to bear arms, though arms we need – not as a call to battle, though embattled we are – but a call to bear the burden of a long twilight struggle, year in and year out, 'rejoicing in hope, patient in tribulation' – a struggle against the common enemies of man: tyranny, poverty, disease and war itself.
>
> . . . With a good conscience our only sure reward, with history the final judge of our deeds, let us go forth to lead the land we love, asking His blessing and His help, but knowing that here on earth God's work must truly be our own.[3]

After presenting this speech Bellah makes two moves, both of which are in my view problematic. First of all he cites the speech as a typical manifestation of activist American eschatology:

> The whole address can be understood as only the most recent statement of a theme that lies very deep in the American tradition, namely the obligation, both collective and individual, to carry out God's will on earth. This was the motivating spirit of those who founded America, and it has been present in every generation since. Just below the surface throughout Kennedy's inaugural address, it becomes explicit in the closing statement that God's work must be our own. That this very activist and non-contemplative conception of the fundamental religious obligation, which has been historically associated with the Protestant position,

---

[2] A formulation used by Will Herberg in *Protestant-Catholic-Jew: An Essay in American Religious Sociology* (London: Doubleday, 1960).

[3] John F. Kennedy's Inaugural Address of 20 January 1961. Quoted in Bellah, *Beyond Belief*, pp. 168–9.

should be enunciated in the first major statement of the first Catholic president seems to underline how deeply established it is in the American outlook.[4]

In his later book, *The Broken Covenant*,[5] Bellah repeats the same claim, arguing that the Kennedy Inaugural is a typical manifestation of a 'public theology' which he identifies as the 'civil millennialism of the revolutionary period',[6] a form of religiously motivated activism which he identifies as responsible for 'most of what is good and most of what is bad in our history . . . from the abolitionists to the social gospel and the early socialist party to the civil rights movement . . . ' along with ' . . . every expansionist war and every form of oppression of racial minorities and immigrant groups'.[7]

A sensitive reading of the Kennedy speech suggests to me that this is wrong. Although using biblical imagery, and calling us to do 'God's work', there are places in the speech where Kennedy is in sharp discord with the Manichean-activist tradition of American eschatology. First of all we are told that we have arrived at an 'end as well as a beginning', a 'renewal as well as change'; this language is more suggestive of a cyclical and Augustinian view of history then the typically millenialist progression of evil over good. We are then explicitly called 'not to arms' but to bear a 'twilight struggle'; a *twilight* is precisely the sort of thing which is *not* invoked in the good and evil, darkness and light tradition of American eschatology discussed here. Talk of twilight and patience evokes a sense of the complexity and frailty spoken of by Augustine. There is a struggle in this twilight, but strikingly our only sure reward is a 'good conscience'; this would be at odds with the likes of Edwards and Adams who can speak with confidence of victory with God's support. This is certainly the conviction of Bush, we remember, with his statement that 'the course of this conflict is not known, yet its outcome is certain' because we know that 'God is not neutral'. 'History' is invoked by Kennedy, but as America's judge ('the final judge of our deeds'), not as that which calls and sanctions America to action. Kennedy would seem to me an example of the diversity in American culture

---

[4] Bellah, *Beyond Belief*, p. 172.
[5] Robert Bellah, *The Broken Covenant* (Chicago and London: University of Chicago Press, 1992).
[6] Bellah, *Broken Covenant*, p. 177.
[7] Bellah, *Broken Covenant*, p. 179.

that I conceded in the last chapter; although the 'American eschatology' as I have outlined it is at least there, there are other vocabularies in place also, with Kennedy offering a fine example. Perhaps Kennedy, as Bellah points out a Catholic, is the most Augustinian of the American presidents.

So Bellah is wrong to use Kennedy as an example of a typical 'civil millennialism', although to grasp the second difficulty with Bellah's thesis, we need temporarily to grant him his claim about Kennedy. We need to concede hypothetically that Kennedy is evidence for a typical Manichean-activist eschatology. My second objection to Bellah is that if he *were* right about Kennedy (which he is not) then he would be quite wrong to say, as he does, that no specific doctrine is invoked, if – that is to say – eschatology is to count as a doctrine. The 'civil millennialism of the revolutionary period' is substantial, controversial and historically saturated in a tradition of American eschatology. It does not espouse a thin contentless theism, but a substantial world-view, with an account of salvation, an ecclesiology, a philosophy of history and an anthropology: substantially that of Protestant interpreters of the founding fathers. We do not have an American 'civil religion' but a 'civil eschatology', the American eschatology, which has a pervasive influence on numerous forms of life in America.

It was, conceptually speaking, predictable that it would be difficult to see how something could both be rich enough to 'require the same care in understanding that any other religion does',[8] while at the same time making very little specific and controversial reference to doctrine or institutions. It is precisely the specific and controversial nature of a religion's doctrines and institutions that require from us care in understanding. Bellah gets into this difficulty because he ultimately wants to endorse and recommend 'civil religion' as an adequate faith for the American public, and foresees – in an extraordinarily eschatological conclusion – a 'world civil religion':[9] hence his desire to make it both serious and substantial (requiring care in understanding), as well as neutral and metaphysically undemanding (so making it inclusive).[10]

Only a non-theologian (and Bellah is a fine sociologist) could accept Bellah's observations concerning American public theology,

---

[8] Bellah, *Broken Covenant*, p. 168.
[9] Bellah, *Broken Covenant*, p. 186.
[10] Bellah, *Broken Covenant*, p. 172.

with the enormous eschatological commitments of such a theology, and still hold that the civil religion was doctrinally sparse or 'formal'. Bellah tries to use a distinct and substantial tradition (the Manichean-activist eschatology originating from eighteenth-century New England) as evidence for a there being a Rousseauistic type 'civil religion' (see Chapter 3) in America, whose doctrines are dictated by the needs of the community alone. In fact, evidence for the former is evidence against the latter; the two are not, as we have seen, compatible.

Clifford Longley's 'Big idea'

Clifford Longley's *Chosen People: The Big Idea that Shapes England and America* is an enjoyable and justifiably popular book on the religious dimension to American and English identity, combining wide reading with an informal and anecdotal style. Longley argues that both the English and Americans have a Protestant ancestral tendency to imagine themselves as a chosen people, a new 'Israel'; this tendency can play itself out in aggressive, militaristic and imperialistic projects. I find myself sympathetic to many of Longley's instincts against such projects, and his inclusive sense of the danger of powerful identifications between nations and religious missions. At the same time, there are a number of differences between the line I am arguing and some of Longley assertions, which it may be useful to spell out.

Longley's methodology is something of a mixture of history and cultural studies, with some occasionally rather journalistic inferences. Missing from the heart of Longley's treatment is a genuine theological understanding or critique of some of the forces behind the 'big idea' of the chosen people. For a very clear example of this, take the way in which Longley deals with the Puritan/Calvinist notion of 'freedom': 'The sense of the word "freedom" New England Puritans were really interested in was the escape from the allegedly Romanising tendencies of the English church, which were thought to threaten the freedom of people like themselves to follow the full Protestant message of John Calvin.'[11] This makes it sound as if 'freedom' for the Puritans was little more than Lockean toleration. In

---

[11] Clifford Longley, *Chosen People: The Big Idea that Shapes England and America* (London: Hodder and Stoughton, 2003), p. 112.

fact, as we have seen, it was much more. It was freedom from sin, a regeneration of the Christian, to an extent removing the frailties and vices which might surround the actions of the unregenerated. This freedom from sin, achieved by the predestined grace of God alone, created the Christian saint, empowered to new levels of political activism, called as he was to help in the historical inauguration of the Kingdom of Heaven on earth. Longley seems not to see this, and consequently almost completely ignores the eschatological dimension to Puritan eschatology. As a result, some of Longley's judgements are not so much wrong, as incidental and a little soapy:

> The creative and destructive powers of the great faiths often go together. Religions bind people together as communities; that is their strength in an age when other structures of meaning and relationship are in disarray. But the very walls we build around ourselves for mutual protection, divide us from those who stand outside; every 'us' creates a 'them'. That is why religions, though they promote peace within their borders, can inspire war across them.
>
>   Can we see God's image in one who is not in our own image? Can we hear His voice in accents unlike our own? Can we learn to love the stranger? God has given us many faiths, but only one world in which to live together, and it is getting smaller all the time.[12]

There is nothing wrong with Longley's general sociological appeal to the cohesive yet excluding powers of 'religion'. Nonetheless, we might suggest that a more focused explanation can be given in terms of a particular anthropology, eschatology and ecclesiology. The Calvinist approach of regeneration from sin (anthropology), combined with a covenental model of Church government (ecclesiology), led to communities confident in their activist responsibilities in overcoming evil (eschatology). This was to be achieved by the purification and perfection of the visible Church, and by extension the nation and the world (ecclesiology). Having identified the theological premises of the movement, we can then offer a critique of such an approach in theological terms, arguing that our natural state is not as wretched as the Calvinists suggest and consequently that our

---

[12] Longley, *Chosen People*, p. 148.

salvation from this state is not so dramatic, complete and politically instrumental. This leads to a more tentative approach to human activism, and a self-wariness and generosity to others when envisaging the boundaries of the invisible Church.

Without this theological dimension Longley resorts to a rather anachronistic refutation of the 'chosen people' idea on historical grounds. 'So our final conclusion about the Chosen People theory has to be that while it is still influential, it is simply not true – and never was. The historical evidence alone refutes it, whatever we make of the theological issue.'[13] The 'historical evidence' offered immediately prior to this conclusion is rather dismal. Longley comments that the Protestant notion of the 'chosen people' was behind the 'Glorious Revolution' of 1688, and then asks 'would it really have been disastrous if James II had been allowed to complete his reign?'.[14] But even if less ambiguous considerations were invoked, Longley could never 'historically refute' the 'chosen people' thesis, because it is not in that sense an historical thesis. A passing acquaintance with the Hebrew Bible teaches us that a really determined 'chosen people' thesis can cope with any amount of defeat, historical complexity, humiliation and suffering, all of which can be explained as part of the intimate historical formation or salvation of a people. To refute the 'chosen people' thesis we must deal head-on with the theological issue, which Longley is happy to say 'whatever' to.

Longley's tendency to overlook the theological leads him to miss some historical and social subtleties. There is a rather high-handed approach taken to the ambivalence of the English Reformation, and the theological tradition of Anglicanism. So the journalistic drive of the 'big idea' is not held up for an instant by the historical reality that the sort of radical Protestant tendencies which Longley is so interested in were systematically repressed and marginalized in England under Elizabeth I, James I and Charles I. They flourished briefly in the interregnum, but were again effectively marginalized at the Restoration. Longley is at his most irritating on this issue. He sees the problem, but shrugs it off in brief comments: 'as to how Romanising the ecclesiastical regimes of James I and Charles I actually were is a discussion for another day'.[15] Why is it a discussion for another day? If we had the discussion today, it might lead indirectly

---

[13] Longley, *Chosen People*, p. 281.
[14] Longley, *Chosen People*, p. 281.
[15] Longley, *Chosen People*, p. 112.

to the heart of the theological issue, in that it could take us to the Anglican theological critique of radical Protestant eschatology, as given by the likes of Richard Hooker. It would also explain why there was an America at all, in Longley's sense: America was the result of the persecution in England of the radical Protestantism which is Longley's target. This immediately suggests that the 'idea' of the chosen people could not have been equally 'big' in England and America; its explosion in the latter was partly the product of its repression in the former.[16]

Longley is not led to this theological and historical complexity, partly because of his rather ungenerous dismissal of Anglicanism, which he sees as a dishonest form of Protestantism:

> Anglicanism stands somewhere between these two poles [Catholicism and Protestantism]. Its act of memory requires a particular version of English history which is now widely held to be far from the whole truth. Its act of will is to bring into existence by a supreme effort of imagination a national church which stands in continuity with the ancient universal church of Christendom. This sense of striving, and with it a corresponding sense of insecurity – what if the striving is not enough? – is characteristically Protestant.[17]

Again we have a distracting appeal to 'history'. Against Longley, I would suggest that the Anglican claim to be in continuity with the ancient universal Church need not at all be based upon dubious and competitive historical genealogies. The continuity – as with any visible Church – is ensured by divine grace, and is rooted in an ecclesiology that understands the invisible Church to be as universal, wide and intimate as the Lordship of Christ. Such an ecclesiology can be found in Hooker, who also considered the Roman Catholic Church as part of the true invisible Church (see Chapter 2). But this ecclesiology is not 'Anglican'. As we saw there, a similar refusal narrowly

---

[16] Of course the British Empire depended upon an enormous degree of historical self-importance and a sense of mission among the English, which Longley explains with his catch-all 'big idea'. But the complex array of factors which went into British Imperialism (including industrialism, commerce, romanticism, patricianism, Anglicanism, evolutionary theory, classicalism) are quite remote from the big seventeenth-century Calvinist idea which motivated America, and still remains in its political rhetoric.

[17] Longley, *Chosen People*, p. 12.

to limit the scope of the invisible Church can be found in both Balthasar and Barth; Hooker's work is simply a specific Anglican application of a broader theological truth.

Longley's notion that Anglicanism must use a (Protestant) 'act of will' to conceive of itself between the two poles of Catholicism and Protestantism is simply bewildering in the face of historical evidence, whatever – as Longley might say – we might make of the theological issue. There have 'been acts of will' attempting to resolve the ambivalence of Anglicanism one way or another, but that there is such an ambivalence is irrefutable. Far from Anglicanism's memory of standing between Catholicism and Protestantism being 'now widely held to be far from the whole truth', the sober and contemporary expert evaluation of the leading Church historian Diarmaid MacCulloch is that 'the seesaw battle between Catholic and Protestant within a single Anglican ecclesial structure' has marked the Church of England from the sixteenth century to the present day.[18] This 'seesaw battle' is still a living source of confusion, creativity and pain for many practising Anglicans today.

The overlooking of historical and theological resistance to the 'big idea' of the Chosen People is also exemplified by the absence of any serious mention of rival traditions in both England and America, such as political liberalism (in the tradition of Burke, Acton and Rawls), universal human rights and the internationalism of an American president such as Kennedy (see above). In these respects the 'chosen people' thesis does too much work. In other respects, it does too little. So for instance, Longley's lack of interest in eschatology makes it hard for him to discern how a similar 'theological' instinct can be behind a wide range of non-Protestant and 'anti-American' movements. Longley's at times aggressive fudging of these issues leads him to perpetuate the very black-and-white cultural and national stereotyping which he finds so objectionable in radical Protestantism.

---

[18] Diarmaid MacCulloch, *The Later Reformation in England 1547–1603* (London: Macmillan, 1990), p. 101.

Select Bibliography

Abbot, G. (ed.) *Lord Acton and His Circle* (London and New York: Gasquet, 1906).

Acton, Lord, *Essays on Freedom and Power* (Boston, Mass.: The Beacon Press, 1948).

Acton, Lord, *Letters of Lord Acton to Mary Gladstone*, ed. Herbert Paul (London and New York: Macmillan, 1904).

Acton, Lord, 'Inaugural Lecture delivered at Cambridge, June 11, 1895', in *Lectures on Modern History* (London: Macmillan, 1906).

Adair, John, *Puritans: Religion and Politics in Seventeenth Century England and America* (Stroud: Sutton Publishing, 1998).

Adams, John, 'A Dissertation on the Canon and the Feudal Law', in *The True Sentiments of America* (London: I. Almon, 1768).

Ames, William, *Medulla Sacrae Theologiae* (London, 1643).

Audi, Robert and Wolterstorff, Nicholas (eds.), *Religion in the Public Square* (Lanham, Md.: Rowman and Littlefield, 1997).

Augustine, *The City of God*, ed. R. Dyson (Cambridge: Cambridge University Press, 1998).

Augustine, *The City of God Against the Pagans*, (Latin Text) Loeb Classical Library (London: Heinemann, 1957), in seven volumes.

Augustine, *Confessions*, trans. F. J. Sheed (London: Sheed and Ward, 1944).

Augustine, *De Libero Arbitrio*, in *Aurelii Augustini Opera, Pars I:2: Contra Academicos* in *Corpus Christianorum, Series Latina 29* (Typographi Brepols Editores Pontificii, 1970).

Ayre, J. (ed.), *The Works of John Whitgift* (Cambridge: Parker Society, 1851–3).

Baker, Ray and Dodd, William (eds.), *Presidential Messages and Addresses, and Public Papers (1917–1924)* (New York and London: Harper & Bros, 1927).

von Balthasar, Hans Urs, *Theo-Drama: Theological Dramatic Theory*, Vol. IV 'The Action' (San Francisco: Ignatius Press, 1981).

von Balthasar, Hans Urs, *Theo-Dramatik III: Die Handlung* (Einsiedeln: Johannes Verlag, 1980).

Barth, Karl, 'The Real Church', in *Against the Stream*, ed. R. G. Smith, trans. E. M. Delacour and Stanley Godman (London: SCM Press, 1954).

Barth, Karl, 'Die Wirkliche Kirche', in *Christliche Gemeinde im Wechsel der Staatsordnungen, Dokumente einer Ungarnreise 1948* (Zollikon: Evangelisher Verlag, 1948).

Barth, Karl, *Church Dogmatics*, 4 vols., ed. G. W. Bromiley and T. F. Torrance (Edinburgh: T. & T. Clark, 1936–77).

Barth, Karl, *Die Kirchliche Dogmatik* (Zollikon: Evangelischer Verlag, 1940–42).

Barth, Karl, *Protestant Theology in the Nineteenth Century* (London: SCM Press, 1972).

Barth, Karl, *Die Protestantische Theologie im 19 Jahrhundert* (Zollikon/Zürich: Evangelisher Verlag AG, 1952).

Bauman, Zygmunt, *In Search of Politics* (Cambridge: Polity Press, 1992).

Beckley, Harlan, 'A Christian Affirmation of Rawl's Idea of Justice as Fairness: Part I', *Journal of Religious Ethics* 13 (1985).

Beckley, Harlan, 'A Christian Affirmation of Rawl's Idea of Justice as Fairness: Part II', *Journal of Religious Ethics* 14 (1986).

Bellah, Robert, *Beyond Belief: Essays on Religion in a Post-Traditional World* (New York: Harper and Row, 1976).

Bellah, Robert, *The Broken Covenant* (Chicago and London: University of Chicago Press, 1992).

Biggar, Nigel, *The Hastening that Waits: Karl Barth's Ethics* (Oxford: Clarendon Press, 1993).

Bouwsma, W., *John Calvin, A Sixteenth Century Portrait* (Oxford: Oxford University Press, 1988).

Bowle, John, *Hobbes and his Critics: A Study in Seventeenth Century Constitutionalism* (London: Frank Cass, 1969).

Burke, Edmund, *The Correspondence of Edmund Burke* (Chicago and Cambridge University Presses, 1958–70).

Burke, Edmund, *The Works and Correspondence of the Rt. Hon. Edmund Burke*, in eight volumes (London: Francis and John Rivington, 1852).

Burke, Edmund, *The Works of the Right Honourable Edmund Burke* (London, Bohn Standard Library, 1877–84).

Calvin, John, *Concerning the Eternal Predestination of God*, trans. J. K. S. Reid (London: James Clark, 1961).

Calvin, John, *Institutes of the Christian Religion* (London: SCM Press, 1960), Library of Christian Classics, Vol. XXI.

Calvin, Jean, *Insitution de la Religion Chrestienne, Livre Troisième*, publiée par Jean-Daniel Benoit (Paris: Librarie Philosophique J. Vrin, 1960).

Cargill, W., 'The Philosopher of the "Politic Society"' in *Studies in Richard Hooker: Essays Preliminary to an Edition of his Works*, ed. W. Speed Hill (Cleveland and London: Press of Case Western Reserve University, 1972).

Coleridge, Samuel Taylor, *On the Constitution of Church and State*, ed. J. Colmer (London: Routledge and Kegan Paul, 1976), Vol. 10 of the Collected Works of Samuel Taylor Coleridge.

Coles, Romand, 'Milbank and Neo-Nitzschean Ethics', *Modern Theology* 8:4, Oct. 1992, pp. 331–51.

Constant, Benjamin, 'The Liberty of the Ancients Compared to that of the Moderns' in *Political Writings*, ed. and trans. B. Fontana (Cambridge: Cambridge University Press, 1988).

Constant, Benjamin, 'De la Liberté des Anciens comparée a celle des Modernes', in *De la Liberté chez les modernes: Écrits politiques*, texts selected and annotated by Marcel Gauchet (Paris: Pluriel, 1980).

Davies, Sir John, *Le primer report des cases & matters en lay* (Dublin, 1615) preface; in David Wootton (ed.), *Divine Right and Democracy: An Anthology of Political Writing in Stuart England* (Harmondsworth: Penguin Books, 1986).

Dombrowski, Daniel A., *Rawls and Religion: The Case for Political Liberalism* (New York: State University of New York Press, 2001).

Dreben, Burton, 'On Rawls and Political Liberalism', in *The Cambridge Companion to Rawls*, ed. S. Freeman (Cambridge: Cambridge University Press, 2003).

Dunn, John, *The Political Thought of John Locke* (Cambridge: Cambridge University Press, 1969).

Dwight, Timothy, *A Discourse on Some Events of the Last Century* (New Haven: Thomas and Samuel Green, 1801).

Dwight, Timothy, *The Duty of Americans at the Present Crisis: Illustrated in a Discourse (on Rev. xvi.15) Preached on the 4th July, 1798* (New Haven: Thomas and Samuel Green, 1798).

Edwards, Jonathan, *Freedom of the Will*, ed. Paul Ramsey (New Haven and London: Yale University Press, 1957).

Edwards, Jonathan, *Religious Affections*, ed. John E. Smith (New Haven and London: Yale University Press, 1959).

Edwards, Jonathan, *The Works of President Edwards in Eight Volumes*, Vol. v, (Leeds: Edward Baines, 1809).

Fergusson, David, *Community, Liberalism and Christian Ethics* (Cambridge: Cambridge University Press, 1998).

Fergusson, David, 'The Reformed Tradition and the Virtue of Tolerance', in *Public Theory for the 21st Century*, eds William Storrar and Andrew Morton (London: T. & T. Clark International, forthcoming, 2004).

Fersch, Seymour, *The View From the White House, A Study of the Presidential State of the Union Messages* (Washington, D.C.: Public Affairs Press, 1961).

Forset, E., *A Comparative Discourse of the Bodies Natural and Politique* (London: John Bill, 1606).

Foster, E. R. (ed.), *Proceedings in Parliament 1610*, 2 vols. (New Haven and London: Yale University Press, 1966).

Freeman, Michael, *Burke and the Critique of Political Radicalism* (Oxford: Blackwell, 1980).

Gilson, Etienne, *The Christian Philosophy of St. Augustine* (London: Victor Gollancz, 1961).

Gray, John, *Endgames: Questions in Late Modern Political Thought* (Cambridge: Polity Press, 1997).

Gray, John, 'The Era of Globalisation is Over', *New Statesman*, 24 September 2001.

Gray, John, *False Dawn: The Illusions of Global Capitalism* (London: Granta Books, 1998).

Gray, John, *Hayek on Liberty* (Oxford: Blackwell, 1984).

Gray, John, *Two Faces of Liberalism* (Cambridge: Polity Press, 2000).

Green, Wayne, 'From Globalisation to Exclusion: Politics, Economics and the UK Churches', forthcoming.

Griswold, Stanley, *The Good Land We Live In. A Sermon Delivered at Suffield (Connecticut) on the Celebration of the Anniversary of American Independence, June 7th 1802* (Suffield: Edward Gray, 1802).

Griswold, Stanley, *Overcoming Evil With Good. A Sermon Delivered at Wallingford, Connecticut, March 11, 1801* (Suffield: Edward Gray, 1801).

Hatch, Nathan, *The Sacred Cause of Liberty* (New Haven: Yale University Press, 1977).

Hauerwas, Stanley, 'Epilogue' in Paul Ramsey, *Speak Up for Just War or Pacifism* (University Park and London: Pennsylvania State University Press, 1988).

Hayek, Friedrich, *The Road to Serfdom* (London: Routledge, 1944).

Heidegger, Martin, 'Letter on Humanism' in *Pathmarks*, ed. W. McNeil, (Cambridge: Cambridge University Press, 1998).

Heidegger, Martin, 'The Question Concerning Technology', in trans. W. Lovitt, *The Question Concerning Technology and Other Essays* (New York: Harper and Row, 1977).

Heimart, Alan, *Religion and the American Mind: From the Great Awakening to the Revolution* (Cambridge, Mass.: Harvard University Press, 1968).

Hemming, Laurence Paul (ed.), *Radical Orthodoxy? – A Catholic Enquiry* (Aldershot: Ashgate Press, 2000).

Herberg, Will, *Protestant–Catholic–Jew: An Essay in American Religious Sociology* (London: Doubleday, 1960).

Hobbes, T., *Behemoth: The History of the Civil Wars of England, From the Year 1640, to 1660* (London, 1680).

Hooker, Richard, *Of the Laws of Ecclesiastical Polity*, ed. A. S. McGrade (Cambridge: Cambridge University Press, 1989).

Hooker, Richard, 'Laws of Ecclesiastical Polity' in *The Works of that Learned and Judicious Divine Mr. Richard Hooker*, ed. John Keble, 7th edn revised by R. Church and F. Paget (Oxford: Clarendon Press, 1888).

Hooker, Thomas, *Soules Preparation* (London, 1632).

Kerr, Fergus, 'Simplicity Itself: Milbank's Thesis', *New Blackfriars*, Vol. 73, no. 861, June 1992.

Kramnick, Isaac, *The Rage of Edmund Burke: Portrait of an Ambivalent Conservative* (New York: Basic Books, 1977).

Kraynak, Robert P., *Christian Faith and Modern Democracy* (Notre Dame, Indiana: University of Notre Dame Press, 2001).

Kundera, Milan, *The Unbearable Lightness of Being* (London: Faber & Faber, 1995).

Lake, Peter, *Anglicans and Puritans: Presbyterian and Conformist Thought from Whitgift to Hooker* (London: Unwin, 1988).

Lash, Nicholas, 'Not Exactly Politics or Power?' *Modern Theology* 8:4, Oct 1992, pp. 354–64.

Lehmann, Paul, *Ethics in a Christian Context* (New York: Harper & Row, 1963).

Lloyd, John, *The Protest Ethic* (London: Demos, 2001).

Locke, John, *An Essay on Human Understanding* (London: Everyman, 1961).

Locke, John, *Four Letters on Toleration* (London: Ward, Lock, 1899).

Longley, Clifford, *Chosen People: The Big Idea that Shapes England and America* (London: Hodder and Stoughton, 2003).

Loughlin, Gerard, 'Christianity at the End of the Story', *Modern Theology* 8:4, Oct. 1992, pp. 365–84.

MacCulloch, Diarmaid, *The Later Reformation in England 1547–1603* (London: Macmillan, 1990).

MacIntyre, Alisdair, *After Virtue: A Study in Moral Theory* (London: Duckworth, 1990).

MacIntyre, Alisdair, *Whose Justice? Which Rationality?* (London: Duckworth, 1988).

Martinich, A. P., *Hobbes: A Biography* (Cambridge: Cambridge University Press, 1999).

Milbank, John, *Being Reconciled: Ontology and Pardon* (London: Routledge, 2003).

Milbank, John, *Theology and Social Theory: Beyond Secular Reason* (Oxford: Blackwell, 2000).

Milbank, John, 'Enclaves, or Where is the Church?', *New Blackfriars*, Vol. 73, no. 861, June 1992.

Milbank, John and Pickstock, Catherine, *Truth in Aquinas* (London: Routledge, 2001).

Miller, Perry, *Errand into the Wilderness* (Cambridge, Mass.: Harvard University Press, 1956).

Milton, John, *The Complete Prose Works of John Milton*, ed. D. M. Wolfe, 8 vols. (New Haven: Yale University Press, 1952–82).

Milton, John, *Of Reformation Touching Church Discipline in England: And the Causes that hitherto have hindered it* (London: Oulton and Gregory Dexter for Thomas Underhill, 1641).

Molesworth, Robert, *An Account of Denmark* (London: 1694).

Morris, Edward, 'The Future of Humanity' in *The Presbyterian Review*, 1880.

Mulhall, Stephen, and Swift, Adam, *Liberals and Communitarians* (Oxford: Blackwell, 1992).

Nancy, Jean-Luc, *The Inoperative Community*, trans. P. Connor (Mineapolis: University of Mineapolis Press, 1991).

Nichols, Aidan, ' "Non tali auxilio": John Milbank's Suasion to Orthodoxy', *New Blackfriars*, Vol. 73, no. 861, June 1992, pp. 326–32.

Niebuhr, Reinold, *The Nature and Destiny of Man* (London: Nisbet, 1943).

Oakeshott, Michael, *Rationalism in Politics and Other Essays* (Indianapolis: Liberty Press, 1991).

O'Brien, Conor Cruise, *Edmund Burke* (London: Vintage, 2002).

O'Donovan, Joan Lockwood, 'Natural Law and Perfect Community:

Contributions of Christian Platonism to Political Theory', *Modern Theology* 14:1, Jan. 1998, pp. 19–42.

O'Donovan, Oliver, *The Desire of the Nations: Rediscovering the Roots of Political Theology* (Cambridge: Cambridge University Press, 1996).

O'Donovan, Oliver, *The Problem of Self-Love in Augustine* (New Haven and London: Yale University Press, 1980).

Paine, Tom, 'The Rights of Man: Part I', in *Political Writings*, ed. B. Kuklick (Cambridge: Cambridge University Press, 1989).

Pickstock, Catherine, *After Writing: On the Liturgical Consummation of Philosophy* (Oxford: Blackwell, 1998).

Rawls, John, *Justice as Fairness: A Restatement*, ed. Erin Kelly (Cambridge, Mass.: Harvard University Press, 2001).

Rawls, John, *Political Liberalism* (New York: Columbia University Press, 1993).

Rawls, John, *A Theory of Justice* (Cambridge Mass.: Harvard University Press, 1971).

Rawls, John, 'The Idea of Public Reason Revisited', in *Collected Papers*, ed. Samuel Freeman (Cambridge, Mass.: Harvard University Press, 1999).

Rogow, Arnold, *Thomas Hobbes: Radical in the Service of Reaction* (London: W.W. Norton, 1986).

Rousseau, Jean-Jacques, *The Social Contract*, trans. Willmoore Kendall (Chicago, Ill.: Gateway, 1954).

Sellars, John, 'Interview' in the *New Left Review*, July/August 2001.

Somerset, H. (ed.), *A Notebook of Edmund Burke* (Cambridge: Cambridge University Press, 1957).

Sommerville, Johann, *Royalists and Patriots: Politics and Ideology in England 1603–1640* (London and New York: Longman, 1999).

Song, Robert, *Christianity and Liberal Society* (Oxford: Clarendon Press, 1997).

Sperry, William, *Religion in America* (New York: Macmillan, 1946).

Strauss, Leo, *Natural Right and Reason* (Chicago: University of Chicago Press, 1953).

Strong, Josiah, *The New Era* (London: Hodder and Stroughton, 1893).

Taylor, Charles, *Human Agency and Language: Philosophical Papers 1* (Cambridge: Cambridge University Press, 1996).

Taylor, Charles, *Philosophy and the Human Sciences: Philosophical Papers 2* (Cambridge: Cambridge University Press, 1999).

Taylor, Charles, *The Sources of the Self: The Making of Modern Identity* (Cambridge: Cambridge University Press, 1989).

Tocqueville, Alexis de, *Democracy in America* (New York: Alfred A. Knopf, 1945).

Tuveson, Ernest Lee, *Redeemer Nation: The Idea of America's Millennial Role* (Chicago: University of Chicago Press, 1968).

Valentine, Henry, *God Save the King: A Sermon Preached in St. Paul's Church on the 27th March 1639, Being the Day of His Majesties Most happy Inauguration, and of His Northern Expedition* (London: John Mariott, 1639).

Vincent, Marvin, *The Lord of War and Righteousness* (Troy, New York, 1864).

Walzer, Michael, *The Revolution of the Saints: A Study in the Origins of Radical Politics* (London: Weidenfeld and Nicolson, 1966).

Ward, Graham, *Cities of God* (London: Routledge, 2000).

Werpehowski, William, 'Political Liberalism and Christian Ethics', *The Thomist* 48 (1984).

Winthrop, John, 'A Modell of Christian Charity', in *The Puritans: A Sourcebook of their Writings*, Vol. 1, ed. P. Miller and T. Johnson (New York: Harper & Row, 1963).

Wittgenstein, Ludwig, *Philosophical Investigations* (Oxford: Basil Blackwell, 1994).

Wolterstorff, Nicholas, 'Why We Should Reject What Liberalism Tells Us about Speaking and Acting in Public for Religious Reasons', in Paul Weithman (ed.), *Religion and Contemporary Liberalism* (South Bend In.: University of Notre Dame Press, 1997).

Woodhouse, A. S. P. (ed.), *Puritanism and Liberty: Being the Army Debates (1647–49) from the Clarke Manuscripts* (London: Everyman, 1986).

Worden, Blair, 'English Republicanism' in J. H. Burns (ed.), *The Cambridge History of Political Thought 1450–1700* (Cambridge: Cambridge University Press, 1991).

Yoder, John, 'Peace Without Eschatology', in *The Original Revolution* (Scottdale, Penn.: Herald Press, 1971).

Index